ActiveBeta
Indexes

Founded in 1807, John Wiley & Sons is the oldest independent publishing company in the United States. With offices in North America, Europe, Australia, and Asia, Wiley is globally committed to developing and marketing print and electronic products and services for our customers' professional and personal knowledge and understanding.

The Wiley Finance series contains books written specifically for finance and investment professionals as well as sophisticated individual investors and their financial advisors. Book topics range from portfolio management to e-commerce, risk management, financial engineering, valuation, and financial instrument analysis, as well as much more.

For a list of available titles, please visit our Web site at www.Wiley Finance.com.

ActiveBeta Indexes

*Capturing Systematic Sources
of Active Equity Returns*

KHALID GHAYUR
RONAN G. HEANEY
STEPHEN A. KOMON
STEPHEN C. PLATT

Foreword by Andrew W. Lo

John Wiley & Sons, Inc.

Published by John Wiley & Sons, Inc., Hoboken, New Jersey.
Published simultaneously in Canada.

ActiveBeta® is a registered trademark of Westpeak Global Advisors, L.P.

The methodologies outlined in the book to create ActiveBeta Indexes, ActiveBeta Custom Indexes, and ActiveBeta Portfolios are the patent-pending intellectual property of Westpeak Global Advisors, L.P.

For general information on our other products and services or for technical support, please contact our Customer Care Department within the United States at (800) 762-2974, outside the United States at (317) 572-3993, or fax (317) 572-4002.

Wiley publishes in a variety of print and electronic formats and by print-on-demand. Some material included with standard print versions of this book may not be included in e-books or in print-on-demand. If this book refers to media such as a CD or DVD that is not included in the version you purchased, you may download this material at http://booksupport.wiley.com. For more information about Wiley products, visit www.wiley.com.

Library of Congress Cataloging-in-Publication Data:

ActiveBeta indexes : capturing systematic sources of active equity returns / Khalid Ghayur ... [et al.].
    p. cm. – (Wiley finance series)
    Includes bibliographical references and indexes.
    ISBN 978-0-470-61002-2 (cloth)
  1. Stock price indexes. 2. Investments. I. Ghayur, Khalid.
    HG4636.A328 2010
    332.63′222–dc22

                            2010000763

ISBN 978-0-470-61002-2

10 9 8 7 6 5 4 3 2 1

*To my wonderful wife, Laura. I thank you
for all your love and support.
To the joy of our lives, Charles and Sophia. The book is
finished. We can jam and hip-hop again!*

Khalid Ghayur

*To my family from whom I have learned so much.
Kari, you have taught me common sense. Sinead, you have
inspired me with your kindness. Brendan, you have shown me
how to Wii. Niamh, you have made me dance, and love it!*

Ronan G. Heaney

*To Lori, for being my very supportive best friend, and
Stevie, for reminding me why all this matters.
I love you both.*

Stephen A. Komon

*To Kim, Madeline, Sarah, and Brady, with love—because you
struggle to understand what Daddy does all day, yet you
faithfully share in the sacrifices.*

Stephen C. Platt

Contents

Foreword

The investment industry is at a crossroads. Never has this fact been more apparent than during the market environment of the past few years. Investors and portfolio managers have seen some of their most cherished investment beliefs fall like dominoes, one after the other. Should we still invest in equities for the long run, given that bonds, and even cash, can outperform stocks for extended periods of time? What are the implications for asset allocation decisions, and what portion of a portfolio should equities comprise? Does any benefit exist to diversifying equity holdings internationally, considering how little diversification benefits were actually offered by international allocations during the recent downturn? And, is there really a consistent trade-off between risk and expected return?

But, one of the biggest challenges to the investment profession is the issue of style investing. How did we end up with growth and value as the canonical dichotomy of investing? Do these current styles reflect legitimate methods employed by active equity managers? If not, are there better ways of defining investment styles?

To a large degree, style investing is a product of empirical observation, in contrast to the theoretically motivated Capital Asset Pricing Model and Efficient Market Hypothesis. While Benjamin Graham did make good use of accounting relationships, economic arguments, and good, old-fashioned common sense to support the wisdom of value investing, it is difficult to understand how investing in growth stocks emerged as its alter ego. This lack of theoretical foundation, and the apparent inconsistency of the value/growth dialectic over time, has bred a new generation of critics—including the authors of this volume—who argue that style investing is based more on hindsight than on foresight.

Khalid Ghayur and his team have taken a different tack with regard to equity styles. The ActiveBeta® Framework described in this book begins with the eminently sensible premise that generic investment styles arise from common (or, in academic jargon, *systematic*) sources of active returns. As such, Active Betas are, first and foremost, a concept. Do systematic sources of active equity returns exist? If so, what are they and why do they persist over time?

By starting with theory, and then providing extensive empirical research to support their hypothesis, Kal and his colleagues reduce the chances of data-snooping that so easily bias and mislead those who rely purely on empirical observation. By focusing on common sources of active equity returns—in particular, the systematic behavior of cash flows and discount rates—the ActiveBeta Framework is able to capture the investment processes of not only value and growth managers, but also of active core managers. In fact, this focus leads naturally to the conclusion that growth is not nearly as compelling a counterweight to value as is momentum. Moreover, with a proper definition of independent styles, Kal and company show that the combination of value and momentum is a better reflection of the style of core managers than just the market-capitalization-based, or size-based, market index. In addressing these issues, Active Betas provide a more transparent and relevant classification of investment approaches than the traditional classifications.

This new framework yields surprisingly broad implications for both active and passive investors, forcing us to look at old problems through new lenses. What is the nature of active equity management returns? Do active equity managers truly add value? Do they have idiosyncratic skill or are they providing only beta-like systematic sources of active return? If Active Betas are truly more representative factors in equity returns than the usual suspects, the answers to these questions—and the fees currently being charged by a number of portfolio managers—will need to be revised.

In developing the Adaptive Markets Hypothesis, I have highlighted the evolutionary nature of the financial markets, and in the dynamic world of professional equity management, the ability to adapt is paramount for survival. Active Betas are an example of the evolution of the investment industry. By providing new answers to some of the oldest questions about investing, this innovative framework offers the investment community a chance to reinvent itself.

On a personal note, I have had the pleasure of interacting with Kal, Ronan, Steve, and Steve for several years as a board member of Westpeak Global Advisors, and I can attest to the passion and expertise they bring to their research. They challenge themselves to find the truth, even when it conflicts with received wisdom. This book, and the ActiveBeta Framework, is the fruit of their labor. I hope you find it as insightful as I did.

ANDREW W. LO

Preface

What if a significant portion of active management returns were driven by systematic sources of active equity returns? What if these systematic active return sources could be captured more efficiently, transparently, and cost-effectively in a passive index structure? Introducing ActiveBeta® Indexes!

THE PROBLEM

The idea for ActiveBeta Indexes, as a conceptual framework and an investment product, developed out of conversations that took place at the start of 2008 between Westpeak Global Advisors and a large pension fund. The investment problem being confronted by this fund was as follows. The equity portion of the fund was equally split between passive index replication and active management. The large size of the fund required an investment in a substantial number of active managers in order to diversify individual manager investment process and business risk. For the three and five years ending 2007, the active managers employed by the fund delivered only benchmark returns, as a group, but the fund paid alpha fees for this outcome. Disappointed by the overall performance of their active managers, the fund's Investment Committee decided to move to a 70 percent allocation to passive index replication. A smaller allocation to active management would allow the fund to concentrate investments in the most skilled active managers, reduce the noise that a large group of active managers inherently creates, and allocate active management fees and risk budgets more efficiently.

Yet, some senior officials at the fund did not necessarily view a higher allocation to passive management as an optimal decision. They believed that common and persistent sources of active returns do exist in the marketplace but that the implementation choices available to capture these sources of active returns were either incomplete and perhaps even misleading (such as value and growth style benchmarks), or inefficient, opaque, and unduly expensive (such as traditional active management). In their view, a clear need existed for an investment solution that better defined the investment styles of active managers (i.e., common sources of active returns) and provided an efficient, transparent, and cost-effective passive capture of a significant portion of traditional active management returns. These senior officials challenged us to develop such an investment solution for the industry.

ActiveBeta Indexes is our attempt at providing this solution.

THE SOLUTION

Three basic questions became the focus of our research efforts.

1. What gives rise to common sources of active returns (investment styles)?
2. How can such active returns persist in highly efficient and adaptive markets?
3. What is the best way to capture the common sources of active returns in an index structure? That is, what is the best way to passively replicate a significant portion of active management returns?

The answers to these questions led to the development of the ActiveBeta Framework and the associated ActiveBeta Indexes.

Current Paradigm of Style Investing

Investment styles have basically emerged out of academic research that focused on discovering stock market anomalies and/or explaining the cross-section of average stock returns. Decades of research and empirical evidence have led to the current industry practice of defining investment styles in terms of value and growth. Index providers and fund consultants have also developed performance benchmarks and fund classification schemes based on the value-growth categorization. However, the current empirical research-driven framework has some limitations. In this framework, so-called market anomalies are first researched, through extensive data crunching, and then an attempt is made to rationalize their existence and persistence. As a result, there is little disagreement on the existence of active returns relating to some strategies, such as value, as these active returns have been well documented. But, because of the lack of a coherent conceptual and theoretical framework, there is little or no agreement on what causes such active returns to exist and persist over time. Similarly, there is no explanation for why growth investing, as it is currently defined, constitutes an investment style of its own.

Furthermore, in the prevailing style framework, the core investment style is defined as the market. That is, the selection universe and performance benchmark for core managers is the market index. Value managers have a value index as a benchmark, rather than the market index, because they are viewed as having a value bias relative to the market. Similarly, growth managers are evaluated against a growth index, not the market index. So, the fact that the core managers' benchmark is the market index implies that these managers have no systematic biases relative to the market. Practitioners know that this is not the case. Core managers do have systematic tilts.

The current paradigm has emerged from the incorrectly defined growth investment style. In its prevailing definition, growth is better classified as non-value, not an independent style of its own. Therefore, the combination of value and growth simply produces the market, which then is used as the performance yardstick for core managers. In the current style framework, both growth managers and core managers are evaluated against inappropriate performance benchmarks.

We approach investment styles from a different conceptual perspective. In our view, an investment style, by definition, represents a source of return common across a large number of active managers. If a common source of return persists over time, despite its widespread exploitation, then it must emanate from fundamental influences that drive stock returns. So, to identify appropriate investment styles, or common and persistent sources of active returns, we have to identify, and study the behavior of, the fundamental drivers of stock returns.

Active Betas: Systematic Sources of Active Equity Returns

Stock prices are fundamentally driven by earnings expectations and interest rates used to discount future earnings. Stock price *changes* are driven by changes in expectations relating to these variables. If changes in expectations depict a systematic behavior, which is not discounted by current prices, then some portion of future returns would also become systematic or predictable. Our research findings, presented in Chapters 3 through 6, indicate that short-term and long-term earnings expectations and discount rates do behave in a systematic or predictable manner over time. Short-term earnings expectations depict positive serial correlation, or an average tendency to trend in the short run. Long-term earnings expectations and discount rates depict negative serial correlation, or an average tendency to mean revert in the long run.

This systematic behavior arises out of the fact that in an open and competitive system, a large group of stocks cannot sustain above-average earnings growth indefinitely. In Chapter 6, we discuss in more detail the influences that explain the systematic behavior of earnings expectations and why it is difficult to fully incorporate this behavior in the formation of current expectations and market prices. Our research further establishes that the payoff to momentum strategies arises from the systematic tendency of short-term earnings expectations to trend in the short run. On the other hand, the payoff to value strategies arises from the systematic tendency of long-term growth expectations to mean revert in the long run. Consequently, we refer to the active returns of momentum and value strategies that are driven partly by the systematic behavior of earnings expectations and discount rates as systematic sources of active equity returns, or *Active Betas*.

Redefining Investment Styles

Based on the ActiveBeta Framework and the associated research, we argue that persistent investment styles arise out of systematic sources of active equity returns that active managers attempt to capture. As such, momentum and value better represent the investment styles of active managers, compared to value and growth.

An analysis of the active returns of the so-called growth managers, presented in Chapter 9, clearly highlights that the so-called growth managers are, in fact, momentum players. That is, they attempt to capture the systematic active return sources associated with the average tendency of short-term expected earnings growth to trend, or to be positively serially correlated. It is not clear what fundamental or systematic source of return the growth investment style, as currently defined by the academic literature and the various growth indexes, attempts to capture. Growth indexes force investors to invest in securities that have high current long-term earnings growth expectations (and, hence, high valuations). But, the systematic behavior of long-term expected earnings growth is to mean revert. Buying securities that are currently classified as high-growth is prone to failure, as these securities subsequently experience decelerating growth expectations (mean reversion), causing their price-earnings (P/E) ratios to contract and future returns to be significantly lower than average. The opposite happens when investors buy value securities. These securities are currently classified in the low-growth category (e.g., low P/E multiples, on average, imply low growth). Going forward, they experience significant expansions in P/E multiples and higher than average returns, as mean reversion of long-term earnings expectations leads to upward revisions in the growth prospects of these companies. It should, therefore, come as no surprise that value indexes systematically outperform and growth indexes systematically underperform the market indexes in the long run in all markets and market segments. The evidence presented in Chapter 9 on the relative performance of value versus growth across a large number of market universes raises serious doubts about the validity of growth as an independent investment style that a large number of active managers follow. With billions of dollars tracking or linked to growth indexes, the research raises concerns regarding the current theory and practice of investment styles.

Further, the active return decomposition analysis presented in Chapter 9 highlights that the so-called core managers are not style-neutral. They have significant combined momentum and value tilts. A large proportion of their portfolio holdings are in stocks that have both high momentum and high value attributes. Given this evidence, how can the market index be the appropriate opportunity set (neutral portfolio) for core managers? Core is a separate investment style with simultaneous biases toward momentum and value.

We need to rethink and revisit the design and structure of investment style indexes.

ActiveBeta Indexes: Capturing Systematic Sources of Active Equity Returns

In order to provide an efficient, transparent, and cost-effective capture of Active Betas, and an alternative to current style indexes, we created an internally consistent family of ActiveBeta Indexes. For any given selection universe, for example, the FTSE All-Share U.K. Index, this family of indexes comprises independent market capitalization-weighted ActiveBeta Momentum and ActiveBeta Value Indexes. The two indexes include high momentum and high value stocks, respectively, and independently target about a 50 percent market capitalization coverage of the selection universe. The two independent indexes are then combined, in equal proportions, to create the ActiveBeta Momentum and Value Index (MVI).

The motivation for creating a combined ActiveBeta MVI is to develop a more representative benchmark for the so-called core managers. The Active-Beta MVI provides roughly 75 percent of the market capitalization coverage of the underlying selection universe. It does not include stocks that have both low-momentum and low-value attributes. These stocks have a negative exposure to the systematic sources of active returns, and they underperform the market on a consistent basis. This group of stocks creates a tremendous performance drag on the market index. These are also the stocks that core managers do not consider for investment. By excluding these stocks, the ActiveBeta MVI better reflects the neutral portfolio of core managers.

The ActiveBeta MVIs outperform the underlying market index or universe on which they are based, in each and every market and market segment we have studied, net of implementation costs. For Developed Markets universes, the after-cost information ratios generated by the ActiveBeta MVIs range from 0.4 to 0.8. The outperformance of the ActiveBeta MVIs has been remarkably consistent, on a year-by-year basis and in each market, during the 1992 through 2008 time period that we have analyzed. The historical performance of the ActiveBeta Indexes is presented in Chapter 8.

The ActiveBeta MVIs outperform because the relative performance of value and momentum is linked to the risk aversion of investors. When risk aversion is high (e.g., in down markets), momentum outperforms value. When risk aversion is low (e.g., in up markets) value outperforms momentum. The link of momentum and value with the risk aversion of investors causes the active returns of the two strategies to become negatively correlated. The negative correlation of momentum and value is observed in all markets and is fairly stable over time. Combining two systematic sources of returns (e.g., momentum and value) that *independently* provide positive active returns but are negatively correlated offers investors an opportunity to realize significant diversification gains without necessarily sacrificing returns. Since value and growth are not independent sources of active returns, and growth, as currently defined, systematically delivers negative active returns in the long run, investors do not have this diversification opportunity in the current value/growth style framework.

ACTIVEBETA INDEX APPLICATIONS

The existence and efficient capture of Active Betas has many investment process applications. Some of these are summarized next.

Decomposing Active Returns

Since ActiveBeta Indexes capture systematic sources of active equity returns, they more accurately represent the generic investment processes of active managers, or investment styles. As such, ActiveBeta Indexes can be used to provide a more accurate decomposition of an active portfolio's returns into a systematic source (Active Beta) component and a skill (pure alpha) component. This analysis, when applied to a large universe of core, value, and growth managers, leads to the conclusion that a significant portion of traditional active management returns comes from the systematic sources of active equity returns, or Active Betas (see Chapter 9).

Revisiting the Alpha-Beta Portfolio Structure

Currently, equity portfolios are structured in terms of a market beta (passive) component and an alpha (active) component. However, if a significant portion of the traditional alpha component comes from Active Betas, then the alpha-beta return separation could be misleading. Therefore, investors should consider moving away from the current alpha-beta return separation portfolio structure to a new structure that comprises three components, namely market beta, Active Betas, and pure alpha.

With ActiveBeta Indexes, investors now have an efficient vehicle for capturing Active Betas, without taking undue investment process risks or paying alpha fees for the delivery of additional forms of beta.

Benchmarking of Active Manager Performance

As discussed, momentum and value better represent the investment styles and processes of active style managers than do value and growth. Similarly, a combination of momentum and value better represents the generic investment process of core managers than does a market index. As such, we argue that the ActiveBeta Momentum Index, ActiveBeta Value Index, and ActiveBeta MVI constitute more appropriate benchmarks for evaluating the performance of growth, value, and core active managers, respectively.

A Fairer Deal on Management Fees

Asset owners have long held the view that active management fees are too high relative to the value-added generated by traditional active management. However, asset owners have lacked the tools to make their argument credible. With ActiveBeta Indexes, investors now have a framework and a tool, through a return decomposition analysis, to argue that the Active Beta component of a manager's alpha should not be compensated at active management fee levels. On the other hand, asset owners should be willing to pay higher management fees to managers who deliver pure alpha that is in addition to and uncorrelated with Active Betas. We realize these suggestions may be viewed as provocative by many, but we believe they represent a step in the right direction and will be beneficial for both asset owners and asset managers in the long run.

Creating Investment Vehicles

An internally consistent family of ActiveBeta Indexes for global equity markets provides a vehicle for investors to capture the systematic sources of active equity returns, either independently through the ActiveBeta Momentum and ActiveBeta Value Indexes or in combination through the ActiveBeta MVI. However, we would also advance the argument that an independent passive replication of an investment style, such as value, may not constitute the optimal long-term active strategy. Investors commonly believe that value is the most powerful and consistent source of active return. This belief is based on the fact that growth, the other (mis-specified) investment style, typically delivers negative active returns. Momentum is currently not viewed as an investment style, partly because the academic literature has yet to agree on a reasonable rationale for the existence of momentum active returns.

The ActiveBeta Framework, in Chapter 6, provides a reasonable rationale for (1) the existence and persistence of momentum and value active returns and (2) the countercyclical (diversifying) nature of momentum and value active returns. In addition, there is no fundamental reason to believe that either momentum or value will provide higher active returns than the other in the long run. In fact, based on the Fama-French Factor Returns, momentum and value have provided similar after-cost risk-adjusted excess returns since 1927 in the United States. Therefore, if no excess return superiority can reasonably be established, then investors might be better served to pursue a combined capture of momentum and value, through the internally consistent ActiveBeta MVI or other such vehicles, to better diversify risk. Stated differently, value investing is characterized by significant downside risk and drawdown relative to the underlying market index. But, this risk can be substantially reduced by combining value with momentum, without sacrificing the active return potential in the long run. The risk-reducing characteristics, and the resulting superior risk-adjusted performance, of the ActiveBeta MVI are clearly evident in all the market universes we have studied. This analysis is presented in Chapter 8.

Customizable Solutions

The ActiveBeta Indexes have been created to demonstrate the working and practical applicability of the ActiveBeta Framework. These indexes provide nearly unlimited capacity and possess other characteristics that we hope will make them widely used as true benchmarks.

However, in addition to the ActiveBeta Index Methodology, we have developed other innovative and patent-pending methods and techniques that provide a more efficient and customizable capture of Active Betas. In particular, we discuss a new portfolio construction technique to create informationally efficient active portfolios. This technique allows for a more efficient capture of the information embedded in a signal, at an active risk level selected by the investor, but without the use of optimizers in order to provide complete transparency in portfolio construction and performance attribution.

We apply this innovative technique to create ActiveBeta Portfolios. An informationally efficient capture of Active Betas results in information ratios that are, on average, 50 percent higher than those achieved by the ActiveBeta Indexes. The historical performance of ActiveBeta Portfolios is presented in Chapter 10.

Summary

In summary, the ActiveBeta Momentum Index, ActiveBeta Value Index, and ActiveBeta MVI more accurately reflect the investment processes of active managers and, as such, constitute more appropriate performance benchmarks for active style and core managers. These indexes also provide a vehicle for an efficient, transparent, and cost-effective passive replication of a significant portion of traditional active management returns, thus allowing asset owners to streamline their portfolio structures and allocate their management fees and active risk budgets more efficiently.

OUR CONTRIBUTION

Through this work, we hope to contribute to the literature and practice of investment management in several ways. First, we present new research and broaden the scope of existing research on the behavior of short-term and long-term earnings expectations and the relationship of momentum and value with earnings expectations by studying and documenting new relationships, not just in the U.S. Large Cap universe but also in other market segments and geographical regions. This comprehensive coverage of markets and market segments, representing many different market environments over the time period studied, makes it possible to ascertain which relationships represent true fundamental influences, as opposed to potentially spurious links specific to a given market and/or a given time period.

Second, we study the various relationships mentioned earlier over a more recent time period, thus providing an out-of-sample confirmation of or challenge to previously published research.

Third, we link independent and narrowly focused pieces of research, both proprietary and published, to create a coherent and new ActiveBeta Framework. This framework establishes the existence of systematic sources of active equity returns and provides a fresh perspective on the rationale for the existence and persistence of active returns associated with broadly diversified momentum and value strategies, something that has been the subject of intense debate and discussion in the world of investments.

Fourth, we design and create an efficient and transparent vehicle, the ActiveBeta Indexes, for investors to implement the capture of systematic sources of active equity returns in actual portfolios. An internally consistent family of market capitalization-weighted momentum indexes, as well as combinations of momentum and value indexes, for various global equity markets and market segments does not currently exist in the marketplace. The ActiveBeta Indexes provide an effective capture of each systematic source, independently as well as in combination, to increase efficiency of capture and ease of implementation. ActiveBeta Indexes make it possible for investors to better understand the nature of active equity management returns and to structure equity portfolios more efficiently by directly capturing the systematic sources of active returns. Active Betas also challenge the current paradigm on style investing and offer a new framework for style replication and performance benchmarking of active style managers.

Finally, in addition to the ActiveBeta Framework and Index Methodology, we present and discuss other proprietary and patent-pending tools and techniques in Chapter 10. We introduce a new methodology for creating ActiveBeta style indexes at varying levels of market coverage and active risk to better suit the investment needs and portfolio structures of asset owners. This customization capability is not available or offered in the design of current style indexes. We also present an innovative portfolio construction technique to implement an informationally efficient capture of systematic sources of active equity returns.

STRUCTURE OF THE BOOK

ActiveBeta Indexes is structured in four main sections, outlined here, to help you navigate the book:

> Section One: Background (Chapters 1 and 2). This section describes the basis for and evolution of market indexes. The discussion is then extended to style indexes, exploring the development and limitations of current style indexes.
>
> Section Two: ActiveBeta Conceptual Framework (Chapters 3 through 6). This section details the theoretical framework behind the ActiveBeta Indexes, as well as the research supporting the framework. The concept of Active Betas is introduced, followed by our research into the nature and relationships of the systematic sources of active equity returns. Lastly, this section delves into the pricing and persistence of the systematic sources of active returns.
>
> Section Three: ActiveBeta Indexes (Chapters 7 through 9). This section discusses the objectives of a style index and illustrates the methodology employed to create the ActiveBeta Indexes. The discussion

then proceeds to a detailed analysis of the historical performance of the ActiveBeta Indexes. This section also demonstrates the various applications of the ActiveBeta Indexes, such as in style investing, performance attribution, portfolio structuring, and asset allocation.

Section Four: ActiveBeta Customizable Solutions (Chapters 10 and 11). This section offers a variety of alternative solutions for capturing the systematic sources of active equity returns. Several innovative techniques are detailed, including the patent-pending informationally efficient ActiveBeta Portfolios.

ACKNOWLEDGMENTS

The development of the ActiveBeta Framework has involved the contributions of numerous individuals, whom we wish to acknowledge. Their assistance to the authors has been invaluable.

Specifically, we wish to thank Jerry Chafkin and Andrew Lo at AlphaSimplex Group. Jerry and Andrew have offered their guidance to us over the past few years, helping to advance our thinking with regard to the theoretical development and practical application of the concepts in this book.

Our partners at FTSE also merit special consideration, particularly Mark Makepeace and Paul Walton. Mark, Paul, and their team provided valuable support and guidance to help with the launch of the FTSE ActiveBeta Indexes.

The ActiveBeta Framework, and this book in particular, could not have been accomplished without the tireless aid of our coworkers at Westpeak Global Advisors. We wish to especially thank Barbara Carlough for dealing with our numerous changes, Anders Fridberg for offering his research insight, Michelle Niemann for making this book more readable with her talent for editing and structuring, and Rachael Sax for producing much of the data and converting it into an understandable format.

Last, but certainly not least, Ingrid Hanson has been instrumental to completing this book. Ingrid kept a group of neophyte authors on track throughout the writing process, making sure the end result matched the original objective. Her attention to detail and organizational skills allowed us to produce the book you hold today.

Background

CHAPTER 1

The Evolution of Market Indexes and Index Funds

Before describing the ActiveBeta concepts and indexes, we need to address why we developed the framework in the first place. What needs do ActiveBeta Indexes fulfill? How do our research and findings advance the discussion on the nature of active equity management or the debate on active versus passive management? Are we reinventing the wheel or taking the next evolutionary step in the life cycle of equity portfolio management?

In later chapters, we detail our rationale for pursuing this research and creating the ActiveBeta Methodology. We introduce the issues and paradoxes that currently exist in the management of equity portfolios, and provide solutions to specific problems and gaps in accepted industry practice. First, however, some background is necessary to place the ensuing discussion in its proper context. How did we reach this point in equity investing?

THE EARLY DAYS OF INDEXING

"How's the market doing?" or "Did you see the market today?" are examples of common investing questions that we take for granted in modern society. Rarely do we stop to ask, "What exactly is the market and how is it defined?" Even novice investors recognize the common definitions of the various asset markets (i.e., the well-publicized market indexes accessible via newspapers, magazines, television, or the Internet). Today, equity indexes are commonplace and sophisticated in their construction, but that was not always the case.

Most observers trace the history of equity indexes back to Charles Dow and 1884. A publisher of news bulletins for traders, Dow set out to provide a benchmark for how stocks performed. Given its importance to the U.S. economy, Dow chose the transportation sector for his first index. The Dow

Transportation Average initially consisted of 11 stocks—9 railroads and 2 nonrail companies. Twelve years later, in 1896, Dow produced his first industrial equity index, the Dow Jones Industrial Average, or DJIA. The DJIA consisted of 12 stocks at first, eventually expanding to the 30 names presently held, and became perhaps the most popular equity index in the world.

While the Dow Averages offered investors some basis to answer the questions that opened this section, the Dow methodology had some well-noted deficiencies. To calculate his Averages, Dow simply added up the prices of the constituent stocks at the end of each day. Thus, these indexes were, and remain, simple price-weighted indexes. That is, the index value is determined by summing the prices of the index constituents, while adjusting for splits and other corporate actions. Changes in the index are the changes in the prices of its constituents. One flaw in this methodology is that a $1 price change in a $10 stock has the same effect on the index as a $1 price change in a $100 stock, despite the former experiencing a 10 percent change, while the latter changed by only 1 percent. In addition, for a representation of the broad or overall equity market, considering only share price seems insufficient. To reflect the activity of the overall equity market more appropriately, company size, or market capitalization, needs to be included in the index. Clearly, changes in the valuations of the companies in the market change the value of the overall market. Yet, the Dow Averages capture only price changes, not value changes.

An additional critique of the Dow Averages is their very limited holdings—30 stocks for the Industrial Average and 20 stocks for the Transportation Average. The small number of names calls into question the match between the returns to these indexes and the returns to the overall market. How can 30 large capitalization stocks represent an overall market that includes thousands of stocks across multiple industries and ranges of market capitalization or size? These price-weighting and coverage issues would be addressed by the next generation of indexes, although not for a number of years.

In 1957, Standard & Poor's introduced its S&P 500 Stock Index, a market-weighted index that would eventually become one of the world's most recognized benchmarks for investors. By weighting its constituent stocks according to their market capitalizations, the S&P 500 Index gave greater weight to the movements of large company stock prices compared to those of small company stock prices. The S&P 500 Index considered changes in market value, not just price. Consequently, the S&P 500 Index better reflected the total value of the overall stock market, as well as overall stock market returns.

Over the years, a myriad of stock indexes have emerged, most of them market capitalization-weighted. Stock indexes now exist for virtually every region, country, sector, or market capitalization range an investor might need. In the United States alone, investors have access to the S&P 500 Index or the Russell 1000 Index for larger stocks, the Russell 2000 Index for smaller stocks, or the Wilshire 5000 Index for all stocks. Globally, index providers such as FTSE and MSCI offer country and regional products across multiple dimensions. With the development of index solutions over the years, particularly during the past decade or two, investors have their choice of tools to answer the question "How's the market doing?" as well as "How are my investments doing compared to the market?" This latter question is important in determining not only personal investment performance, but also the performance of professional investment advisers and mutual funds.

THE INCEPTION OF THE MUTUAL FUND INDUSTRY

For several years starting in the late 1800s, public and private investors in the United States could participate in the pooled vehicles known as investment trusts. These investment trusts traded just as stocks traded, similar to the closed-end mutual funds of today. With a set number of shares and no redemption provision, supply and demand for a given investment trust determined its price. The price could offer a premium or discount to the value of the assets included in the investment trust. While investment trusts did provide access for smaller investors, a lack of controls and securities regulations damaged the reputation of this type of investment vehicle by the 1920s.

More modern mutual fund structures also emerged at this time. For example, the first closed-end fund, the Boston Personal Property Trust, was formed in 1893. Then, in the 1920s, Wall Street began to explore how to mitigate problems with the early investment trusts and, to some extent, closed-end funds. In particular, investors needed a vehicle that could better match the price of the trust with its underlying assets. The solution came in the form of the now well-known open-end mutual fund. The redemption at the net asset value feature of these funds basically eliminated the problems with discounts and premiums, as well as the additional issue of price manipulation seen in investment trusts. Since these open-end mutual funds also invested in publicly traded common stock, investors could track the performance and value of the mutual fund, thus providing greater transparency and confidence.

Massachusetts Investors (now MFS) took this new open-end concept to fruition, creating the Massachusetts Investment Trust in 1924. Initially holding 46 stocks and offering redemption at net asset value on demand, the Massachusetts Investment Trust set the stage for a new investment industry, one that would cater to individual investors. Shortly thereafter, Incorporated Investors produced what is now called Putnam Investors A, and State Street Investment Corporation offered the current State Street Research Investment S. Thus, the open-end mutual fund industry was born.

As the Great Depression approached, closed-end funds still dominated the investment industry, with almost 700 closed-end funds known to exist, compared to 19 open-end funds. The ensuing stock market crash more heavily affected the closed-end side of the business, as these funds tended to be highly leveraged, and thus more vulnerable to a sharp decline in the value of their holdings. Meanwhile, the smaller, unlevered, open-end funds survived.

Once the world moved past the Great Depression and World War II, the open-end fund industry began to thrive. Investors began to revisit the idea of investing in stocks, and over 100 open-end funds existed by the early 1950s. Growth continued through the next two decades, as more and more individual investors embraced the equity markets. Today, investors can choose from literally thousands of open-end mutual fund offerings.

Still, the only alternatives for small investors, prior to mid-1970, were buying individual stocks or investing in mutual funds run by active managers. Already, some had begun to question the efficacy of active equity management. Could active managers consistently beat the market, as defined by the broad indexes? Did active managers actually earn their management fees? Many academic researchers studied these questions in earnest, and their conclusions changed the evolution of the investment management industry.

ENTER ACADEMIA

The nascent active equity management industry almost immediately faced challenges to its basic premise of providing superior performance for a fee. With the onset of the Great Depression, and the massive loss of investor wealth, research contesting the added value of professional management became more relevant. Alfred Cowles, who lost significant money during the market crash, established the Cowles Commission to study economics and securities markets. In 1933, the Commission produced a report titled "Can Stock Market Forecasters Forecast?" The conclusion, after researching 16 financial services firms, was that they could not. The over 7,000 recommendations used in the research performed no better, and perhaps slightly worse, than what would be randomly expected.

As the investment industry evolved, so did the research and theories of economists, or, more specifically, financial academics. In the 1950s, academic theory focused on the efficiency of markets, in particular, how effectively security prices incorporate new information. Research began to rebut prior beliefs about the power of fundamental or technical analysis. Paul Samuelson of MIT and others conducted significant research on the topic. Samuelson circulated the work of French mathematician Louis Bachelier from 1900, in which, among other things, Bachelier first expressed the idea of an efficient market and the inability of speculators to consistently profit.

The idea that the market reacted quickly to new information and that stocks followed a random walk gained credence over the ensuing two decades. Eugene Fama, coincident with Samuelson, established the Efficient Market Hypothesis (EMH) to provide a theoretical framework around the various empirical studies of the time. One important conclusion of the EMH pertaining to mutual funds was that stock picking could not yield economic profit, on average, after costs were considered, a point essentially noted by Bachelier (1900). Given this conclusion, chasing performance by trying to pick the best active managers seemed futile. The EMH, combined with further studies showing the general underperformance of mutual funds compared to market indexes, suggested that the logical path for investors was to invest in "the market," or index funds.

Meanwhile, Harry Markowitz's development of modern portfolio theory, and William Sharpe's refinement of this theory into the Capital Asset Pricing Model (CAPM), influenced the direction of the mutual fund industry as well. A key point by Markowitz illustrated that investing in a diversified portfolio, as opposed to a single or limited number of stocks, could reduce risk without sacrificing return. Sharpe then broke down risk into systematic risk (i.e., risk related to the movement of the overall market) and unsystematic risk (i.e., risk idiosyncratic to a specific stock). Diversification could basically eliminate unsystematic risk, leaving the investor exposed to only systematic risk. This again led to the idea of investing in indexes, since what could be more diversified than a broad market index?

One problem existed, however. Where were the index funds?

THE ADVENT OF INDEX/PASSIVE MUTUAL FUNDS

Burton Malkiel wrote *A Random Walk Down Wall Street*, published in 1973, making an early call for a publicly available index fund in light of the underperformance of actively managed mutual funds. Samuelson furthered the effort in a 1974 article for the *Journal of Portfolio Management* titled "Challenge to Judgment." Samuelson suggested that, at the very least, some respected entity should establish an S&P 500 Index tracking strategy, thus offering a real-world benchmark for active equity managers. Shortly thereafter, some would take up Samuelson's challenge and help reshape the investment management industry.

As the works of Malkiel and Samuelson were published, early attempts were made to establish an index-tracking or broad-market equity portfolio. The initial efforts focused on the institutional marketplace. Wells Fargo Bank, under the leadership of John McQuown and William Fouse, designed a strategy in 1971 for Samsonite Corporation. The idea was to buy equal-weighted positions of the stocks on the New York Stock Exchange, which sounded very simple and straightforward, but ended up being a nightmare to manage.

The next moves toward index tracking used the S&P 500 Index as a benchmark. Batterymarch Financial Management in Boston pursued this avenue starting in 1971, but, despite the academic research, their idea lacked institutional support until 1974. Meanwhile, American National Bank created a high-minimum ($100,000) common trust fund that also tracked the S&P 500. Still, the industry awaited an index-tracking solution for the individual investor.

INDEX MUTUAL FUNDS FOR THE PUBLIC

John Bogle provided this solution in 1976, offering an index fund for the masses. Bogle had begun considering the concept in the late 1940s/early 1950s as a Princeton undergraduate. His senior thesis, "The Economic Role of the Investment Company," had several recommendations for the fund industry. The most relevant for our purposes was that funds should "make no claim for superiority over the market averages" nor create "expectations of miracles from management." As Bogle himself has noted, this thesis marked the start of the journey that culminated in the Vanguard S&P 500 Index Fund.

By 1975, Bogle was chairman of a new firm, Vanguard Group. Given Bogle's aversion to making any claims of outperformance, Vanguard unsurprisingly focused much of its attention on reducing costs and fees. Bogle then set out to create the first low-cost index fund for the public. The First Index Investment Trust (the "Trust"), an S&P 500 Index fund, opened for business on August 31, 1976. This fund later changed its name to the well-known Vanguard S&P 500 Index Trust in 1980.

Initially, the Trust was sold through brokers with a front-end load charge, although a lower charge than was customary at the time. Still, the front-end load fell short of the low-cost goal. In addition, any extra fees weighed upon performance and, thus, made the Trust less of the true index alternative craved by academics. In February 1977, distribution of the Trust was moved away from the commissioned broker network, and the Trust became a no-load fund.

The investing public, thus, had a real chance to decide between active and passive management. What had been a nice theoretical discussion now had empirical evidence. Which fund performed better, index tracking or actively managed? Samuelson's challenge to the industry had been taken on by Vanguard, and an entire index fund industry would soon develop as a result.

Active managers, of course, did not see the attraction of this new index fund concept for the masses. Outperformance was the name of the game in their minds, since no one wanted to be just "average." In fact, Fidelity Chairman Edward C. Johnson III said at the time, "I can't believe that the great mass of investors is going to be satisfied with just receiving average returns."

The initial reaction by investors was tepid at best, as the Trust had only $17 million in assets by mid-1977. Performance didn't help, either, as the S&P 500 Index trailed most mutual funds from 1977 to 1979. Acceptance, however, was just around the corner. By 1982, the Trust surpassed $100 million in assets, and by 1986 the Trust was in the top quintile of equity funds by size. This success was clearly just the beginning, as the Vanguard 500 Index Investor (the current name) now includes assets of over $87 billion (as of October 31, 2009).

Today, virtually every market, region, sector, or style that can be benchmarked has an index fund alternative. Many major investment firms run index portfolios, including former critic Fidelity. In fact, a Pensions & Investments/Watson Wyatt report listed Barclays Global Investors, State Street Global Advisors, and Vanguard Group, all noted managers of index-tracking mutual funds, among the top nine largest international money managers at the end of 2008.

CONCLUSION

Clearly, the rise in popularity of index mutual funds over the past three decades demonstrated the need that existed in the marketplace. Investors and academics wanted a vehicle to understand how their active managers performed, as well as an alternative to high active fees. With the advent of low-cost index mutual funds, investors had an obvious benchmark by which to gauge the results of active managers. This passive investment alternative provided a choice. No longer were investors faced with having to decide between active management and no management. Today, individuals as well as institutions can opt for low cost or seek out superior skill. They can implement Samuelson's challenge on their own portfolios.

While this chapter walked us through the path to the pervasive indexing seen today, one key topic was left untouched. What if simple, straightforward ways exist for managers to beat market indexes? What if the EMH is incomplete and other sources of systematic risk/return exist and can be captured? Index mutual fund providers have an alternative for this as well. In the next chapter, we discuss the evolution of style indexes and how they may or may not better reflect the actual portfolio construction processes of active managers.

CHAPTER 2

The Evolution of Equity Style Indexes

The advent and expansion of equity indexation has given investors some valuable tools. The market indexes fulfill many investor needs, such as:

- Asset class and asset allocation research and implementation
- Performance benchmarking of active core managers
- Vehicles for implementing passive replication strategies

The market indexes we focused on in Chapter 1 represent an important development in equity investing. However, questions still remain. Are core market indexes enough? What improvements can be made to better reflect active managers' investment processes? Do investors need more precise information upon which to base their decisions? Are core index returns easy for active managers to outperform, and, if so, why?

In this chapter, we consider these and other questions and analyze where the answers have taken the equity index industry. In particular, we look at the driving forces behind the development of more specific equity indexes, especially style-based equity indexes. We further discuss the pitfalls of the current index offerings and how these issues might be rectified.

EMPIRICAL CHALLENGES TO FINANCIAL THEORIES

In Chapter 1, we discuss some of the academic arguments that fostered the movement toward equity indexation and the various uses of the indexation concept. In that discussion, we note that the Capital Asset Pricing Model (CAPM) represents one of the central theories in the evolution of equity indexes. In the CAPM, since any idiosyncratic portfolio risk unrelated to the market can be eliminated by diversification, stock returns are defined by their exposure to a single risk factor, the market, which is called market beta.

Combining the CAPM with the Efficient Market Hypothesis (EMH) leads to certain conclusions. If markets are efficient, then trying to beat the market by finding new information or analyzing information better than others seems challenging, if not futile. Meanwhile, if all risk, except market risk, can be diversified away, then any risk taken other than market risk should not be rewarded with excess return. These ideas led to investing in the most diversified portfolio available, the market itself. This, in turn, encouraged the development of broad equity indexes and index funds for both investment and benchmark purposes.

Of course, as the CAPM and the EMH grew in acceptance and popularity, people began to search for holes in these ideas. Among the key questions were:

- How efficient are markets? Do markets fully incorporate all available information?
- Is market risk, or beta, the only risk that drives return? Do other systematic risks exist, beyond the market beta?

Economic researchers soon found empirical evidence of various "anomalies" left unexplainable, in their view, by the CAPM and the EMH. One of the first anomalies was discovered by Rolf Banz in 1979—the Size effect. Banz found that stocks with smaller market capitalizations outperformed stocks with larger market capitalizations. This result held true for these differing groups of stocks even after adjusting for their Beta, or exposure to the overall market. In other words, the single-factor systematic risk, the market beta, did not account for the excess returns of small cap stocks.

Around the same time, a second critical anomaly was found—the Valuation effect. Detailed by Sanjoy Basu in 1977, this exception to the CAPM showed that stocks with lower price-earnings (P/E) ratios outperformed stocks with higher P/E ratios. That is, cheaper stocks provide better returns than expensive stocks, again after adjusting for market beta. Later studies confirmed this Valuation effect, including the use of other factors, such as price-book value.

The research into these various anomalies initially involved little *ex-ante* framework or hypothesis. Academics appeared more focused on testing the basic premise of the one-factor CAPM. The question seemed more "Does it work?," not "Why do exceptions exist?" The answers to the "why" question proved diverse, and the debate over which explanation is most correct continues to this day.

THEORETICAL EXPLANATIONS OF ANOMALIES

So, if markets are efficient and the CAPM, in some form, holds, what exactly are these anomalies? The first, and perhaps most obvious, explanation is that markets are not efficient, or at least not completely efficient. In this case, the Size and Valuation effects represent market inefficiencies. These effects arise from the inability of the market to correctly interpret and fully incorporate all available information. Thus, practitioners can tilt their portfolios toward smaller or cheaper stocks to beat the market without taking undue risk.

Economic theory offers a critique of the inefficiency explanation that is hard to refute. If the Size and Valuation effects exist solely due to the inability of market participants to price in information, and this situation is widely known and understood, why do these effects persist? Arbitrage (i.e., risk-free profit opportunity) should arise from this informational disconnect. Over time, and with enough arbitraging investors, these effects should become negligible and unprofitable in the face of transaction costs. However, the Size and Valuation effects remain, even after the publicized research of Banz, Basu, and others.

Another thought on these effects is that they are simply time-period-specific observations. This explanation suggests that researchers discovered anomalies like Size and Valuation by picking a particular time period and trying whatever factors they could find until they "fit" the data for that time period. Presumably, by using this data-mining approach, factors found to outperform in one period would have no reason to do so in another, independent time period. The long-term (out-of-sample) evidence of the power of Size and Valuation makes this explanation difficult to accept.

Behavioral finance also attempts to explain various anomalies, including Size and Valuation. In broad strokes, behavioral finance believes that investors can behave irrationally, not always as the rational operators portrayed by the EMH. As an example of this biased behavior, investors may favor buying stocks of companies they know, leading to the overpricing of larger, well-known stocks and underpricing of their smaller brethren. In another illustration, individuals may overestimate the rapid growth of certain companies, thus causing their stocks to become expensive on a P/E basis and to underperform when these extrapolated expectations are not met.

A fourth explanation of the Size and Valuation effects is that these factors represent some additional risk taken by investors. In essence, this idea suggests that the one-factor CAPM is incomplete and that factors beyond market exposure require consideration. Academics espousing the EMH prefer this explanation because it does not call into question market efficiency. Rather, this risk premium idea allows for a more robust version of the CAPM that better captures the systematic risks that are priced by the market.

Economic theorists and financial practitioners continue to debate the behavioral and risk premium explanations for the discovered anomalies, particularly Size and Valuation. We will weigh in on this discussion, especially with regard to Valuation, in later chapters. For now, we will consider how these effects, and the questions regarding why they exist, influenced the evolution of equity style indexes. If the one-factor CAPM is insufficient, then perhaps solely employing core market indexes is also insufficient. These findings led to the next steps in the development of equity indexes based on factors, or investment styles.

ESTABLISHING EQUITY STYLES

Whether behavioral or risk premium, the idea that investors needed to consider more than market beta gained credence. Equity style management increased in popularity, with managers becoming classified according to size segment or value/growth, as growth emerged as the counterpart to value. Investment consultants began to advise clients to add small-cap and value- and growth-oriented strategies to their overall portfolios to increase diversification.

In the late 1980s, William Sharpe, the father of the CAPM, used regression analysis to determine the exposure of portfolios, such as mutual funds, to various style factors. He published his "returns-based style analysis" methodology in 1988, with further refinements being released in 1992. Sharpe focused on large cap, small cap, value, and growth as the style choices for his analysis, a key step in establishing the popular equity styles seen today in the marketplace.

Sharpe's approach took the returns over time of a given portfolio or fund and regressed these returns against the selected style benchmarks. In this way, returns-based style analysis can shed light on how a portfolio tilts in reality, whether intentionally or unintentionally. Generally, portfolios are combinations of the various styles, not purely one or two styles. Sharpe's analytical technique thus gave investors a clearer picture of how their investments actually were managed, not just what the fund description stated.

Sharpe's methodology also provided a basis for assessing a manager's ability to provide true alpha. By deriving a relevant combination of styles for comparison purposes, investors could evaluate whether active management returns came from manager skill or simply one or more styles that could be captured passively. This point is critical not only in manager selection but also in determining the appropriate nature of management fees, in light of potential passive style index alternatives.

Moving further down the equity style path, Eugene Fama and Kenneth French produced an influential paper in 1992. Fama and French considered the performance and power of Size and Valuation, determining that these factors are significant in the explanation of stock returns, as well as the prediction of these returns. In fact, the information found in Size and Valuation largely overwhelmed Beta as an explanatory factor. However, Beta still had power in certain time periods, leading Fama and French to retain it in their model. The Fama-French three-factor model thus incorporated Size, Valuation, and Beta to explain returns. The inclusion of Size and Valuation built upon Sharpe's work and further solidified styles as an important part of equity investing.

Given the academic stature of the authors, the Fama-French three-factor model was quickly accepted in the marketplace. Mutual fund analysts and consultants, such as Morningstar, often categorize managers based on "style boxes" related to the Sharpe methodology or Fama-French three-factor model. A typical style box for equities is shown in Figure 2.1.

As one can see in this style box, large-cap stocks represent one end of the stock spectrum, with small-cap stocks representing the opposite end. By the same token, value stocks (based on high book value-price ratios, earnings-price ratios, etc.) find their mirror image in growth stocks.

With the advent of styles and style boxes, consultants and investors uncovered a tool to classify managers. Mutual funds, consequently, began to market themselves according to the best match of their investing methods and these styles. Equity style indexes achieved increased popularity as a

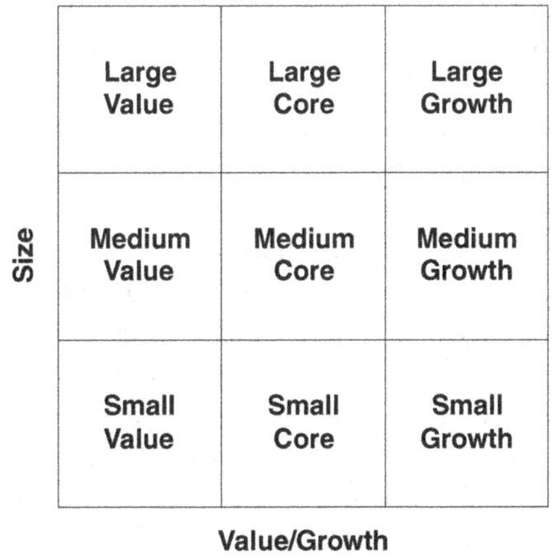

Large Value	Large Core	Large Growth
Medium Value	Medium Core	Medium Growth
Small Value	Small Core	Small Growth

Size

Value/Growth

FIGURE 2.1   Equity Style Box
Source: Westpeak.

more specific measure of performance for managers, as well as an investment alternative through passive-replication mutual funds.

EQUITY STYLE INDEX METHODOLOGY

In the mid-1980s, providers of core equity indexes moved into the style index arena. The Frank Russell Company and Wilshire Associates created the first of these styles indexes, with several competitors soon to follow. Long-time index standard-bearers Standard & Poor's, in conjunction with the factor model firm Barra, and Dow Jones also entered the style fray. These indexes became particularly popular in the United States, and investors soon had several equity style choices.

Size indexes were quite straightforward. Index providers took their broad universe of stocks, for example the Russell 3000 Index, and divided the constituents according to market capitalization. Thus, the Russell 3000 Index breaks down into the Russell 1000 Index of large cap stocks and the Russell 2000 Index of small cap stocks. While index providers have made adjustments to market capitalization, such as available shares or float, the Size indexes are basically reflective of the market value of stocks.

With Size classifications established, index providers initially took a similar tack to Sharpe and Fama-French when creating their value and growth style indexes. Early style indexation saw index providers divide the overall, or core, universe in half according to a single factor, such as book value-price. The high book value-price half became the value index. The other half became the growth index. Thus, the value and growth indexes are defined in terms of each other, and the combination of the two style halves equals the whole core index. This value/growth classification scheme was then applied to the various broad large cap and small cap equity indexes.

More recently, equity style index construction has become somewhat more sophisticated. The process has evolved to define growth more explicitly, in terms of long-term realized growth and/or expected growth, thus creating a two-dimensional process for dividing the core universe into growth and value. In addition, many index providers now establish both value and growth classifications using multiple descriptors, not just a single factor, such as book value-price. Today, the value nature of a stock may result from its scores on additional factors relating to earnings, sales, or dividend yield. Furthermore, stocks generally are not either value or growth, but rather can have characteristics of both styles. Still, the two style halves continue to be defined in terms of each other and together cover fully and exactly the market capitalization and constituents of the broader core index, in most cases.

PITFALLS OF CURRENT EQUITY STYLE INDEXES

The development of styles in this fashion, particularly those pertaining to value or growth characteristics, has created a number of difficulties for the investment management industry. We will address some of these in more depth later in the book, but a brief overview is appropriate in this chapter to connect where indexes are to where indexes need to be.

The first challenge is the use of growth. As this factor initially emerged as the opposite of value, it may be more precise to call these style indexes non-value instead of growth. The usefulness of a non-value, or growth, equity index is questionable as a practical matter. Our research indicates that growth does not represent a systematic source of return, while value clearly does represent such a source. Also, while growth managers do exist, growth benchmarks do not appear to capture their investment methodologies. It is hard to imagine many managers explicitly or implicitly seeking out expensive non-value stocks for their own sake. Lastly, growth benchmarks, as currently and historically defined, have often trailed value and core indexes by significant margins. This performance makes tracking a growth index, or measuring managers against said index, a somewhat irrational decision.

A second question that arises in style index construction is coverage of the core index. Does the entire market capitalization and constituency of the core index need to be present in the combination of the value and growth indexes? While some "pure" style indexes exist, most index providers employ a complete coverage philosophy in their style index construction. This policy forces stocks that may have little or no real value or growth qualities into one camp or the other. While this method does account for all the stocks in the universe, it is not the most efficient way to obtain the returns to a core style. Yet, fullness of coverage continues to override purity of capture in the most popular equity style indexes.

Another test for style indexes is how to incorporate the most recent and relevant information in the index. A common belief of index providers is that indexes need to be as stable, and have as little turnover, as possible. While this idea makes some sense, it can cause a mismatch between indexes and higher-turnover active management strategies. More frequent rebalancing of equity style indexes can alleviate this problem if the transaction costs can be contained. We will discuss how this can be achieved later in the book.

CONCLUSION

Academic research called into question the sole use of a single-factor CAPM and, consequently, the focus on only core equity indexes. Consultants rapidly picked up on this research, as they sought better ways to measure the performance of active equity managers. To meet this need, index providers built suites of equity style indexes based largely on Size and Valuation. The construction methodology of these style indexes has evolved over the years, bringing the industry to its current stage of development.

Still, improvements in the framework of equity style indexes seem necessary for the industry to take the next steps. Indexes need to better reflect the activities of portfolio managers in order to serve as appropriate benchmarks. This is especially true of the growth indexes, which essentially emerged only as a counterpart to value, not as a stand-alone systematic source of active equity returns. In the next chapter, we introduce a framework to address this and other issues in building a better suite of equity style and core indexes.

ActiveBeta
Conceptual Framework

Introducing Active Betas

In order to better define the investment styles of active managers and create style indexes that reflect what active style managers actually do, we need to develop a framework to explain what influences could give rise to common sources of active equity returns, that is, equity styles. In this chapter, we introduce Active Betas as the primary common sources of active equity returns. In Chapters 4 through 6, we develop further the concepts and relationships that provide the foundation for the proposed ActiveBeta Framework.

DEFINING ACTIVE BETAS

Many investors believe that markets are highly efficient and highly adaptive. In a highly efficient market, pure alpha could exist, but it should be difficult to find and require significant investment skill. In a highly adaptive market, a particular source of alpha, once discovered and documented, should lose its effectiveness over time as it becomes commoditized or is arbitraged away.

Yet, sources of positive active returns (returns in excess of the market), which do not require a high level of investment skill to capture, have been easily found. These include size (market capitalization), value (e.g., price-book value), momentum (relative returns), and so forth. Even more surprisingly, some sources of positive active returns have persisted over time despite the fact that they were discovered and documented decades ago.

Consider Figure 3.1. It depicts the cumulative excess returns over cash generated by the Fama-French 12-month price momentum factor and the price-book value factor for U.S. stocks since 1927. These returns reflect the performance of long-short, market-neutral factor portfolios generated by subtracting the returns of high momentum and value stocks from the returns

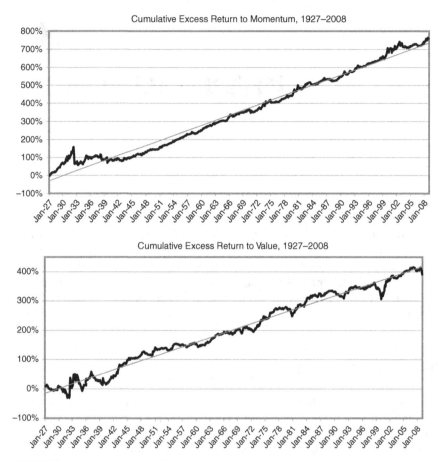

FIGURE 3.1 Performance of Fama-French Momentum and Value Factors for U.S. Stocks, 1927 through 2008
Note: This figure illustrates the monthly excess return for Momentum and Value portfolios. The accumulation is a straight addition of the monthly returns.
Source: Westpeak, based on data from Kenneth French (http://mba.tuck.dartmouth. edu/pages/faculty/ken.french/data_library.html).

of low momentum and value stocks. From 1927 through 2008, a total of 82 years, momentum and value have provided significant excess returns, despite their well-known existence and straightforward definitions. It should be noted that since these excess returns are not adjusted for transaction costs, it appears that momentum, a high turnover strategy, has delivered better performance than value, a low turnover strategy. Once implementation costs are considered, the two strategies generate almost identical Sharpe ratios.

Interestingly, the value effect was documented as far back as 1977 by Basu. Value as an investment style gained greater industry-wide popularity after Fama and French published their research in 1992. Meanwhile, the success of medium-term momentum was documented by Jegadeesh and Titman in 1993. However, value and momentum have shown no evidence of losing their excess return generation capability since the 1990s, as depicted by the slope of the two lines in Figure 3.1.

How can these publicly documented excess returns coexist with a basic acceptance of the highly efficient and adaptive nature of equity markets? While many theories have been offered to explain the nature of momentum and value active returns (as we discuss in Chapter 6), our research provides some fresh insights on how to reconcile this conflict between core investment beliefs and observed facts. It highlights that simple and publicly known sources of active returns that persist over time emanate from systematic sources of active equity returns.

By "systematic" we mean a system that adheres to an intuitive, fundamental law, which gives rise to predictable and consistent behavior of the variables that drive stock prices, such as earnings and discount rates. This predictable behavior, when captured in appropriate investment strategies, gives rise to persistent sources of active equity returns.

A basic law characterizes the behavior of earnings (and discount rates) in open, competitive, free-market economies. That is, *earnings for large groups of stocks cannot grow at above-average rates indefinitely.* Competitive forces cause both prior fast and slow growers to revert toward the mean over time. This is the fundamental behavior of the earnings of a large group of stocks in open, competitive systems. Predictable patterns of trends and mean reversion in the behavior of earnings over different time horizons are thus created. Earnings growth exhibits an average tendency to trend in the short run and mean revert in the long run, as we show in Chapters 4 and 5. We refer to this as the "systematic" behavior of earnings, which makes it possible to use current forecasts to estimate future growth prospects.

The systematic sources of active equity returns arise from the systematic behavior of earnings (and discount rates) over time. Investment strategies that are closely linked to short-term (e.g., momentum) and long-term (e.g., value) earnings growth prospects provide a basic mechanism for exploiting and benefiting from the systematic behavior of earnings.

Therefore, the active returns associated with momentum and value strategies constitute systematic sources of active equity returns. This is why they have persisted over time, despite being heavily researched and documented and having significant amounts of money linked to them.

These active return sources have been improperly characterized as "alpha" emanating from manager skill. Since they represent systematic sources of active equity returns, they should be viewed as additional forms of beta, which we refer to as *Active Betas*. Once these systematic sources of active equity returns are taken into account as betas, "pure" alpha does become harder to find and retain, which is consistent with the basic premise of a highly efficient and adaptive market.

Active Betas provide a conceptual framework for understanding what gives rise to systematic sources of active equity returns, why these systematic sources persist over time, and how best to capture them. The systematic sources of active equity returns also give rise to investment styles. Next, we begin developing an ActiveBeta Framework by identifying and verifying the drivers of equity returns.

IDENTIFYING THE DRIVERS OF EQUITY RETURNS

Investors commonly employ cash flow discount models to value equities. Cash flows can be specified in terms of dividends, free cash flow, earnings, and so forth. For example, a simple constant-growth earnings discount model specifies the price of a security at time t as:

$$P_t = E_t^n/(k_t - g_t) \qquad (3.1)$$

where: P_t = Price of a security at time t

E_t^n = Expected earnings per share for period n at time t (for example, expected earnings for next fiscal year at time t)

k_t = Expected rate of return for the security, given the risk associated with it, at time t (also referred to as the discount rate)

g_t = Long-term (steady-state) expected growth in earnings at time t

Rearranging Equation 3.1 provides the following approximation for change in price levels, which is the variable of interest.

$$\Delta P_{t,t+1} \approx \Delta E_{t,t+1}^n - \Delta (k - g)_{t,t+1} \qquad (3.2)$$

where: $\Delta P_{t,t+1}$ = Change in price between time t and $t + 1$

$\Delta E_{t,t+1}^n$ = Change in expected earnings per share for period n between time t and $t + 1$ (for example, change in next fiscal year earnings between time t and $t + 1$)

$\Delta (k - g)_{t,t+1}$ = Change in the difference between the discount rate and the long-term expected growth in earnings between time t and $t + 1$

Furthermore, from Equation 3.1 we can specify the earnings-price (E/P) ratio as:

$$E_t^n / P_t = k_t - g_t \qquad (3.3)$$

The change in the E/P ratio is then defined as:

$$\Delta(E_t^n / P_t)_{t,t+1} \approx \Delta(k_t - g_{t,})_{t,t+1} \qquad (3.4)$$

Substituting Equation 3.4 in Equation 3.2 we get:

$$\Delta P_{t,t+1} \approx \Delta E_{t,t+1}^n - \Delta(E_t^n / P_t)_{t,t+1}$$

or

$$\Delta P_{t,t+1} \approx \Delta E_{t,t+1}^n + \Delta(P_t / E_t^n)_{t,t+1} \qquad (3.5)$$

Equation 3.5 stipulates that security returns are fundamentally driven by change in consensus short-term earnings expectation and change in valuation. The change in valuation component of price return is, in turn, a function of the change in the difference between the consensus estimate of the discount rate and the consensus expected long-term earnings growth rate.

Driver #1: Change in Expectation

Equation 3.5 tells us that price changes are driven primarily by how consensus earnings estimates for a given short-term future earnings horizon change over time, rather than by growth in actual earnings. To make this important point clear, let us assume that, for a given stock at time t, the past 12-month realized earnings are $5 per share and the consensus expectation for next fiscal year earnings is $6 per share. At time $t + 1$, the past 12-month realized earnings are $5 and the consensus expectation for next fiscal year earnings is $9. The growth in 12-month realized earnings is 0 percent. The change in consensus expectation for next fiscal year earnings, the same look-ahead period at each point in time, is +50 percent between time t and $t + 1$. Equation 3.5 states that this +50 percent change in consensus expectation is one driver of price changes.

Driver #2: Change in Valuation

The other driver is change in valuation (price-earnings [P/E] ratio). Equation 3.3 specifies that the level of the P/E ratio is driven by the difference between the consensus estimate of the discount rate and the consensus long-term growth expectation $(k - g)$. Thus, changes in the P/E ratio are a function of the changes in this difference.

VERIFICATION

Even though Equation 3.5 simply states a straightforward intuition, and approximates an identity, it has important implications for the identification of systematic sources of active equity returns. Therefore, the real-life relevance of these results requires verification. However, one problem is that true consensus market expectations are unobservable. These expectations are reflected in market prices, but cannot be disentangled from other influences impacting them.

To overcome this problem, we use the analyst estimates provided by Institutional Brokers' Estimate System (IBES) in place of true market expectations. In particular, we use changes in IBES fiscal-year-two estimates (FY2) as a proxy for the change in consensus expectation component of Equation 3.5 and to calculate the P/E ratio.

Figure 3.2 presents an analysis that supports the intuitive conclusions of Equation 3.5. It reports the contemporaneous relationship of one-year price change with one-year change in IBES FY2 estimates and one-year change in valuation for the U.S. Large Cap universe (defined as the top 500 U.S. stocks by size). From 1985 to 2008, the average univariate rank correlation

$t - 1$	t	Price Change Past Year vs.	Correlation	t-Stat
P_{t-1}	P_t			
Price Change		FY2 Estimate Change Past Year	0.54	27.00
$FY2_{t-1}$	$FY2_t$	P/E Change Past Year	0.43	10.37
Expectation Change				
P/E_{t-1}	P/E_t			
Valuation Change				

FIGURE 3.2 Relationship of Price Change with Change in Analyst Expectation and Change in Valuation for U.S. Large Cap Universe, 1985 through 2008
Note: This figure contains the results of a rank correlation between the previous year price change and the previous year change in estimates and the previous year change in P/E for stocks in the U.S. Large Cap universe. The earnings estimates used in the analysis are the IBES FY2 estimates.
Source: Westpeak, based on data from IBES and MSCI Barra.

coefficient between price change and change in short-term expectation and change in valuation is 0.54 and 0.43, respectively. Thus, on average, change in expectation and change in valuation relate to price returns roughly equally over a one-year change horizon.

Equation 3.3 also implies that the P/E ratio is influenced by the market estimate of the discount rate and the market long-term earnings expectation. Verifying this relationship presents the same problem, in that the market expectations for these two variables are not observable in real life. However, as before, we can use the analyst estimates of long-term expected growth provided by IBES as a proxy for true market expectations. Further, we can consider a few commonly used risk measures, such as leverage, earnings variability, and volatility of returns, as proxies for risk variables that may influence the discount rate, k.

Figure 3.3 analyzes the relationship between the current level of the P/E ratio and IBES long-term growth estimates and risk measures for the U.S. Large Cap universe. The univariate rank correlation analysis shows that these factors independently have an influence on the level of the P/E ratio, with the strongest influence coming from the analyst long-term growth

P/E Current vs.	Univariate Correlation	*t*-Stat	Multiple Regression	*t*-Stat
Long-Term Growth Expectation	0.41	22.50	0.40	15.00
Leverage	−0.28	−13.80	−0.12	−7.20
Earnings Variability	−0.24	−16.70	−0.20	−10.90
Volatility	0.07	2.60	0.03	0.70

Quintile	P/E Curent (%)	Long-Term Growth Expectation (%)	Leverage	Earnings Variability	Volatility
1	9.8	9.9	0.4	0.1	28.5
2	12.6	10.7	0.2	−0.2	27.3
3	15.4	11.9	−0.1	−0.3	28.6
4	18.6	13.1	−0.2	−0.3	28.9
5	25.5	15.3	−0.2	−0.1	33.4
High-Low Spread	15.7	5.4	0.5	0.2	4.9

FIGURE 3.3 Relationship of P/E Ratio with Analyst Long-Term Growth Expectation and Various Risk Factors for U.S. Large Cap Universe, 1985 through 2008

Note: This figure contains the results of a univariate rank correlation and multiple regression between the current P/E ratio and estimated long-term growth, leverage, earnings variability, and volatility in the U.S. Large Cap universe. The long-term earnings estimate used in the analysis is the IBES Long-Term Forecast at time t. In the quintile analysis, we sort companies into five groups with an equal number of constituents, covering the entire universe. Quintiles are established according to the variable in the first column of numbers and are the cross-sectional median value of the stocks within each quintile. The bars on the quintile charts are the relative statistics depicted as differences from the median value for each column variable.

Source: Westpeak, based on data from IBES and MSCI Barra.

expectation. The univariate rank correlations can, however, be somewhat misleading if the various factors are highly correlated amongst themselves. Therefore, we also conduct a multiple regression analysis to identify the true influences. This analysis shows that the significance of the analyst long-term expected growth remains stable, with a rank correlation coefficient of 0.40, while the significance of leverage and return volatility drops substantially. Figure 3.3 also shows a quintile analysis, in which the universe of the top 500 U.S. stocks is sorted by the P/E ratio, from low to high, and then divided into five quintiles containing around 100 stocks each. This analysis highlights that when a universe is sorted by P/E quintiles, the most linear relationship is obtained with long-term growth expectation quintiles. Thus, investing in low P/E stocks is similar to investing in low long-term expected growth stocks. The influence of risk factors, on the other hand, appears to be driven by the extremes, that is, Quintile 1 for leverage and earnings variability and Quintile 5 for volatility of returns.

The main conclusion from Figure 3.3 is that valuation ratios are a proxy for current estimates of long-term growth prospects.

EXPLORING THE BEHAVIOR OF RETURN DRIVERS

We have identified change in analyst expectation and the level of long-term analyst growth expectation as two variables that influence equity returns. We have also established the link between change in analyst expectation and price change and between the level of long-term analyst growth expectation and value. The next step is to consider the behavior of these two drivers.

Chapter 4 examines the behavior of short-term earnings expectations and further explores the association with momentum (price change). Chapter 5 studies the behavior of long-term earnings growth expectations and further investigates the connection with value. We provide research into these behaviors and relationships that builds upon the theoretical framework in this chapter. We extend the analyses shown in Figure 3.2 and Figure 3.3 to establish the ActiveBeta Framework.

Furthermore, in Chapter 6, we explore the persistence of these relationships and how they are incorporated into stock prices. We consider to what extent current prices discount the systematic behavior of the return drivers. We also provide a review of the existing explanations of these phenomena, while offering the ActiveBeta perspective on the debate.

Behavior of Short-Term Earnings Expectation and the Link with Price Momentum

In this chapter, we focus on the behavior of analyst short-term earnings expectation for the next one- and two-year time frames, and further explore its link with price momentum. First, we document the strong contemporaneous relationship between one-year stock return and one-year change in analyst short-term earnings expectation. Second, we show that the change in analyst short-term expectation is positively serially correlated. Finally, we study price momentum and find that it also exhibits similar positive serial correlation properties. The purpose of this chapter is not to delve into the potential reasons for the existence of these relationships, but rather to document their existence in various global equity market universes. In Chapter 6, we offer an explanation of the reasons for short-term earnings expectation trends and discuss why such trends are not fully incorporated in current expectations and prices.

ANALYSIS METHODOLOGY

Before exploring the behavior of earnings expectations, we first provide an overview of the methodology we use to analyze the various relationships presented in this chapter and in Chapter 5.

The primary statistic we use to assess the overall strength of the relationship between two variables is the Spearman rank correlation coefficient. The values of the correlation coefficient range from -1 to 1, where -1 implies a perfectly negative relationship, $+1$ implies a perfectly (linear) positive relationship, and 0 implies no relationship. (The Appendix in this chapter provides a discussion of the rank correlation and its link to regression analysis.) Reporting just a correlation coefficient, however, is typically not sufficient. A companion statistic is necessary to indicate if the correlation coefficient is significant, that is, meaningfully different from 0. To determine significance, we use a technique pioneered by Fama and MacBeth, which involves calculating yearly correlation coefficients and then performing a statistical analysis on those yearly observations. Specifically, at the end of June of each year, we calculate the rank correlation between the variables of interest. This calculation is repeated for each year of the analysis period, resulting in a time series of correlation coefficients. We then calculate the average correlation and use the standard deviation of the correlations to calculate a t-statistic. A t-statistic value exceeding two is considered statistically significant, implying that a relationship exists between the variables.

While the rank correlation is a useful statistic, it assumes a linear relationship between the ranked dependent and independent variables. In order to determine if there is any nonlinear behavior, we employ a technique known as fractile analysis. Fractile analysis provides an important complement to the correlation statistics. The basic method of fractile analysis is to group the stocks in a given universe based on the dependent variable and then report the values of the independent variable within each group. As in the case of the correlation coefficient, we calculate yearly fractile values and then average them over time. Specifically, at the end of June of each year, we sort the stocks from low to high based on the dependent variable. We then group the stocks into five equal-sized buckets (quintiles) and calculate the median value of the dependent and independent variables in each group. This calculation is repeated for each year of the analysis period, resulting in a time series of values for both the dependent variable and independent variables for each quintile. Then, the average value is calculated for each variable and quintile. From a practical perspective, each quintile can be viewed as an equal-weighted portfolio of stocks that is rebalanced each June.

The results in Chapter 4 and Chapter 5 are presented in figures that follow an identical format. The top left corner of each figure graphically depicts the relationship being studied. The top right corner reports the average rank correlation coefficient between the dependent and independent variables and the corresponding statistical significance. The graph in the middle plots the cross-sectional rank correlation coefficient for each year. The bottom part of each figure shows the quintile analysis. The quintiles are formed based on a ranking of the universe on the dependent variable, from low to high, which is represented by the first column of numbers. The values reported for each quintile are the averages of the yearly median values. The other columns contain the median values of the dependent variables within each quintile. The bar graphs next to the median values graphically depict the linear or nonlinear nature of the relationship. The bars for each quintile are calculated relative to the median value of the quintiles.

For the United States, we study the time period from 1985 through 2008. We present the results for two market universes. One is the U.S. Large Cap universe, which is defined as the top 500 stocks by market capitalization, and the second is the U.S. Small Cap universe, which is defined as the stocks that have ranks between 1,001 and 3,000 according to market capitalization. Thus, our U.S. Large Cap and Small Cap universes closely approximate the constituents of the S&P 500 Index and the Russell 2000 Index, respectively.

For European markets, we analyze the time period from 1994 through 2008. Our U.K. and Europe excluding U.K. universes are a close approximation of the FTSE 350 Index and the MSCI Europe ex-U.K. Index, respectively. For Japan, our universe approximates the Tokyo Stock Price Index (TOPIX), and we cover the period from 1996 through 2008. The reason for these differing time periods has to do with the quality and coverage of the available analyst expectation data for various markets.

RELATIONSHIPS STUDIED

The three relationships explored in this chapter are graphically represented in Figure 4.1. These are:

1. The relationship between price momentum and change in analyst expectation.
2. The relationship between past change in analyst expectation and future change in analyst expectation.

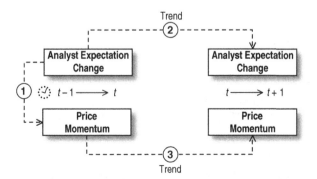

FIGURE 4.1 Relationships Studied
Source: Westpeak.

3. The relationship between past price momentum and future price momentum.

Price Momentum and Change in Analyst Expectation

The relationship studied in this section is depicted in Figure 4.2.

As documented in Chapter 3, change in expectation is an important component of price change. In this section, we provide more detailed analysis of this relationship.

Since true market expectations are not directly observable in the marketplace, we use analyst estimates from the Institutional Brokers' Estimate System (IBES) Global Aggregates database as a proxy. More specifically, we use fiscal-year-two (FY2) analyst projections from IBES. These estimates are the arithmetic average of individual analyst estimates collected over the trailing four weeks for the next fiscal year. We chose the FY2 analyst estimate instead of FY1 because FY2 always represents a pure forecast extending at least one full year into the future. The FY1 forecast, on the other hand, may represent a combination of reported and estimated quarterly earnings, depending on where the company is within its fiscal year.

The results are presented in Figures 4.3 through 4.7 for the five universes studied. In general, across all markets, the results reveal a strong contemporaneous relationship between stock return (momentum) and change in analyst short-term earnings expectation. The average correlation coefficients are substantial and range from a high of 0.54 for U.S. Large Cap (Figure 4.3) to a low of 0.42 for the United Kingdom (Figure 4.5). In the field of financial econometrics, achieving a correlation of this magnitude is rare

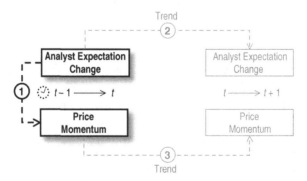

FIGURE 4.2   Relationship between Price Momentum and Change in Analyst Expectation
Source: Westpeak.

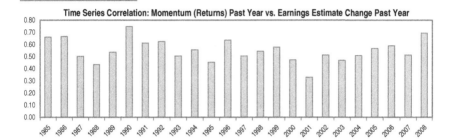

Momentum (Returns) Past Year vs.	Correlation	*t*-Stat
Earnings Estimate Change Past Year	0.54	27.00

Time Series Correlation: Momentum (Returns) Past Year vs. Earnings Estimate Change Past Year

Quintile	Momentum Past Year (%)	Earnings Estimate Change Past Year (%)
1	−22.9	−13.2
2	−2.6	1.9
3	10.2	7.8
4	23.7	12.2
5	49.0	21.0
High-Low Spread	71.9	34.2

FIGURE 4.3 Relationship between Price Momentum and Change in Analyst Short-Term Expectation for U.S. Large Cap Universe, 1985 through 2008
Note: This figure contains the results of a rank correlation between the previous year returns and the previous year change in earnings estimates for stocks in the universe. The earnings estimates used in the analysis are the IBES FY2 estimates. In the quintile analysis, we sort companies into five groups with an equal number of constituents, covering the entire universe. Quintiles are established according to the variable in the first column of numbers, and the numbers reported are the cross-sectional median value of the stocks within each quintile. The bars on the quintile charts depict the difference between the quintile value and the median value of the quintiles.
Source: Westpeak, based on data from IBES and MSCI Barra.

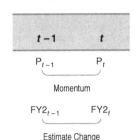

Momentum (Returns) Past Year vs.	Correlation	*t*-Stat
Earnings Estimate Change Past Year	0.52	50.00

Quintile	Momentum Past Year (%)		Earnings Estimate Change Past Year (%)	
1	−36.4		−20.7	
2	−10.7		−3.6	
3	6.9		5.3	
4	26.0		13.2	
5	64.1		26.9	
High-Low Spread	100.5		47.6	

FIGURE 4.4 Relationship between Price Momentum and Change in Analyst Short-Term Expectation for U.S. Small Cap Universe, 1985 through 2008
Note: This figure contains the results of a rank correlation between the previous year returns and the previous year change in earnings estimates for stocks in the universe. The earnings estimates used in the analysis are the IBES FY2 estimates. In the quintile analysis, we sort companies into five groups with an equal number of constituents, covering the entire universe. Quintiles are established according to the variable in the first column of numbers, and the numbers reported are the cross-sectional median value of the stocks within each quintile. The bars on the quintile charts depict the difference between the quintile value and the median value of the quintiles.
Source: Westpeak, based on data from IBES and MSCI Barra.

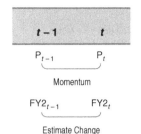

Momentum (Returns) Past Year vs.	Correlation	*t*-Stat
Earnings Estimate Change Past Year	0.42	16.00

Quintile	Momentum Past Year (%)		Earnings Estimate Change Past Year (%)	
1	−24.1		−5.2	
2	−4.2		3.6	
3	8.5		7.6	
4	21.5		11.7	
5	47.0		19.0	
High-Low Spread	71.1		24.2	

FIGURE 4.5 Relationship between Price Momentum and Change in Analyst Short-Term Expectation for U.K. Universe, 1994 through 2008
Note: This figure contains the results of a rank correlation between the previous year returns and the previous year change in earnings estimates for stocks in the universe. The earnings estimates used in the analysis are the IBES FY2 estimates. In the quintile analysis, we sort companies into five groups with an equal number of constituents, covering the entire universe. Quintiles are established according to the variable in the first column of numbers, and the numbers reported are the cross-sectional median value of the stocks within each quintile. The bars on the quintile charts depict the difference between the quintile value and the median value of the quintiles.
Source: Westpeak, based on data from IBES and MSCI Barra.

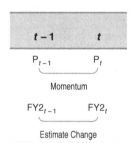

Momentum (Returns) Past Year vs.	Correlation	*t*-Stat
Earnings Estimate Change Past Year	0.44	12.00

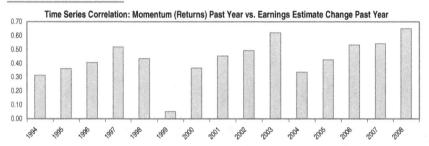

Quintile	Momentum Past Year (%)	Earnings Estimate Change Past Year (%)
1	−25.7	−13.2
2	−5.5	−2.8
3	7.6	3.2
4	21.4	7.2
5	46.9	17.0
High-Low Spread	72.6	30.2

FIGURE 4.6   Relationship between Price Momentum and Change in Analyst Short-Term Expectation for Europe ex-U.K. Universe, 1994 through 2008
Note: This figure contains the results of a rank correlation between the previous year returns and the previous year change in earnings estimates for stocks in the universe. The earnings estimates used in the analysis are the IBES FY2 estimates. In the quintile analysis, we sort companies into five groups with an equal number of constituents, covering the entire universe. Quintiles are established according to the variable in the first column of numbers, and the numbers reported are the cross-sectional median value of the stocks within each quintile. The bars on the quintile charts depict the difference between the quintile value and the median value of the quintiles.
Source: Westpeak, based on data from IBES and MSCI Barra.

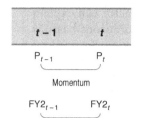

	Momentum (Returns) Past Year vs.	Correlation	*t*-Stat
	Earnings Estimate Change Past Year	0.46	12.55

Quintile	Momentum Past Year (%)	Earnings Estimate Change Past Year (%)
1	−28.4	−18.1
2	−12.4	−5.6
3	−0.7	0.3
4	12.2	8.6
5	37.7	22.3
High-Low Spread	66.1	40.4

FIGURE 4.7 Relationship between Price Momentum and Change in Analyst Short-Term Expectation for Japan Universe, 1996 through 2008

Note: This figure contains the results of a rank correlation between the previous year returns and the previous year change in earnings estimates for stocks in the universe. The earnings estimates used in the analysis are the IBES FY2 estimates. In the quintile analysis, we sort companies into five groups with an equal number of constituents, covering the entire universe. Quintiles are established according to the variable in the first column of numbers, and the numbers reported are the cross-sectional median value of the stocks within each quintile. The bars on the quintile charts depict the difference between the quintile value and the median value of the quintiles.

Source: Westpeak, based on data from IBES and MSCI Barra.

when a price variable is involved. The fact that a single factor can explain such a high degree of price variation, even on a contemporaneous basis, is truly remarkable.

The t-statistic values indicate high statistical significance ranging from 50 in U.S. Small Cap (Figure 4.4) to 12 in Continental Europe (Figure 4.6). The t-statistic value in U.S. Small Cap is noteworthy. U.S. Small Cap has a correlation coefficient similar to U.S. Large Cap and the international markets, but its t-statistic indicates the relatively high stability of the yearly observations. The correlations have a very tight range of 0.40 to 0.65. Contrast this with Continental Europe, where the correlations range from a low of 0.05 in 1999 to a high of 0.65 in 2008. The relatively high stability of the correlation coefficient in U.S. Small Cap may indicate the importance of change in analyst expectation and earnings growth in that segment of the market.

The quintile analyses confirm the strong linear relationship that exists between the two variables. In every market, when quintiles are formed based on a ranking of past one-year price momentum, a clear monotonic (linear) relationship emerges between momentum and expectation change. A number of observations can be made from the quintile results that are not captured by the simple rank correlation coefficient.

First, the quintiles of return indicate the degree of differentiation between the best- and worst-performing stocks on a one-year change basis. For example, in U.S. Small Cap, the top 20 percent of stocks outperform the bottom 20 percent by a staggering 100 percent a year. Clearly, an investment process with even small predictive ability has the potential to generate abnormal returns. This point will be addressed when we visit the section on serial correlation in price momentum. A second observation is how much larger the spread in return and expectations change is for the U.S. Small Cap universe compared to all the large cap universes. The larger spread confirms that small cap stocks have higher volatility and also that the volatility appears to be driven by higher volatility in earnings expectations. We suspect that looking at small cap universes in other regions would yield similar results. Lastly, the Japan quintile analysis is of interest in that it shows expectations dispersion (40.4 percent) that is higher than the other large cap markets. This is interesting because, strangely, the larger spread in expectations does not lead to a larger spread in returns. We will revisit this observation when we investigate the serial correlation of expectation change.

In summary, there is a very strong contemporaneous relationship between price momentum and change in analyst short-term expectation in all markets under review. This implies that price changes are driven by changes in expectation and that investing in high momentum stocks is similar to investing in high current change in expectation stocks.

Change in Analyst Expectation Trends

The relationship studied in this section is depicted in Figure 4.8.

How do analyst short-term earnings expectations behave over time? To answer this question, we investigate the relationship between past one-year change in analyst FY2 estimates and future one-year and two-year changes in analyst FY2 estimates. This type of correlation, in which a variable's own past observations are regressed on future observations, is typically called either auto-correlation or serial correlation.

The results are presented in Figures 4.9 through 4.13. In general, across all markets except Japan, there is a very strong positive serial correlation in FY2 estimate changes one year forward. We characterize this behavior as a trending behavior for ease of comprehension of the concept. The correlations range from a high of 0.23 in the United Kingdom to a low of 0.05 in Japan. Though the correlations have dropped significantly in magnitude from the previous section, we note that we have moved from explaining a contemporaneous relationship to a predictive one. It is interesting to note that the one-year correlation in U.S. Large Cap (0.21) is considerably larger than U.S. Small Cap (0.14). This is unusual since predictive relationships are typically stronger in small cap universes. One explanation for this result may be the lack of sufficient analyst coverage in small cap stocks. Fewer analysts covering a stock may lead to noisier estimates, which, in turn, may lead to lower correlations. By the second year, the correlations have dropped to almost zero, except in the case of Japan.

The Japan universe is particularly interesting. In Japan, contrary to other developed markets, there appears to be a weak serial correlation (0.05) in analyst growth expectations. In the second year, the correlation coefficient

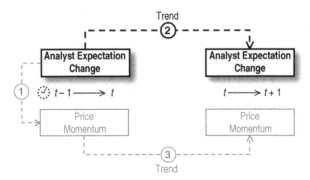

FIGURE 4.8 Relationship between Past and Future Change in Analyst Expectation
Source: Westpeak.

	FY2 Earnings Estimate Change Past Year vs.	Correlation	t-Stat
	Earnings Estimate Change 1 Year Forward	0.21	9.70
	Earnings Estimate Change 2 Years Forward	0.02	1.27

Time Series Correlation: FY2 Earnings Estimate Change Past Year vs. 1-Year Forward Change

Quintile	Earnings Estimate Change Past Year (%)	Earnings Estimate Change 1 Year Forward (%)	Earnings Estimate Change 2 Years Forward (%)
1	−23.3	0.9	6.7
2	−1.1	2.8	5.9
3	8.8	6.5	6.7
4	17.2	11.3	8.8
5	38.9	12.7	8.2
High-Low Spread	62.2	11.8	1.5

FIGURE 4.9 Relationship between Past and Future Change in Analyst Expectation for U.S. Large Cap Universe, 1985 through 2008

Note: This figure contains the results of a rank correlation between the previous year change in earnings estimates and the one- and two-year forward change in earnings estimates for stocks in the universe. The earnings estimates used in the analysis are the IBES FY2 estimates at time $t - 1$, t, $t + 1$, and $t + 2$. In the quintile analysis, we sort companies into five groups with an equal number of constituents, covering the entire universe. Quintiles are established according to the variable in the first column of numbers, and the numbers reported are the cross-sectional median value of the stocks within each quintile. The bars on the quintile charts depict the difference between the quintile value and the median value of the quintiles.

Source: Westpeak, based on data from IBES.

actually turns negative (-0.06), indicating a reversal in earnings growth expectations. This result may be due to the inability of Japanese companies to maintain high relative earnings growth from one year to the next because of the deflationary environment experienced by Japan during this time period.

The time-series graph of correlations in U.S. Large Cap (Figure 4.9) is worth highlighting. The graph indicates that the serial correlation in estimates was high except for a few years, namely 1991, 2000, and 2001. These were periods of recession and times of economic shocks in the United

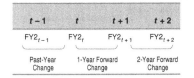

	$t-1$	t	$t+1$	$t+2$
	FY2$_{t-1}$	FY2$_t$	FY2$_{t+1}$	FY2$_{t+2}$
	Past-Year Change	1-Year Forward Change	2-Year Forward Change	

FY2 Earnings Estimate Change Past Year vs.	Correlation	*t*-Stat
Earnings Estimate Change 1 Year Forward	0.14	9.60
Earnings Estimate Change 2 Years Forward	0.00	−0.13

Time Series Correlation: FY2 Earnings Estimate Change Past Year vs. 1-Year Forward Change

Quintile	Earnings Estimate Change Past Year (%)	Earnings Estimate Change 1 Year Forward (%)	Earnings Estimate Change 2 Years Forward (%)
1	−38.7	−1.7	4.4
2	−7.5	0.0	4.4
3	7.3	4.2	5.0
4	22.6	9.7	6.7
5	60.2	11.4	4.6
High-Low Spread	98.9	13.1	0.2

FIGURE 4.10   Relationship between Past and Future Change in Analyst Expectation for U.S. Small Cap Universe, 1985 through 2008
Note: This figure contains the results of a rank correlation between the previous year change in earnings estimates and the one- and two-year forward change in earnings estimates for stocks in the universe. The earnings estimates used in the analysis are the IBES FY2 estimates at time $t-1$, t, $t+1$, and $t+2$. In the quintile analysis, we sort companies into five groups with an equal number of constituents, covering the entire universe. Quintiles are established according to the variable in the first column of numbers, and the numbers reported are the cross-sectional median value of the stocks within each quintile. The bars on the quintile charts depict the difference between the quintile value and the median value of the quintiles.
Source: Westpeak, based on data from IBES.

States, which would have caused a dislocation between past and future earnings growth. This observation, together with the weak correlations in Japan, suggests that the correlation results partially capture a fundamental relationship between prior and future earnings growth and that the results cannot be totally attributed to analyst behavior.

The quintile analysis results presented at the bottom of each figure corroborate the correlation statistics. The quintiles are formed based on a ranking, from low to high, of past one-year change in analyst FY2 estimates. The change in FY2 estimates one year forward and two years forward are

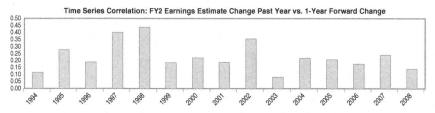

$t-1$	t	$t+1$	$t+2$
$FY2_{t-1}$	$FY2_t$	$FY2_{t+1}$	$FY2_{t+2}$
Past-Year Change	1-Year Forward Change	2-Year Forward Change	

FY2 Earnings Estimate Change Past Year vs.	Correlation	t-Stat
Earnings Estimate Change 1 Year Forward	0.23	8.65
Earnings Estimate Change 2 Years Forward	0.06	1.85

Time Series Correlation: FY2 Earnings Estimate Change Past Year vs. 1-Year Forward Change

Quintile	Earnings Estimate Change Past Year (%)	Earnings Estimate Change 1 Year Forward (%)	Earnings Estimate Change 2 Years Forward (%)
1	−18.1	−1.5	1.3
2	0.2	1.2	2.4
3	9.2	5.0	3.6
4	18.4	9.2	5.1
5	38.1	12.2	5.0
High-Low Spread	56.2	13.7	3.7

FIGURE 4.11 Relationship between Past and Future Change in Analyst Expectation for U.K. Universe, 1994 through 2008

Note: This figure contains the results of a rank correlation between the previous year change in earnings estimates and the one- and two-year forward change in earnings estimates for stocks in the universe. The earnings estimates used in the analysis are the IBES FY2 estimates at time $t-1$, t, $t+1$, and $t+2$. In the quintile analysis, we sort companies into five groups with an equal number of constituents, covering the entire universe. Quintiles are established according to the variable in the first column of numbers, and the numbers reported are the cross-sectional median value of the stocks within each quintile. The bars on the quintile charts depict the difference between the quintile value and the median value of the quintiles.

Source: Westpeak, based on data from IBES.

then reported for each of these quintiles. As the correlation coefficients suggest, there is a clear monotonic relationship between one-year past estimate change and one-year forward estimate change. This is true for all markets except Japan. The linear relationship disappears in the second year for all other markets.

In summary, there is statistically significant evidence that analyst expectations depict a systematic behavior, or average tendency, to trend over a one-year time horizon in all markets, except Japan. To the contrary, in Japan, there is some evidence that change in analyst short-term earnings expectation mean reverts between year one and year two.

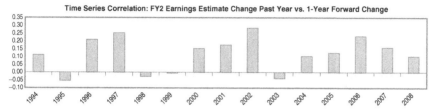

	$t-1$	t	$t+1$	$t+2$
	$FY2_{t-1}$	$FY2_t$	$FY2_{t+1}$	$FY2_{t+2}$
	Past-Year Change	1-Year Forward Change	2-Year Forward Change	

FY2 Earnings Estimate Change Past Year vs.	Correlation	*t*-Stat
Earnings Estimate Change 1 Year Forward	0.12	4.05
Earnings Estimate Change 2 Years Forward	0.01	0.18

Time Series Correlation: FY2 Earnings Estimate Change Past Year vs. 1-Year Forward Change

Quintile	Earnings Estimate Change Past Year (%)	Earnings Estimate Change 1 Year Forward (%)	Earnings Estimate Change 2 Years Forward (%)
1	−25.0	−4.3	0.0
2	−5.9	−0.4	1.5
3	5.0	0.8	2.8
4	17.8	2.5	1.4
5	52.1	5.2	1.2
High-Low Spread	77.1	9.5	1.2

FIGURE 4.12 Relationship between Past and Future Change in Analyst Expectation for Europe ex-U.K. Universe, 1994 through 2008

Note: This figure contains the results of a rank correlation between the previous year change in earnings estimates and the one- and two-year forward change in earnings estimates for stocks in the universe. The earnings estimates used in the analysis are the IBES FY2 estimates at time $t-1$, t, $t+1$, and $t+2$. In the quintile analysis, we sort companies into five groups with an equal number of constituents, covering the entire universe. Quintiles are established according to the variable in the first column of numbers, and the numbers reported are the cross-sectional median value of the stocks within each quintile. The bars on the quintile charts depict the difference between the quintile value and the median value of the quintiles.

Source: Westpeak, based on data from IBES.

Price Momentum Trends

The relationship studied in this section is depicted in Figure 4.14.

In the previous section, we reported a significant positive serial correlation in analyst growth expectation. We used analyst expectations as a proxy for true market expectations. If market expectations, which drive market pricing, behave like analyst expectations, then we should observe a similar positive serial correlation (or trend) in stock returns. We study this relationship by correlating past one-year return (price momentum) with one-year forward and two-year forward price momentum.

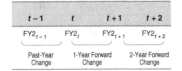

$t-1$	t	$t+1$	$t+2$
$FY2_{t-1}$	$FY2_t$	$FY2_{t+1}$	$FY2_{t+2}$
Past-Year Change	1-Year Forward Change	2-Year Forward Change	

FY2 Earnings Estimate Change Past Year vs.	Correlation	t-Stat
Earnings Estimate Change 1 Year Forward	0.05	1.99
Earnings Estimate Change 2 Years Forward	−0.06	−2.11

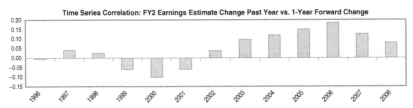

Time Series Correlation: FY2 Earnings Estimate Change Past Year vs. 1-Year Forward Change

Quintile	Earnings Estimate Change Past Year (%)	Earnings Estimate Change 1 Year Forward (%)	Earnings Estimate Change 2 Years Forward (%)
1	−34.6	−0.1	3.2
2	−9.4	−2.6	4.4
3	6.0	1.2	0.8
4	22.4	3.7	0.0
5	68.4	3.7	−2.8
High-Low Spread	103.0	3.8	6.0

FIGURE 4.13 Relationship between Past and Future Change in Analyst Expectation for Japan Universe, 1996 through 2008

Note: This figure contains the results of a rank correlation between the previous year change in earnings estimates and the one- and two-year forward change in earnings estimates for stocks in the universe. The earnings estimates used in the analysis are the IBES FY2 estimates at time $t − 1$, t, $t + 1$, and $t + 2$. In the quintile analysis, we sort companies into five groups with an equal number of constituents, covering the entire universe. Quintiles are established according to the variable in the first column of numbers, and the numbers reported are the cross-sectional median value of the stocks within each quintile. The bars on the quintile charts depict the difference between the quintile value and the median value of the quintiles.

Source: Westpeak, based on data from IBES.

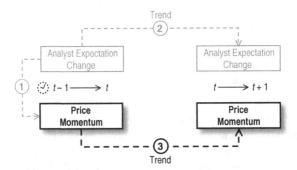

FIGURE 4.14 Relationship between Past and Future Price Momentum
Source: Westpeak.

$t-1$	t	$t+1$	$t+2$
P_{t-1}	P_t	P_{t+1}	P_{t+2}
Momentum Past-Year	Momentum 1 Year Forward	Momentum 2 Years Forward	

Price Momentum Past Year vs.	Correlation	t-Stat
Price Momentum 1 Year Forward	0.06	1.80
Price Momentum 2 Years Forward	−0.01	−0.35

Time Series Correlation: Price Momentum Past Year vs. Price Momentum 1 Year Forward

Quintile	Price Momentum Past Year (%)	Price Momentum 1 Year Forward (%)	Price Momentum 2 Years Forward (%)
1	−21.4	6.3	7.1
2	−1.2	8.7	8.8
3	11.5	9.1	9.6
4	24.7	10.4	7.5
5	48.6	10.7	7.4
High-Low Spread	70.0	4.4	0.3

FIGURE 4.15 Relationship between Past and Future Price Momentum for U.S. Large Cap Universe, 1985 through 2008
Note: This figure contains the correlations of the past one-year price momentum to the one-year and two-year forward price momentum in the universe. Price momentum is the total return from $t-1$ to t, t to $t+1$, and $t+1$ to $t+2$. In the quintile analysis, we sort companies into five groups with an equal number of constituents, covering the entire universe. Quintiles are established according to the variable in the first column of numbers, and the numbers reported are the cross-sectional median value of the stocks within each quintile. The bars on the quintile charts depict the difference between the quintile value and the median value of the quintiles.
Source: Westpeak, based on data from MSCI Barra.

The results are presented in Figures 4.15 through 4.19. The first, most striking observation is the magnitude of the correlations compared to those presented in the previous section. The maximum correlation is seen in Continental Europe and is only 0.10. The magnitude of the correlation, however, is not unusual when correlating a variable with future stock returns. As was noted in the discussion on contemporaneous return correlations, only a small correlation is needed for a predictive signal to be successful. This is a direct consequence of the large spread in return between top- and bottom-performing quintiles over a one-year horizon (for example, about 100 percent in U.S. Small Cap).

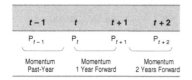

Price Momentum Past Year vs.	Correlation	t-Stat
Price Momentum 1 Year Forward	0.09	3.41
Price Momentum 2 Years Forward	0.03	2.19

Quintile	Price Momentum Past Year (%)	Price Momentum 1 Year Forward (%)	Price Momentum 2 Years Forward (%)
1	−35.4	−6.5	−3.6
2	−9.6	1.5	3.3
3	7.9	5.9	5.6
4	27.0	6.5	4.7
5	65.1	3.0	−1.0
High-Low Spread	100.5	9.5	2.6

FIGURE 4.16 Relationship between Past and Future Price Momentum for U.S. Small Cap Universe, 1985 through 2008
Note: This figure contains the correlations of the past one-year price momentum to the one-year and two-year forward price momentum in the universe. Price momentum is the total return from $t-1$ to t, t to $t+1$, and $t+1$ to $t+2$. In the quintile analysis, we sort companies into five groups with an equal number of constituents, covering the entire universe. Quintiles are established according to the variable in the first column of numbers, and the numbers reported are the cross-sectional median value of the stocks within each quintile. The bars on the quintile charts depict the difference between the quintile value and the median value of the quintiles.
Source: Westpeak, based on data from MSCI Barra.

In correlations with future price return, achieving a 0.10 correlation is quite meaningful. A correlation on the order of only 0.05 is typically necessary for a strategy to be economically significant. Take U.S. Large Cap as an example. The correlation of 0.06 may seem low at first glance, but it represents an economically exploitable relationship. This is confirmed by studying the fractile returns. The spread in one-year forward return between high past momentum companies (Quintile 5) and low past momentum companies (Quintile 1) averaged 4.4 percent a year over the analysis period.

Across all markets, price momentum appears to exhibit behavior similar to analyst expectations. For all markets, except Japan, positive serial correlation exists at the one-year forward horizon. Beyond the first year,

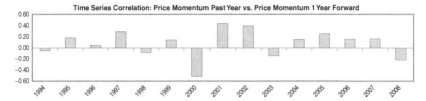

$t-1$	t	$t+1$	$t+2$
P_{t-1}	P_t	P_{t+1}	P_{t+2}

Momentum Past-Year	Momentum 1 Year Forward	Momentum 2 Years Forward

Price Momentum Past Year vs.	Correlation	*t*-Stat
Price Momentum 1 Year Forward	0.08	1.25
Price Momentum 2 Years Forward	0.04	0.97

Time Series Correlation: Price Momentum Past Year vs. Price Momentum 1 Year Forward

Quintile	Price Momentum Past Year (%)	Price Momentum 1 Year Forward (%)	Price Momentum 2 Years Forward (%)
1	−22.5	−0.3	1.0
2	−2.8	4.5	5.5
3	9.9	8.1	6.6
4	22.9	6.5	5.9
5	48.7	7.0	6.3
High-Low Spread	71.2	7.3	5.3

FIGURE 4.17   Relationship between Past and Future Price Momentum for U.K. Universe, 1994 through 2008
Note: This figure contains the correlations of the past one-year price momentum to the one-year and two-year forward price momentum in the universe. Price momentum is the total return from $t-1$ to t, t to $t+1$, and $t+1$ to $t+2$. In the quintile analysis, we sort companies into five groups with an equal number of constituents, covering the entire universe. Quintiles are established according to the variable in the first column of numbers, and the numbers reported are the cross-sectional median value of the stocks within each quintile. The bars on the quintile charts depict the difference between the quintile value and the median value of the quintiles.
Source: Westpeak, based on data from MSCI Barra.

there is little evidence of any influence of past momentum on future returns. In other words, the horizon of momentum as an investment strategy is consistent with the horizon over which short-term earnings trend.

   Japan shows no evidence of serial correlation, whether looking at one-year forward or two-year forward returns. The results, however, are consistent with the serial correlation of analyst expectations. The results provide fresh insight into why momentum, as a strategy, has not worked in Japan over the 1996 through 2008 period. Researchers who advocate behavioral inefficiencies for explaining momentum active returns characterize this finding as puzzling. Our research suggests that the failure of momentum in Japan can be simply explained by the lack of positive serial correlation in the growth of short-term earnings expectations.

$t-1$	t	$t+1$	$t+2$
P_{t-1}	P_t	P_{t+1}	P_{t+2}
Momentum Past-Year	Momentum 1 Year Forward	Momentum 2 Years Forward	

Price Momentum Past Year vs.	Correlation	*t*-Stat
Price Momentum 1 Year Forward	0.10	2.18
Price Momentum 2 Years Forward	0.04	0.84

Time Series Correlation: Price Momentum Past Year vs. Price Momentum 1 Year Forward

Quintile	Price Momentum Past Year (%)	Price Momentum 1 Year Forward (%)	Price Momentum 2 Years Forward (%)
1	−24.1	−0.9	4.7
2	−3.6	5.9	7.2
3	9.7	6.7	7.7
4	23.6	7.3	9.5
5	49.9	10.0	8.0
High-Low Spread	74.0	10.9	3.3

FIGURE 4.18 Relationship between Past and Future Price Momentum Europe ex-U.K. Universe, 1994 through 2008
Note: This figure contains the correlations of the past one-year price momentum to the one-year and two-year forward price momentum in the universe. Price momentum is the total return from $t-1$ to t, t to $t+1$, and $t+1$ to $t+2$. In the quintile analysis, we sort companies into five groups with an equal number of constituents, covering the entire universe. Quintiles are established according to the variable in the first column of numbers, and the numbers reported are the cross-sectional median value of the stocks within each quintile. The bars on the quintile charts depict the difference between the quintile value and the median value of the quintiles.
Source: Westpeak, based on data from MSCI Barra.

In summary, across all markets, price momentum exhibits a behavior that is very similar to analyst expectations. Thus, momentum is a short investment horizon strategy, and the investment horizon is consistent with the horizon over which change in analyst short-term earnings expectation trends.

DECOMPOSING MOMENTUM RETURNS

We have established (1) a strong relationship between momentum and change in expectation and (2) the systematic behavior of change in

t − 1	*t*	*t* + 1	*t* + 2
P_{t-1}	P_t	P_{t+1}	P_{t+2}
Momentum Past-Year	Momentum 1 Year Forward	Momentum 2 Years Forward	

Price Momentum Past Year vs.	Correlation	*t*-Stat
Price Momentum 1 Year Forward	0.00	−0.09
Price Momentum 2 Years Forward	0.00	−0.02

Time Series Correlation: Price Momentum Past Year vs. Price Momentum 1 Year Forward

Quintile	Price Momentum Past Year (%)	Price Momentum 1 Year Forward (%)	Price Momentum 2 Years Forward (%)
1	−27.3	−5.0	−4.7
2	−11.2	−4.3	−2.4
3	0.6	−4.0	−1.5
4	13.7	−4.3	−2.3
5	39.9	−6.9	−4.7
High-Low Spread	67.2	1.9	0.0

FIGURE 4.19 Relationship between Past and Future Price Momentum for Japan Universe, 1996 through 2008

Note: This figure contains the correlations of the past one-year price momentum to the one-year and two-year forward price momentum in the universe. Price momentum is the total return from *t* − 1 to *t*, *t* to *t* + 1, and *t* + 1 to *t* + 2. In the quintile analysis, we sort companies into five groups with an equal number of constituents, covering the entire universe. Quintiles are established according to the variable in the first column of numbers, and the numbers reported are the cross-sectional median value of the stocks within each quintile. The bars on the quintile charts depict the difference between the quintile value and the median value of the quintiles.

Source: Westpeak, based on data from MSCI Barra.

expectation to trend in the short run. These results would suggest that momentum active returns are driven, and explained, partly by the average tendency of change in expectation to trend in the short term. Therefore, referring back to Equation 3.5 and the two drivers of price change, momentum appears to be an investment strategy that captures the systematic portion of the change in expectation component of future price changes.

Using Equation 3.5, we can decompose momentum returns into the change in expectation and change in valuation component to verify that momentum returns are indeed coming from the change in expectation component of future returns.

Figure 4.20 provides a decomposition of momentum returns for the various universes. In this figure, the quintiles are formed on the basis of past 12-month price momentum. Quintile 1 represents the lowest past 12-month price momentum stocks, and Quintile 5 comprises the highest past momentum stocks. Then, the total one-year forward median return of each quintile is decomposed into a return attributed to the change in expectation component and a return attributed to the change in valuation component.

As can be seen from this figure, the future one-year return of the highest past momentum stocks (Quintile 5) is driven primarily by the change in expectation component, implying that these stocks, which are selected on

Momentum$_{(t-1,t)}$ Quintile	Earnings Estimate Change 1 Year Forward (%)	P/E Change 1 Year Forward (%)
U.S. Large Cap		
1	−6	11
2	3	4
3	7	1
4	11	−2
5	16	−6
U.S. Small Cap		
1	−12	12
2	−2	4
3	4	1
4	10	−3
5	17	−10
United Kingdom		
1	−7	6
2	2	−3
3	6	−4
4	8	−4
5	13	−7
Europe ex-UK		
1	−8	5
2	−1	1
3	0	−2
4	5	−5
5	9	−8
Japan		
1	−9	−1
2	−3	−4
3	2	−7
4	3	−10
5	8	−15

FIGURE 4.20 Decomposing Momentum Returns for Various Universes
Source: Westpeak, based on data from IBES and MSCI Barra.

the basis of high past change in expectation, continue to experience high positive change in expectation going forward. These stocks also experience negative contributions from the change in valuation component, but these contractions in valuations are smaller in magnitude than the increases in expectation. Again, the only exception is Japan, where the results are explained by the lack of positive serial correlation, or trend, in change in expectation.

CONCLUSION

The main findings reported in this chapter can be summarized (and generalized) as follows:

- Momentum is contemporaneously linked to change in analyst short-term earnings expectation. This relationship is highly significant in all markets.
- Change in short-term earnings expectation trends in the short run (up to one year). True market expectations embedded in market prices are likely to follow a similar pattern.
- Momentum exhibits a behavior identical to that of change in analyst expectation. That is, it trends in the short run (up to one year). This is why momentum is a short investment horizon strategy.
- The failure of momentum in Japan over the recent past is explained partly by the lack of positive serial correlation in change in short-term expectation.

In summary, momentum active returns appear to be driven, and explained, partly by the average tendency of change in expectation to trend in the short term. Therefore, momentum is an investment strategy that provides an effective capture of the systematic portion of the change in expectation component of future price changes.

APPENDIX: REGRESSION ANALYSIS AND CORRELATION COEFFICIENT

The goal of regression analysis is to determine how well the changes in one variable, known as the dependent variable, can be explained by changes in one or more other variables, typically called the independent variables. When there is only one independent variable, this is called a univariate regression. When there are multiple independent variables, it is appropriately called a multiple regression. Both approaches are used in this book. The most frequently used regression technique is the linear regression. As its name suggests, the basic assumption of the linear regression is that the relationship between the dependent and independent variables is linear.

When we perform a linear regression, a number of statistics help us understand the relationship, such as the R-squared and beta coefficient. The R-squared statistic indicates how well changes in the dependent variable are explained by changes in the independent variables. The R-squared values range from 0 to 1. A beta coefficient is reported for each independent variable, and it indicates how much the dependent variable changes when the independent variable changes by one unit.

The linear regression works well when a linear relationship exists. Since the properties of linear regression are well understood, it is typical to transform variables suspected of having a nonlinear relationship, and then run a linear regression. One such transformation is ordinal ranking, which we employ extensively in our research.

Conveniently, the beta coefficient reported in a univariate regression (of ranked variables) is identical to a more commonly recognized statistic, known as the Spearman rank correlation coefficient. This statistic is also used extensively throughout the book.

An advantage of understanding the rank correlation coefficient from a regression viewpoint occurs when we move from a univariate to multiple regression framework. The beta coefficients reported from a multiple regression of ranked variables can be conveniently compared to the rank correlation coefficients from prior univariate analyses.

CHAPTER 5

Behavior of Long-Term Earnings Expectation and the Link with Value

In this chapter, we focus on the behavior of analyst long-term earnings expectation for the next one-, three-, and five-year time frames, and further investigate their link with value. We demonstrate that analyst long-term earnings expectations depict a negative serial correlation, or an average tendency to mean revert, in the long run. Since valuation ratios are a proxy for growth prospects, they too depict an average tendency to mean revert in the long run. The purpose of this chapter is not to investigate the reasons for the mean-reverting behavior of long-term earnings estimates and valuations, but rather to document their existence in a comprehensive manner in the various global equity market universes. In Chapter 6, we offer an explanation for the systematic behavior of long-term earnings and discuss why such behavior is not fully incorporated in current expectations and prices.

RELATIONSHIPS STUDIED

The three relationships explored in this chapter are graphically represented in Figure 5.1. These are:

1. The relationship between current valuation and analyst long-term growth expectation.
2. The relationship between current level of analyst long-term growth expectation and future change in that growth expectation.
3. The relationship between current valuation level and future changes in valuation.

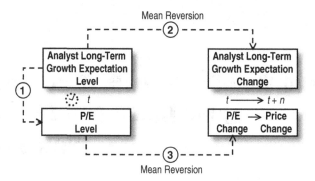

FIGURE 5.1   Relationships Studied
Source: Westpeak.

To analyze and document these various relationships, we employ the same market universes, time periods, and types of analysis introduced and discussed in Chapter 4.

Objective: Forecasting Change in Valuation

To provide a context for the motivation for studying these various relationships, we briefly revisit the basic concepts that Chapter 3 establishes. As we discuss in that chapter, price change is driven by change in expectation and change in valuation. In Chapter 4, we document the strong contemporaneous influence of change in expectation on change in price. We now move on to the connection between change in valuation and change in price.

Figures 5.2 through 5.6 detail the contemporaneous relationship that exists between change in valuation (price-earnings [P/E] ratio) and change in price. To calculate the P/E ratios, we use the IBES FY2 estimates.

As one would expect, there is a strong relationship in all markets, since price changes over a given horizon are driven by valuation changes, or vice versa. The average rank correlation coefficients range from a high of 0.56 for the United Kingdom to a low of 0.28 for Japan. All correlation coefficients are highly significant, and, as depicted by the bar graphs, the relationship is stable over time, except for Japan, where two years, 1996 and 2005, experienced a fall in the significance of this relationship.

In the quintile analysis, we attempt to verify the nature of this relationship, particularly its linearity. The quintile analyses show that change in valuation and change in price have a direct and linear relationship across quintiles in all markets. That is, in each market, the stocks with the lowest price change over the past year have the lowest, or most negative, change in

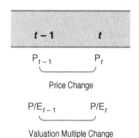

$t-1$	t
P_{t-1}	P_t

Price Change

P/E_{t-1}	P/E_t

Valuation Multiple Change

Price Change (Returns) Past Year vs.	Correlation	*t*-Stat
P/E Change Past Year	0.43	10.37

Time Series Correlation: Price Change (Returns) Past Year vs. P/E Change Past Year

Quintile	Price Change Past Year (%)		P/E Change Past Year (%)	
1	−22.9		−13.8	
2	−2.6		−6.3	
3	10.2		0.1	
4	23.7		6.8	
5	49.0		16.8	
High-Low Spread	71.9		30.6	

FIGURE 5.2 Relationship between Price Change and Change in Valuation for U.S. Large Cap Universe, 1985 through 2008

Note: This figure contains the rank correlations between the previous year price change and the previous year change in P/E for the universe. Price change is the total return from $t-1$ to t. In the quintile analysis, we sort companies into five groups with an equal number of constituents, covering the entire universe. Quintiles are established according to the variable in the first column of numbers, and the numbers reported are the cross-sectional median value of the stocks within each quintile. The bars on the quintile charts depict the difference between the quintile value and the median value of the quintiles.

Source: Westpeak, based on data from MSCI Barra.

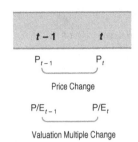

Price Change (Returns) Past Year vs.	Correlation	*t*-Stat
P/E Change Past Year	0.44	21.13

Quintile	Price Change Past Year (%)		P/E Change Past Year (%)	
1	−36.4		−24.0	
2	−10.7		−9.3	
3	6.9		−1.3	
4	26.0		7.6	
5	64.1		22.1	
High-Low Spread	100.5		46.1	

FIGURE 5.3 Relationship between Price Change and Change in Valuation for U.S. Small Cap Universe, 1985 through 2008
Note: This figure contains the rank correlations between the previous year price change and the previous year change in P/E for the universe. Price change is the total return from $t - 1$ to t. In the quintile analysis, we sort companies into five groups with an equal number of constituents, covering the entire universe. Quintiles are established according to the variable in the first column of numbers, and the numbers reported are the cross-sectional median value of the stocks within each quintile. The bars on the quintile charts depict the difference between the quintile value and the median value of the quintiles.
Source: Westpeak, based on data from MSCI Barra.

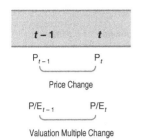

		Price Change (Returns) Past Year vs.	Correlation	*t*-Stat
t − 1	*t*			
P$_{t-1}$	P$_t$	P/E Change Past Year	0.56	14.93
____Price Change____				
P/E$_{t-1}$	P/E$_t$			
__Valuation Multiple Change__				

Quintile	Price Change Past Year (%)		P/E Change Past Year (%)	
1	−24.1		−19.7	
2	−4.2		−10.2	
3	8.5		−2.2	
4	21.5		5.4	
5	47.0		18.3	
High-Low Spread	71.1		38.0	

FIGURE 5.4 Relationship between Price Change and Change in Valuation for U.K. Universe, 1994 through 2008

Note: This figure contains the rank correlations between the previous year price change and the previous year change in P/E for the universe. Price change is the total return from *t* − 1 to *t*. In the quintile analysis, we sort companies into five groups with an equal number of constituents, covering the entire universe. Quintiles are established according to the variable in the first column of numbers, and the numbers reported are the cross-sectional median value of the stocks within each quintile. The bars on the quintile charts depict the difference between the quintile value and the median value of the quintiles.

Source: Westpeak, based on data from MSCI Barra.

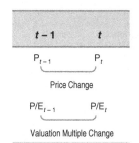

Price Change (Returns) Past Year vs.	Correlation	*t*-Stat
P/E Change Past Year	0.47	11.01

Quintile	Price Change Past Year (%)		P/E Change Past Year (%)	
1	−25.7		−18.2	
2	−5.5		−9.6	
3	7.6		−3.7	
4	21.4		3.2	
5	46.9		15.7	
High-Low Spread	72.6		33.9	

FIGURE 5.5   Relationship between Price Change and Change in Valuation for Europe ex-U.K. Universe, 1994 through 2008

Note: This figure contains the rank correlations between the previous year price change and the previous year change in P/E for the universe. Price change is the total return from $t - 1$ to t. In the quintile analysis, we sort companies into five groups with an equal number of constituents, covering the entire universe. Quintiles are established according to the variable in the first column of numbers, and the numbers reported are the cross-sectional median value of the stocks within each quintile. The bars on the quintile charts depict the difference between the quintile value and the median value of the quintiles.

Source: Westpeak, based on data from MSCI Barra.

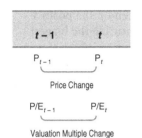

Price Change (Returns) Past Year vs.	Correlation	t-Stat
P/E Change Past Year	0.28	8.52

Quintile	Price Change Past Year (%)		P/E Change Past Year (%)	
1	−28.4		−20.1	
2	−12.4		−12.9	
3	−0.7		−5.0	
4	12.2		−0.9	
5	37.7		7.4	
High-Low Spread	66.1		27.5	

FIGURE 5.6 Relationship between Price Change and Change in Valuation for Japan Universe, 1996 through 2008

Note: This figure contains the rank correlations between the previous year price change and the previous year change in P/E for the universe. Price change is the total return from $t - 1$ to t. In the quintile analysis, we sort companies into five groups with an equal number of constituents, covering the entire universe. Quintiles are established according to the variable in the first column of numbers, and the numbers reported are the cross-sectional median value of the stocks within each quintile. The bars on the quintile charts depict the difference between the quintile value and the median value of the quintiles.

Source: Westpeak, based on data from MSCI Barra.

valuation over the same period. This connection is also seen on the positive side, with the best-returning stock quintile, Quintile 5, featuring the biggest gains in valuation.

If change in valuation is an important and stable component of price change, then forecasting changes in valuation might also lead to an ability to predict and capture future price changes. So, is it possible to forecast future changes in valuation? To answer this question, we have to start by identifying the factors that might influence valuations at a given point in time.

Value Represents Growth Expectation and Anticipated Risk

The simple constant-growth earnings discount model, introduced in Chapter 3, highlights that value is a function of the market estimate of the discount rate, k, and the consensus long-term expected growth rate of earnings, as shown:

$$E/P = (k - g) \qquad (5.1)$$

The discount rate, k, the required return on a security, given its anticipated risk, can be further decomposed as follows:

$$k = Rf + MRP + SRP \qquad (5.2)$$

where: Rf = Risk-free rate of return
   MRP = Market risk premium (the traditional equity risk premium)
   SRP = Stock risk premium, the excess return over MRP required to compensate for stock-specific risk

Substituting Equation 5.2 in Equation 5.1 yields the following:

$$E/P = (Rf + MRP + SRP) - g \qquad (5.3)$$

The Rf and MRP components in Equation 5.3 are common across all stocks in a given universe and, hence, can be ignored in a cross-sectional analysis. With this adjustment, Equation 5.3 provides a simple, but useful, insight. The level of consensus long-term growth expectation and stock-specific risk influence the level of the E/P ratio. More specifically, value represents the long-term (steady-state earnings) growth-adjusted stock risk premium, that is:

$$E/P = SRP - g \qquad (5.4)$$

and

$$\Delta(E/P) \approx \Delta(SRP - g) \qquad (5.5)$$

Therefore, one way of forecasting future changes in valuation would be to study the behavior of consensus long-term growth expectation, g, and stock-specific risk, SRP, over time. If these two variables depict a predictable behavior over time, then they could be used to forecast future valuation changes. However, a problem again presents itself. Neither the consensus long-term steady-state earnings growth expectation nor the stock-specific risk premium is directly observable in the marketplace. So, what observable factors might influence the level of a valuation ratio, and might explain its behavior over time?

In the remainder of this chapter, we explore the relationship of value with observable growth expectation and risk factors, and study the systematic behavior of both growth expectation and value over time.

Value Reflects Long-Term Growth Expectations

The relationship reviewed in this section is depicted in Figure 5.7.

Since true market expectations are unknown, we use analyst long-term expected growth estimates provided by IBES as a proxy for market

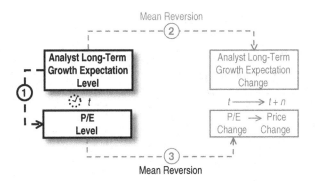

FIGURE 5.7 Relationship between Value and Long-Term Growth Expectations
Source: Westpeak.

expectations of long-term growth. Further, we consider commonly used risk factors, such as leverage, earnings variability, and volatility of returns, as a proxy for stock-specific risk.

As theory would suggest, and practitioners commonly know, we do find a strong relationship between valuation ratios and growth prospects, and valuation ratios and stock-specific risk. This relationship has already been documented in Figure 3.3, which analyzes the relationship between the current level of the P/E ratio and IBES long-term growth estimates, and the current level of the P/E ratio and the three risk factors, for the U.S. Large Cap universe. The univariate correlation analysis in this table showed that these factors independently have an influence on the level of the P/E ratio, with the strongest influence coming from the analyst long-term growth expectation. The multiple regression analysis, on the other hand, showed that long-term growth is a more powerful and stable influence on valuation than the three risk factors studied, namely leverage, earnings variability, and volatility of returns.

The main conclusion from Figure 3.3 is that valuation ratios are a proxy for current estimates of long-term growth prospects. That is, low P/E companies have low long-term growth expectation, and vice versa. Thus, cross-sectional differences in valuation ratios across stocks are explained primarily by cross-sectional differences in long-term growth prospects.

Analyst Long-Term Growth Expectation Mean Reverts

The relationship studied in this section is depicted in Figure 5.8.

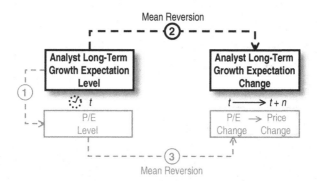

FIGURE 5.8 Relationship between Current Analyst Long-Term Growth Expectation and Future Changes in Analyst Long-Term Growth Expectation
Source: Westpeak.

To study the behavior of long-term earnings expectations, we again employ the IBES long-term analyst projections* as a proxy for true market expectations. The relationship investigated is the correlation between the current level of analyst long-term growth expectation and future percentage changes in that growth expectation. Figures 5.9 through 5.13 analyze this relationship.

Estimated Long-Term Growth Current vs.	Correlation	t - Stat
Estimated Long-Term Growth 1-Year Change	−0.24	−13.38
Estimated Long-Term Growth 3-Year Change	−0.38	−23.90
Estimated Long-Term Growth 5-Year Change	−0.45	−39.08

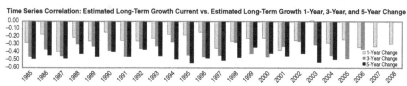

Time Series Correlation: Estimated Long-Term Growth Current vs. Estimated Long-Term Growth 1-Year, 3-Year, and 5-Year Change

Quintile	Estimated Long-Term Growth Current (%)	Estimated Long-Term Growth 1-Year Change (%)	Estimated Long-Term Growth 3-Year Change (%)	Estimated Long-Term Growth 5-Year Change (%)
1	7.0	2.3	9.8	15.0
2	10.1	−0.5	0.6	1.7
3	11.9	−1.9	−4.1	−5.5
4	14.0	−3.3	−7.5	−9.8
5	18.7	−7.3	−17.7	−23.2
High-Low Spread	11.7	9.6	27.5	38.2

FIGURE 5.9   Relationship between Current Analyst Long-Term Growth Expectation and Future Changes in Analyst Long-Term Growth Expectation for the U.S. Large Cap Universe, 1985 through 2008
Note: This figure contains the correlations between the current level of long-term expected growth and the one-year, three-year, and five-year forward change in estimated long-term growth for the universe. The long-term earnings estimates used in the analysis is the IBES Long-Term Forecast. In the quintile analysis, we sort companies into five groups with an equal number of constituents, covering the entire universe. Quintiles are established according to the variable in the first column of numbers, and the numbers reported are the cross-sectional median value of the stocks within each quintile. The bars on the quintile charts depict the difference between the quintile value and the median value of the quintiles.
Source: Westpeak, based on data from IBES.

---

*IBES Terms and Conventions states that "Long-Term Growth Forecasts are received directly from contributing analysts, they are not calculated by IBES. While different analysts apply different methodologies, the Long-Term Growth Forecast generally represents an expected annual increase in operating earnings over the company's next full business cycle. In general, these forecasts refer to a period between three to five years. Due to the variance in methodologies for Long-Term Growth calculations, IBES uses the median value for Long-Term Growth Forecast as opposed to mean value. The median value is less affected by outlier forecasts."

t	$t+1$	$t+3$	$t+5$
G_t			
G_t	G_{t+1}	G_{t+3}	G_{t+5}

1-Year Change

3-Year Change

5-Year Change

Estimated Long-Term Growth Current vs.	Correlation	t-Stat
Estimated Long-Term Growth 1-Year Change	−0.28	−28.05
Estimated Long-Term Growth 3-Year Change	−0.43	−42.05
Estimated Long-Term Growth 5-Year Change	−0.49	−53.59

Time Series Correlation: Estimated Long-Term Growth Current vs. Estimated Long-Term Growth 1-Year, 3-Year, and 5-Year Change

Quintile	Estimated Long-Term Growth Current (%)	Estimated Long-Term Growth 1-Year Change (%)	Estimated Long-Term Growth 3-Year Change (%)	Estimated Long-Term Growth 5-Year Change (%)
1	7.9	0.2	4.6	13.6
2	12.2	−0.1	−1.4	−0.6
3	16.0	−1.2	−6.7	−9.4
4	21.1	−4.4	−14.7	−19.5
5	31.6	−10.0	−28.2	−35.1
High-Low Spread	23.6	10.2	32.8	48.7

FIGURE 5.10   Relationship between Current Analyst Long-Term Growth Expectation and Future Changes in Analyst Long-Term Growth Expectation for U.S. Small Cap Universe, 1985 through 2008
Note: This figure contains the correlations between the current level of long-term expected growth and the one-year, three-year, and five-year forward change in estimated long-term growth for the universe. The long-term earnings estimates used in the analysis is the IBES Long-Term Forecast. In the quintile analysis, we sort companies into five groups with an equal number of constituents, covering the entire universe. Quintiles are established according to the variable in the first column of numbers, and the numbers reported are the cross-sectional median value of the stocks within each quintile. The bars on the quintile charts depict the difference between the quintile value and the median value of the quintiles.
Source: Westpeak, based on data from IBES.

Results for the U.S. Large Cap universe provide a clear example of this relationship. As illustrated in Figure 5.9, the current level of analyst long-term growth expectation has a highly significant negative correlation of −0.24, −0.38, and −0.45 with one-year forward, three-year forward, and five-year forward change in analyst long-term growth expectation, respectively. For ease of comprehension, we characterize this behavior as mean reversion. The data indicates that an increasing degree of mean reversion occurs the further we look into the future. The declining rate of increase in the correlation coefficient, however, also suggests that the bulk of the mean reversion takes place within a three- to five-year period.

The average correlation figures for the other universes studied produce very similar patterns of behavior. The correlations with one-year forward

t	t + 1	t + 3	t + 5
G_t			
G_t	G_{t+1}	G_{t+3}	G_{t+5}

1-Year Change
3-Year Change
5-Year Change

Estimated Long-Term Growth Current vs.	Correlation	t-Stat
Estimated Long-Term Growth 1-Year Change	−0.26	−8.99
Estimated Long-Term Growth 3-Year Change	−0.41	−24.78
Estimated Long-Term Growth 5-Year Change	−0.47	−35.77

Time Series Correlation: Estimated Long-Term Growth Current vs. Estimated Long-Term Growth 5-Year Change

Quintile	Estimated Long-Term Growth Current (%)	Estimated Long-Term Growth 1-Year Change (%)	Estimated Long-Term Growth 3-Year Change (%)	Estimated Long-Term Growth 5-Year Change (%)
1	7.0	0.5	23.3	46.8
2	10.2	0.0	−0.9	−2.4
3	12.0	−0.6	−11.0	−14.5
4	14.1	−2.7	−16.0	−26.4
5	18.7	−7.4	−36.6	−52.7
High-Low Spread	11.7	7.9	59.9	99.5

FIGURE 5.11 Relationship between Current Analyst Long-Term Growth Expectation and Future Changes in Analyst Long-Term Growth Expectation for U.K. Universe, 1994 through 2008
Note: This figure contains the correlations between the current level of long-term expected growth and the one-year, three-year, and five-year forward change in estimated long-term growth for the universe. The long-term earnings estimates used in the analysis is the IBES Long-Term Forecast. In the quintile analysis, we sort companies into five groups with an equal number of constituents, covering the entire universe. Quintiles are established according to the variable in the first column of numbers, and the numbers reported are the cross-sectional median value of the stocks within each quintile. The bars on the quintile charts depict the difference between the quintile value and the median value of the quintiles.
Source: Westpeak, based on data from IBES.

change in analyst long-term growth expectation vary between −0.22 and −0.29. For five-year forward change, the correlation range is −0.45 to −0.51. This consistency of correlation across the various regions of the world, as well as between size categories in the United States, emphasizes the strong connection between the current level of analyst long-term growth expectation and future changes in this growth expectation.

The bar graphs in Figures 5.9 through 5.13 further highlight the strong and stable nature of this relationship. Across the five universes studied, the correlation between current level of analyst growth expectation and future change in growth expectation is negative in each and every year of the time period. This negative correlation holds whether we consider one-year, three-year, or five-year forward changes in analyst long-term expected growth.

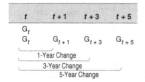

t	$t+1$	$t+3$	$t+5$
G_t			
G_t	G_{t+1}	G_{t+3}	G_{t+5}

1-Year Change
3-Year Change
5-Year Change

Estimated Long-Term Growth Current vs.	Correlation	t-Stat
Estimated Long-Term Growth 1-Year Change	−0.29	−15.78
Estimated Long-Term Growth 3-Year Change	−0.43	−21.89
Estimated Long-Term Growth 5-Year Change	−0.51	−25.40

Time Series Correlation: Estimated Long-Term Growth Current vs. Estimated Long-Term Growth 5-Year Change

[Bar chart, years 1994 through 2008, values ranging from 0.00 to −0.70. Legend: 1-Year Change, 3-Year Change, 5-Year Change]

Quintile	Estimated Long-Term Growth Current (%)	Estimated Long-Term Growth 1-Year Change (%)	Estimated Long-Term Growth 3-Year Change (%)	Estimated Long-Term Growth 5-Year Change (%)
1	3.9	2.7	19.0	48.2
2	7.5	1.4	3.5	5.8
3	10.3	−2.7	−7.9	−13.8
4	13.6	−5.3	−21.2	−28.7
5	21.3	−11.9	−37.2	−49.0
High-Low Spread	17.3	14.6	56.2	97.2

FIGURE 5.12 Relationship between Current Analyst Long-Term Growth Expectation and Future Changes in Analyst Long-Term Growth Expectation for Europe ex-U.K. Universe, 1994 through 2008
Note: This figure contains the correlations between the current level of long-term expected growth and the one-year, three-year, and five-year forward change in estimated long-term growth for the universe. The long-term earnings estimates used in the analysis is the IBES Long-Term Forecast. In the quintile analysis, we sort companies into five groups with an equal number of constituents, covering the entire universe. Quintiles are established according to the variable in the first column of numbers, and the numbers reported are the cross-sectional median value of the stocks within each quintile. The bars on the quintile charts depict the difference between the quintile value and the median value of the quintiles.
Source: Westpeak, based on data from IBES.

While magnitudes may vary from year to year, the directional reliability of the relationship indicates its power.

Moving on to the quintile analysis, we again consider the nature of the relationship between current analyst long-term growth expectation and future changes. The quintiles appearing in the first column are formed based on a ranking, from low to high, of the current analyst long-term growth expectation. The other three columns show the median percentage change in long-term expected growth experienced by each quintile over time.

Through quintile analysis, another consistent pattern emerges across the regional universes. This analysis shows that companies with low (high) current analyst long-term growth expectation, that is, Quintile 1 (Quintile 5)

t	$t + 1$	$t + 3$	$t + 5$
G_t			
G_t	G_{t+1}	G_{t+3}	G_{t+5}

1-Year Change
3-Year Change
5-Year Change

Estimated Long-Term Growth Current vs.	Correlation	*t*-Stat
Estimated Long-Term Growth 1-Year Change	−0.22	−5.72
Estimated Long-Term Growth 3-Year Change	−0.38	−8.15
Estimated Long-Term Growth 5-Year Change	−0.49	−10.38

Time Series Correlation: Estimated Long-Term Growth Current vs. Estimated Long-Term Growth 1 Year, 3 Year, and 5 Year Change

Quintile	Estimated Long-Term Growth Current (%)	Estimated Long-Term Growth 1-Year Change (%)	Estimated Long-Term Growth 3-Year Change (%)	Estimated Long-Term Growth 5-Year Change (%)
1	−0.3	4.9	20.8	71.6
2	5.2	0.8	18.1	50.9
3	9.1	0.0	2.6	7.9
4	14.1	−2.0	−9.9	−12.6
5	27.9	−5.7	−21.1	−45.8
High-Low Spread	28.2	10.6	41.9	117.4

FIGURE 5.13 Relationship between Current Analyst Long-Term Growth Expectation and Future Changes in Analyst Long-Term Growth Expectation for Japan Universe, 1996 through 2008
Note: This figure contains the correlations between the current level of long-term expected growth and the one-year, three-year, and five-year forward change in estimated long-term growth for the universe. The long-term earnings estimates used in the analysis is the IBES Long-Term Forecast. In the quintile analysis, we sort companies into five groups with an equal number of constituents, covering the entire universe. Quintiles are established according to the variable in the first column of numbers, and the numbers reported are the cross-sectional median value of the stocks within each quintile. The bars on the quintile charts depict the difference between the quintile value and the median value of the quintiles.
Source: Westpeak, based on data from IBES.

companies, tend to experience positive (negative) changes in their long-term growth forecasts over the next year, three years, and five years. This relationship is linear across quintiles for the three forward periods and provides further evidence of mean reversion in long-term expected growth estimates.

The quintile analyses suggest that the mean reversion of long-term expectations happens in two stages. First, the one-year mean reversion is generally muted, with the effect most significant in stocks that had the highest expected long-term growth (Quintile 5) at the start of the period. Then, in the three-year and five-year cases, the mean reversion spreads across the entire universe and depicts an even more linear profile across all the quintiles.

In summary, we see clear evidence of mean reversion in analyst long-term growth expectation in all markets.

Value Mean Reverts

The relationship studied in this section is depicted in Figure 5.14.

Does current value predict future changes in valuation, and, if so, how far into the future? To answer this question, we study the relationship between the current level of valuation (P/E ratio) and one-year, three-year, and five-year forward change in valuation (change in the P/E ratio).

Figures 5.15 through 5.19 show a strong tendency for P/E ratios to mean revert in all markets. This behavior of P/E ratios is highlighted by significant, highly-negative average rank correlation coefficients in all markets. As with analyst long-term growth expectation, the bulk of the mean reversion occurs within three to five years. These relationships are remarkably consistent across the various universes. For example, the correlation coefficient between current valuation and three-year change in valuation ranges from −0.35 for the U.K. universe to −0.44 for the Europe ex-U.K. universe.

As with analyst long-term expected growth, the relationship between current P/E ratio and future change in P/E ratio is remarkably consistent across time. We again note that correlations using one-year, three-year, and five-year forward changes remain reliably negative at each point in time, although the magnitude does vary to some degree. This effect is stable across the universes studied, supporting the premise that P/E ratios systematically mean revert.

The quintile analyses confirm the strength of the relationship, as well as its linear nature. Also consistent in all the universes, low P/E stocks see their

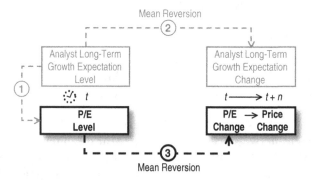

FIGURE 5.14 Relationship between Current Level of Valuation and Future Changes in Valuation
Source: Westpeak.

				P/E Current vs.	Correlation	t-Stat
t	$t+1$	$t+3$	$t+5$			
P/E_t P/E_t	P/E_{t+1}	P/E_{t+3}	P/E_{t+5}	P/E 1-Year Change	−0.27	−9.50
				P/E 3-Year Change	−0.40	−12.00
1-Year Change				P/E 5-Year Change	−0.44	−12.60
3-Year Change						
5-Year Change						

Time Series Correlation: P/E Current vs. P/E 1-Year, 3-Year, and 5-Year Change

□ 1-Year Change ■ 3-Year Change ■ 5-Year Change

Quintile	P/E Current (%)	P/E 1-Year Change (%)	P/E 3-Year Change (%)	P/E 5-Year Change (%)
1	10.0	10.0	21.4	27.9
2	13.0	3.8	6.7	11.9
3	15.7	−0.1	1.6	5.5
4	19.0	−2.2	−4.9	−4.0
5	26.0	−10.4	−19.6	−20.4
High-Low Spread	15.9	20.4	41.0	48.3

FIGURE 5.15 Relationship between Current Level of Valuation and Future Changes in Valuation for U.S. Large Cap Universe, 1985 through 2008
Note: This figure contains the correlations between the current P/E ratio and the one-year, three-year, and five-year forward P/E ratio in the universe. One-year, three-year, and five-year earnings estimates are the IBES FY2 earnings estimates and are calculated from t to $t+1$, t to $t+3$, and t to $t+5$, respectively. In the quintile analysis, we sort companies into five groups with an equal number of constituents, covering the entire universe. Quintiles are established according to the variable in the first column of numbers, and the numbers reported are the cross-sectional median value of the stocks within each quintile. The bars on the quintile charts depict the difference between the quintile value and the median value of the quintiles.
Source: Westpeak, based on data from MSCI Barra.

valuation ratios expand on average over time. Meanwhile, high P/E stocks witness a contraction in their ratios, as mean reversion takes effect.

The mean reversion increases over time, as confirmed by the spreads between the low P/E (Quintile 1) stocks and the high P/E (Quintile 5) stocks. Using the U.S. Large Cap universe to demonstrate (Figure 5.15), low P/E stocks experience a 10.0 percent expansion in P/E in the first year, compared to a −10.4 percent contraction for the high P/E stocks. By the fifth year, however, this 20.4 percent difference between low and high P/E stocks jumps to a 48.3 percent spread, or 27.9 percent versus −20.4 percent. The compounding of the mean reversion effect is found consistently in each of our universes.

To summarize, in all markets, we see clear evidence of mean reversion in valuation ratios.

t	$t+1$	$t+3$	$t+5$
P/E_t			
P/E_t	P/E_{t+1}	P/E_{t+3}	P/E_{t+5}

1-Year Change
3-Year Change
5-Year Change

P/E Current vs.	Correlation	t - Stat
P/E 1-Year Change	−0.32	−12.80
P/E 3-Year Change	−0.43	−20.00
P/E 5-Year Change	−0.47	−21.60

Time Series Correlation: P/E Current vs. P/E 1-Year, 3-Year, and 5-Year Change

Quintile	P/E Current (%)	P/E 1-Year Change (%)	P/E 3-Year Change (%)	P/E 5-Year Change (%)
1	9.5	12.8	27.5	41.4
2	12.5	4.7	11.2	18.5
3	15.2	−0.9	0.9	5.0
4	19.1	−6.4	−8.9	−8.0
5	29.0	−19.3	−27.4	−29.0
High-Low Spread	19.5	32.1	54.9	70.4

FIGURE 5.16 Relationship between Current Level of Valuation and Future Changes in Valuation for U.S. Small Cap Universe, 1985 through 2008
Note: This figure contains the correlations between the current P/E ratio and the one-year, three-year, and five-year forward P/E ratio in the universe. One-year, three-year, and five-year earnings estimates are the IBES FY2 earnings estimates and are calculated from t to $t+1$, t to $t+3$, and t to $t+5$, respectively. In the quintile analysis, we sort companies into five groups with an equal number of constituents, covering the entire universe. Quintiles are established according to the variable in the first column of numbers, and the numbers reported are the cross-sectional median value of the stocks within each quintile. The bars on the quintile charts depict the difference between the quintile value and the median value of the quintiles.
Source: Westpeak, based on data from MSCI Barra.

INVESTMENT HORIZON OF VALUE STRATEGIES

As previously shown, change in valuation is an important component of price change. If, as suggested earlier, current value predicts change in valuation, then current value should also predict future change in price.

Does current value predict future change in price, and, if so, how far into the future? Figures 5.20 to 5.24 answer these questions by analyzing the relationship between current level of valuation (P/E ratio) and one-year, three-year, and five-year forward price change.

Across the various universes, the correlations between the current level of P/E ratio and forward price returns are consistently negative. This result is similar to the relationship between current P/E and forward change in P/E.

t	t + 1	t + 3	t + 5
P/E_t			
P/E_t	P/E_{t + 1}	P/E_{t + 3}	P/E_{t + 5}
1-Year Change			
3-Year Change			
5-Year Change			

P/E Current vs.	Correlation	t-Stat
P/E 1-Year Change	−0.26	−5.40
P/E 3-Year Change	−0.35	−6.86
P/E 5-Year Change	−0.44	−7.40

Time Series Correlation: P/E Current vs. P/E 1-Year, 3-Year, and 5-Year Change

Quintile	P/E Current (%)	P/E 1-Year Change (%)	P/E 3-Year Change (%)	P/E 5-Year Change (%)
1	9.5	7.0	17.4	23.2
2	12.7	−0.8	1.5	2.8
3	15.1	−4.3	−8.3	−10.1
4	18.2	−6.8	−11.5	−19.6
5	25.1	−13.3	−23.8	−31.5
High-Low Spread	15.7	20.3	41.2	54.7

FIGURE 5.17 Relationship between Current Level of Valuation and Future Changes in Valuation for U.K. Universe, 1994 through 2008

Note: This figure contains the correlations between the current P/E ratio and the one-year, three-year, and five-year forward P/E ratio in the universe. One-year, three-year, and five-year earnings estimates are the IBES FY2 earnings estimates and are calculated from t to $t + 1$, t to $t + 3$, and t to $t + 5$, respectively. In the quintile analysis, we sort companies into five groups with an equal number of constituents, covering the entire universe. Quintiles are established according to the variable in the first column of numbers, and the numbers reported are the cross-sectional median value of the stocks within each quintile. The bars on the quintile charts depict the difference between the quintile value and the median value of the quintiles.

Source: Westpeak, based on data from MSCI Barra.

However, and as expected, the connection between P/E and price change is less in magnitude. While these correlation coefficients may appear low, they represent economically exploitable relationships when considered in the context of predicting future returns.

The average correlation coefficients become stronger, and more significant, as the horizon is lengthened. The correlation range is −0.03 to −0.09 when considering one-year forward price change, and it increases significantly to −0.08 to −0.19 in the five-year time frame. The enhanced connection when moving from one-year to five-year forward price returns indicates that the effect accumulates over longer stretches of time.

The time series of cross-sectional correlations are negative for most of the time periods studied. It is apparent that the shorter the horizon, the higher the volatility. This result is expected since returns in shorter periods

t	$t+1$	$t+3$	$t+5$
P/E_t			
P/E_t	P/E_{t+1}	P/E_{t+3}	P/E_{t+5}

1-Year Change
3-Year Change
5-Year Change

P/E Current vs.	Correlation	t-Stat
P/E 1-Year Change	−0.33	−7.60
P/E 3-Year Change	−0.44	−8.40
P/E 5-Year Change	−0.52	−11.30

Time Series Correlation: P/E Current vs. P/E 1-Year, 3-Year, and 5-Year Change

Quintile	P/E Current (%)	P/E 1-Year Change (%)	P/E 3-Year Change (%)	P/E 5-Year Change (%)
1	10.0	9.9	22.7	24.9
2	13.2	2.3	5.1	1.3
3	15.9	−3.5	−3.5	−7.6
4	19.4	−7.5	−12.8	−23.5
5	27.0	−14.0	−25.2	−38.4
High-Low Spread	17.0	23.9	47.9	63.3

FIGURE 5.18 Relationship between Current Level of Valuation and Future Changes in Valuation for Europe ex-U.K. Universe, 1994 through 2008
Note: This figure contains the correlations between the current P/E ratio and the one-year, three-year, and five-year forward P/E ratio in the universe. One-year, three-year, and five-year earnings estimates are the IBES FY2 earnings estimates and are calculated from t to $t+1$, t to $t+3$, and t to $t+5$, respectively. In the quintile analysis, we sort companies into five groups with an equal number of constituents, covering the entire universe. Quintiles are established according to the variable in the first column of numbers, and the numbers reported are the cross-sectional median value of the stocks within each quintile. The bars on the quintile charts depict the difference between the quintile value and the median value of the quintiles.
Source: Westpeak, based on data from MSCI Barra.

tend to be more volatile than in longer-term periods (as return patterns smooth out over time).

The quintile analyses also depict that the forecasting ability of value increases with longer investment horizons, as evidenced by the spread between Quintile 1 and Quintile 5 returns for the one-year, three-year, and five-year forward change horizons. For example, in the United Kingdom (Figure 5.22), the spread using one-year forward price returns is 8.3 percent, while the difference between Quintile 1 and Quintile 5 using five-year returns is 48.3 percent. The high-low spread pattern is consistent in the other universes as well.

In the case of the U.S. Large Cap, U.S. Small Cap, and Continental Europe universes, the quintile returns also highlight that the returns to value

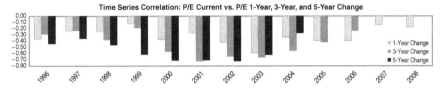

P/E Current vs.	Correlation	*t*-Stat
P/E 1-Year Change	−0.31	−8.57
P/E 3-Year Change	−0.42	−7.24
P/E 5-Year Change	−0.50	−9.50

Time Series Correlation: P/E Current vs. P/E 1-Year, 3-Year, and 5-Year Change

Quintile	P/E Current (%)	P/E 1-Year Change (%)	P/E 3-Year Change (%)	P/E 5-Year Change (%)
1	13.8	8.2	17.5	21.0
2	18.7	0.1	1.6	−5.3
3	22.9	−3.9	−10.9	−18.9
4	27.9	−10.6	−20.8	−31.2
5	36.4	−20.5	−33.2	−44.6
High-Low Spread	22.6	28.7	50.7	65.6

FIGURE 5.19 Relationship between Current Level of Valuation and Future Changes in Valuation for Japan Universe, 1996 through 2008

Note: This figure contains the correlations between the current P/E ratio and the one-year, three-year, and five-year forward P/E ratio in the universe. One-year, three-year, and five-year earnings estimates are the IBES FY2 earnings estimates and are calculated from t to $t + 1$, t to $t + 3$, and t to $t + 5$, respectively. In the quintile analysis, we sort companies into five groups with an equal number of constituents, covering the entire universe. Quintiles are established according to the variable in the first column of numbers, and the numbers reported are the cross-sectional median value of the stocks within each quintile. The bars on the quintile charts depict the difference between the quintile value and the median value of the quintiles.

Source: Westpeak, based on data from MSCI Barra.

(or quintile spread differences) were primarily driven by high P/E stocks (Quintile 5) experiencing significantly lower returns than stocks in other quintiles. This result is largely due to the dot-com bubble, which produced much more pronounced swings in P/E ratios in certain sectors. In contrast, improving valuation for low P/E stocks drove forward returns in the United Kingdom and Japan, although Japanese results are more linear than those of other universes.

These correlation and quintile results are reasonably consistent across the various universes in terms of explanatory power and investment horizon. In general, the investment horizon of a simple P/E ratio–based value strategy appears to be consistent with the mean reversion horizon of long-term earnings expectations and valuations.

P/E Current vs.	Correlation	t-Stat
Return 1 Year Forward	−0.03	−0.73
Return 3 Years Forward	−0.08	−2.72
Return 5 Years Forward	−0.10	−2.97

Time Series Correlation: P/E Current vs. Return 1 Year, 3 Years, and 5 Years Forward

Quintile	P/E Current (%)	Return 1 Year Forward (%)	Return 3 Years Forward (%)	Return 5 Years Forward (%)
1	9.1	9.7	35.5	69.9
2	11.5	11.6	32.4	60.7
3	13.7	9.8	31.5	59.8
4	16.3	9.7	31.9	60.9
5	21.7	6.6	18.6	39.4
High-Low Spread	12.6	3.1	16.9	30.5

FIGURE 5.20   Investment Horizon of Value Strategies for U.S. Large Cap
Universe, 1985 through 2008
Note: This figure contains the correlations between the current P/E ratio and the
one-year, three-year, and five-year forward total returns in the universe. One-year,
three-year, and five-year returns are calculated from t to $t + 1$, t to $t + 3$, and t to $t
+ 5$, respectively. In the quintile analysis, we sort companies into five groups with an
equal number of constituents, covering the entire universe. Quintiles are established
according to the variable in the first column of numbers, and the numbers reported
are the cross-sectional median value of the stocks within each quintile. The bars on
the quintile charts depict the difference between the quintile value and the median
value of the quintiles.
Source: Westpeak, based on data from MSCI Barra.

In summary, the global evidence presented in this section suggests that
value is a long investment horizon strategy, and the investment horizon is
consistent with the horizon over which analyst long-term growth expectations and valuations mean revert.

IMPLICATIONS FOR STOCK RISK PREMIUM

We have documented two relationships that can be used to draw inferences
regarding the behavior of the unobservable stock risk premium (SRP). One,
there is a strong relationship between current valuation (P/E ratios) and
analyst long-term growth expectation. Two, long-term growth expectation

t	$t+1$	$t+3$	$t+5$
P/E_t			
P_t	P_{t+1}	P_{t+3}	P_{t+5}

1-Year Forward Return
3-Year Forward Return
5-Year Forward Return

P/E Current vs.	Correlation	t-Stat
Return 1 Year Forward	–0.04	–1.14
Return 3 Years Forward	–0.06	–2.06
Return 5 Years Forward	–0.08	–3.07

Time Series Correlation: P/E Current vs. Return 1 Year, 3 Years, and 5 Years Forward

Quintile	P/E Current (%)	Return 1 Year Forward (%)	Return 3 Years Forward (%)	Return 5 Years Forward (%)
1	8.2	3.6	17.7	41.0
2	10.9	5.8	24.5	49.7
3	13.0	5.7	23.1	44.3
4	16.1	2.4	13.8	32.6
5	23.7	–2.2	0.0	5.2
High-Low Spread	15.5	5.8	17.7	35.8

FIGURE 5.21 Investment Horizon of Value Strategies for U.S. Small Cap Universe, 1985 through 2008

Note: This figure contains the correlations between the current P/E ratio and the one-year, three-year, and five-year forward total returns in the universe. One-year, three-year, and five-year returns are calculated from t to $t+1$, t to $t+3$, and t to $t+5$, respectively. In the quintile analysis, we sort companies into five groups with an equal number of constituents, covering the entire universe. Quintiles are established according to the variable in the first column of numbers, and the numbers reported are the cross-sectional median value of the stocks within each quintile. The bars on the quintile charts depict the difference between the quintile value and the median value of the quintiles.

Source: Westpeak, based on data from MSCI Barra.

and valuation exhibit a strong mean-reverting behavior over the same horizon. The power of these relationships, in the absence of the SRP, could imply the following for the behavior of the SRP over time. First, cross-sectional differences in the SRP may be much smaller than cross-sectional differences in long-term growth expectation. Second, changes in the SRP over time may be much smaller than changes in long-term earnings expectation. Third, long-term growth expectation might itself influence the perceived riskiness of a company. That is, all else being equal, lower (higher) long-term expected growth of earnings may imply higher (lower) relative expected risk, such as default risk. This may cause the growth-adjusted stock risk premium (SRP – g) to be higher and P/E ratios to be lower for value stocks.

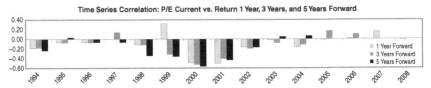

t	t + 1	t + 3	t + 5
P/E_t			
P_t	P_{t+1}	P_{t+3}	P_{t+5}

1-Year Forward Return
3-Year Forward Return
5-Year Forward Return

P/E Current vs.	Correlation	t-Stat
Return 1 Year Forward	−0.09	−1.58
Return 3 Years Forward	−0.13	−2.24
Return 5 Years Forward	−0.19	−2.96

Time Series Correlation: P/E Current vs. Return 1 Year, 3 Years, and 5 Years Forward

Quintile	P/E Current (%)	Return 1 Year Forward (%)	Return 3 Years Forward (%)	Return 5 Years Forward (%)
1	8.6	10.7	36.5	63.5
2	11.4	5.8	22.7	43.1
3	13.4	5.9	17.5	31.7
4	16.1	4.5	18.1	29.4
5	22.3	2.4	14.7	15.2
High-Low Spread	13.6	8.3	21.8	48.3

FIGURE 5.22 Investment Horizon of Value Strategies for U.K. Universe, 1994 through 2008
Note: This figure contains the correlations between the current P/E ratio and the one-year, three-year, and five-year forward total returns in the universe. One-year, three-year, and five-year returns are calculated from t to $t + 1$, t to $t + 3$, and t to $t + 5$, respectively. In the quintile analysis, we sort companies into five groups with an equal number of constituents, covering the entire universe. Quintiles are established according to the variable in the first column of numbers, and the numbers reported are the cross-sectional median value of the stocks within each quintile. The bars on the quintile charts depict the difference between the quintile value and the median value of the quintiles.
Source: Westpeak, based on data from MSCI Barra.

Given the strength of the various reported relationships, it would be reasonable to conclude that the strong mean reversion in long-term growth expectation, g, over the three- to five-year horizon causes both the growth-adjusted stock risk premium (SRP − g) and valuation (P/E) to mean revert over the same horizon.

DECOMPOSING VALUE RETURNS

The strong relationship between value and long-term growth expectation, and the systematic behavior of long-term growth expectation to mean revert, makes current valuation a reasonably good and systematic predictor of future change in valuation and, hence, price returns. This would suggest that

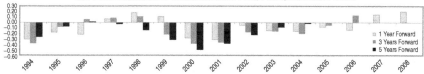

t	t + 1	t + 3	t + 5
P/E_t			
P_t	P_{t+1}	P_{t+3}	P_{t+5}

1-Year Forward Return
3-Year Forward Return
5-Year Forward Return

P/E Current vs.	Correlation	t-Stat
Return 1 Year Forward	−0.08	−1.71
Return 3 Years Forward	−0.12	−2.44
Return 5 Years Forward	−0.18	−3.56

Time Series Correlation: P/E Current vs. Return 1 Year, 3 Years, and 5 Years Forward

(chart, 1994 through 2008) — legend: 1 Year Forward, 3 Years Forward, 5 Years Forward

Quintile	P/E Current (%)	Return 1 Year Forward (%)	Return 3 Years Forward (%)	Return 5 Years Forward (%)
1	8.8	7.6	36.8	63.6
2	11.5	9.4	41.2	64.7
3	13.7	6.8	35.4	53.5
4	16.8	6.1	28.8	40.3
5	23.3	1.9	17.5	20.7
High-Low Spread	14.5	5.7	19.3	42.9

FIGURE 5.23   Investment Horizon of Value Strategies for Europe ex-U.K. Universe, 1994 through 2008
Note: This figure contains the correlations between the current P/E ratio and the one-year, three-year, and five-year forward total returns in the universe. One-year, three-year, and five-year returns are calculated from t to $t + 1$, t to $t + 3$, and t to $t +5$, respectively. In the quintile analysis, we sort companies into five groups with an equal number of constituents, covering the entire universe. Quintiles are established according to the variable in the first column of numbers, and the numbers reported are the cross-sectional median value of the stocks within each quintile. The bars on the quintile charts depict the difference between the quintile value and the median value of the quintiles.
Source: Westpeak, based on data from MSCI Barra.

value active returns are driven, and explained, partly by the average tendency of long-term growth expectation to mean revert in the long run. Therefore, referring back to Equation 3.5 and the two drivers of price change, value appears to be an investment strategy that provides an effective capture of the systematic portion of the change in valuation component of future price changes.

As in the case of momentum, we can decompose value returns into the change in expectation and change in valuation component to verify that value returns are indeed coming from the change in valuation component of future returns.

Figure 5.25 provides a decomposition of value returns for the various universes. In this figure, the quintiles are formed on the basis of the level

t	t + 1	t + 3	t + 5
P/E_t			
P_t	P_{t+1}	P_{t+3}	P_{t+5}

1-Year Forward Return
3-Year Forward Return
5-Year Forward Return

P/E Current vs.	Correlation	t-Stat
Return 1 Year Forward	−0.04	−0.94
Return 3 Years Forward	−0.09	−1.83
Return 5 Years Forward	−0.12	−2.74

Time Series Correlation: P/E Current vs. Return 1 Year, 3 Years, and 5 Years Forward

Quintile	P/E Current (%)	Return 1 Year Forward (%)	Return 3 Years Forward (%)	Return 5 Years Forward (%)
1	12.5	−1.7	10.9	23.5
2	17.2	−3.3	8.5	19.8
3	21.0	−3.7	3.1	10.5
4	25.3	−4.8	−0.7	8.4
5	33.4	−4.8	−2.1	1.8
High-Low Spread	20.8	3.1	13.0	21.7

FIGURE 5.24 Investment Horizon of Value Strategies for Japan Universe, 1996 through 2008
Note: This figure contains the correlations between the current P/E ratio and the one-year, three-year, and five-year forward total returns in the universe. One-year, three-year, and five-year returns are calculated from t to $t + 1$, t to $t + 3$, and t to $t + 5$, respectively. In the quintile analysis, we sort companies into five groups with an equal number of constituents, covering the entire universe. Quintiles are established according to the variable in the first column of numbers, and the numbers reported are the cross-sectional median value of the stocks within each quintile. The bars on the quintile charts depict the difference between the quintile value and the median value of the quintiles.
Source: Westpeak, based on data from MSCI Barra.

of the P/E ratio at time t. Quintile 1 represents the lowest P/E stocks, and Quintile 5 comprises the highest P/E stocks. Then, the total one-year forward median return of each quintile is decomposed into a return attributed to the change in expectation component and a return attributed to the change in valuation component.

As can be seen from this figure, the future one-year return of the high value companies (Quintile 1) is driven primarily by the change in valuation component, implying that these stocks, which are selected on the basis of their current P/E ratios, experience expansions in P/E ratios going forward. These stocks also experience negative contribution from the change in expectation component, but this contribution is smaller in magnitude than the increases in valuations, except for Japan.

P/E $_{(t-1,t)}$ Quintile	Earnings Estimate Change 1 Year Forward (%)	P/E Change 1 Year Forward (%)
U.S. Large Cap		
1	−1	8
2	5	4
3	7	1
4	11	−1
5	13	−7
U.S. Small Cap		
1	−3	11
2	3	4
3	6	0
4	9	−4
5	14	−12
United Kingdom		
1	0	8
2	2	0
3	5	−3
4	9	−6
5	10	−11
Europe ex-UK	−4	
1	−2	8
2	1	3
3	4	−2
4	6	−6
5	9	−11
Japan		
1	−6	5
2	−3	−2
3	0	−4
4	3	−9
5	7	−15

FIGURE 5.25 Decomposing Value Returns for Various Universes
Source: Westpeak, based on data from IBES and MSCI Barra.

CONCLUSION

The main findings reported in this chapter can be summarized (and generalized) as follows:

- Value is contemporaneously linked to analyst long-term growth expectation.
- Analyst long-term growth expectation mean reverts in the long run (three to five years). The tendency to mean revert is very strong in every market studied. True market expectations embedded in market prices are likely to follow a similar pattern.

- Valuations exhibit a pattern similar to long-term growth expectations and also mean revert in the long run (three to five years).
- Value is a long investment horizon strategy (three to five years). Its horizon is consistent with the horizon over which long-term growth expectations mean revert.

Therefore, value active returns appear to be driven, and explained, partly by the average tendency of long-term growth expectation to mean revert in the long run (three to five years). The strong mean reversion of long-term growth expectation results in the mean reversion of the growth-adjusted stock risk premium ($SRP - g$), which, in turn, leads to the mean reversion in valuation. As such, value is an investment strategy that provides an effective capture of the systematic portion of the change in valuation component of future price changes.

Before we tie together all the relationships we have established so far into a cohesive ActiveBeta Framework, we have to answer two further questions:

1. Is the systematic future behavior of earnings discounted in current expectations and prices?
2. What explains the persistence of systematic sources of active equity returns?

We discuss these two topics in the next chapter.

CHAPTER 6

Pricing and Persistence of Systematic Sources of Active Equity Returns

In this chapter, we explore two topics. First, we discuss the pricing of the systematic behavior of short-term and long-term earnings growth by studying the extent to which this systematic behavior is discounted in current prices and expectations. Second, we approach the question of the persistence of systematic sources of active equity returns by reviewing the explanations offered for the existence of the momentum premium and value premium in the current literature, and advancing this debate by providing an ActiveBeta perspective. Finally, we conclude the chapter by summarizing all the relationships in Chapters 3 through 6, which provide the conceptual foundation for the proposed ActiveBeta Framework and Indexes.

PRICING OF THE SYSTEMATIC SOURCES OF ACTIVE EQUITY RETURNS

In previous chapters, we have argued that momentum and value active returns originate from the average tendency of the change in short-term expectation to trend and long-term growth expectation to mean revert, respectively. This would imply that the systematic future behavior of earnings expectations is not incorporated in current expectations and market pricing. So, a reasonable challenge to our arguments might be that if the systematic behavior of earnings expectations is known, then why is it not reflected in current expectations and market prices?

Formation of Analyst Earnings Expectations

Using analyst expectations as a proxy for true market expectations, we have already documented the significant positive serial correlation in change in analyst short-term expectation and the negative serial correlation in analyst long-term growth expectation. If the systematic tendency for analyst expectations to trend and mean revert were incorporated in current expectations, we would not see these strong relationships. So, why isn't the future systematic behavior of earnings expectations reflected in current expectations?

Current analyst expectations may not fully reflect the systematic behavior of those expectations for the following reasons. First, analysts face uncertainty with regard to the magnitude of the average systematic behavior. For instance, in a given economic environment, would the tendency for change in short-term expectation to trend and long-term growth expectation to mean revert be strong or muted? Second, the timing of the systematic behavior is also uncertain. Will the short-term trend persist over one quarter, two quarters, or one year? Will the long-term mean reversion take one, three, or five years?

Consider the graphs in Figure 6.1. These graphs show the R-squared, over time, of the regression between the current level of IBES long-term growth estimates and one-year, three-year, and five-year forward change in those growth estimates. In general, the graphs highlight that the mean reversion of analyst long-term earnings growth is the most pronounced (highest negative R-squared) over a five-year period in all markets. However, as can be seen from these graphs, there are many points in time when the mean reversion becomes more pronounced over a three-year or even one-year forward horizon.

Indeed, it is difficult to anticipate the systematic behavior of earnings in terms of magnitude or timing without some new information or catalyst. The risk of poorly estimating the magnitude or timing of the trend or mean-reverting behavior, based purely on historical relationships, may overwhelm the expected benefit from trying to impound this average behavior in prices. Perhaps some of the average behavior could be considered, but trying to fully account for the average historical behavior would add estimation risk to the analysis.

Additionally, the average tendency for earnings to trend, and then mean revert, may be difficult to incorporate in the pricing of individual securities. Individual securities are primarily priced based on security-specific growth prospects and risk considerations. A value stock, with a high probability of default, may be difficult to price at the average tendency for value stocks to experience increases in long-term growth rates and expansions in price-earnings (P/E) multiples.

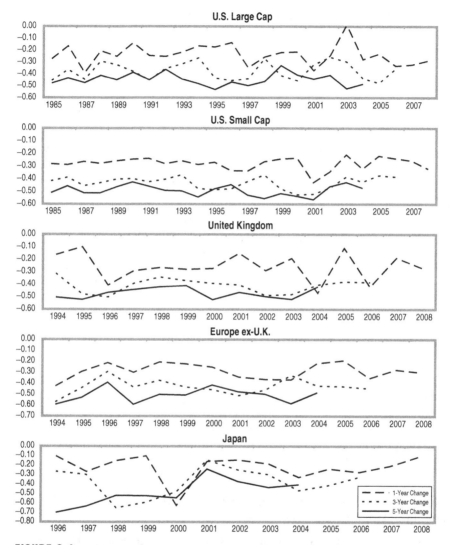

FIGURE 6.1 Horizon of Mean Reversion in Analyst Long-Term Growth Expectation for Various Universes

Note: This figure shows the correlations between the current level of long-term expected growth and the one-year, three-year, and five-year forward change in long-term expected growth for the U.S. Large Cap, U.S. Small Cap, U.K., Europe ex-U.K., and Japan universes. The long-term earnings estimates used in the analysis are the IBES Long-Term Forecast.

Source: Westpeak, based on data from IBES.

TABLE 6.1 Pricing of the Systematic Behavior of Change in Analyst Short-Term Expectation for Various Universes

Universe	R-Squared (Adj.)	Price Change Past Year		Expectations Change Past Year	
		Beta	t-Stat	Beta	t-Stat
U.S. Large Cap	0.16	0.29	14.80	0.14	5.56
U.S. Small Cap	0.13	0.26	15.60	0.15	9.62
United Kingdom	0.15	0.26	8.40	0.18	6.40
Europe ex-U.K.	0.13	0.25	4.90	0.11	3.80
Japan	0.06	0.20	7.30	0.04	1.46

Note: This table contains the results of a multiple regression that analyzes changes in the IBES FY2 estimate over the next year (t to $t + 1$) as the dependent variable versus the independent variables that include changes in the IBES FY2 estimate over the past year ($t - 1$ to t) and price changes over the past year ($t - 1$ to t). All variables are scored (ranked). For the U.S. Large Cap and U.S. Small Cap universes, the analysis period is from June 1986 through June 2009. For the U.K. and Europe ex-U.K. universes, the analysis period is from June 1995 through June 2009. For the Japan universe, the analysis period is from June 1997 through June 2009. The regression uses an annual frequency.
Source: Westpeak, based on data from IBES and MSCI Barra.

Under conditions of uncertainty, therefore, market participants adopt a conservative approach toward the formation of their expectations. As such, current analyst expectations reflect the systematic behavior of underlying earnings only slowly over time, as new information becomes available, which sheds light on the expected magnitude and timing of the average systematic behavior.

Pricing of the Systematic Behavior of Analyst Earnings Expectations

It appears that market pricing and market expectations follow the same conservative pattern. That is, market prices discount the systematic behavior of analyst earnings expectations only slowly over time. The evidence is presented in Tables 6.1 through 6.3. In general, the analysis contained in these tables indicates that market prices appear to incorporate some of the future systematic behavior of analyst earnings expectations, but not all of it.

Table 6.1 presents a multiple regression analysis to explore whether current momentum discounts the systematic trending behavior of change in analyst short-term expectation for the major developed markets. In this

TABLE 6.2 Pricing of the Systematic Behavior of Analyst Long-Term Growth Expectation for Various Universes, One-Year Forward Change

Universe	R-Squared (Adj.)	Long-Term Growth Expectation Level		P/E Level	
		Beta	*t*-Stat	Beta	*t*-Stat
U.S. Large Cap	0.09	−0.33	−17.92	0.23	13.78
U.S. Small Cap	0.10	−0.34	−19.00	0.14	12.26
United Kingdom	0.09	−0.27	−8.30	0.11	4.70
Europe ex-U.K.	0.09	−0.29	−11.80	0.14	6.88
Japan	0.08	−0.24	−2.60	0.06	1.64

Note: This table contains the results of a multiple regression that analyzes changes in the IBES Long-Term Growth (LTG) forecast estimate over the next year (*t* to *t* + 1) as the dependent variable versus the independent variables that include the LTG forecast level (at time *t*) and the P/E level (at time *t*). The earnings variable used in the P/E ratio is the IBES FY1 estimate (at time *t*). All variables are scored (ranked). For the U.S. Large Cap and U.S. Small Cap universes, the analysis period is from June 1986 through June 2009. For the U.K. and Europe ex-U.K. universes, the analysis period is from June 1995 through June 2009. For the Japan universe, the analysis period is from June 1997 through June 2009. The regression uses an annual frequency.
Source: Westpeak, based on data from IBES and MSCI Barra.

regression, the dependent variable is one-year forward change in IBES FY2 earnings estimates. The independent variables are one-year past change in IBES FY2 estimates and one-year past price momentum (return). The objective of this analysis is to determine whether past change in FY2 estimates is useful in explaining forward change in FY2 estimates in the presence of past momentum. Stated differently, we know that, on its own, one-year past change is positively serially correlated with one-year forward change in FY2 estimates. When we include one-year past momentum in price as another independent variable, does the significance of one-year past change in FY2 estimates disappear? If it does, then it would imply that past year momentum discounts contemporaneous changes in analyst expectation as well as future changes in analyst expectation.

As can be seen in Table 6.1, the one-year past momentum has highly significant beta coefficients, with the *t*-statistic values ranging from 15.60 to 4.90, in all markets. This finding, in conjunction with the highly significant relationship reported in Chapter 4 between momentum and changes in analyst expectation, suggests that past returns discount both the contemporaneous change in FY2 estimates as well as at least some of the one-year

TABLE 6.3 Pricing of the Systematic Behavior of Analyst Long-Term Growth Expectation for Various Universes, Three-Year Forward Change

Universe	R-Squared (Adj.)	Long-Term Growth Expectation Level		P/E Level	
		Beta	t-Stat	Beta	t-Stat
U.S. Large Cap	0.13	−0.42	−20.50	0.15	7.90
U.S. Small Cap	0.18	−0.50	−35.00	0.11	12.00
United Kingdom	0.18	−0.47	−14.90	0.18	5.55
Europe ex-U.K.	0.16	−0.43	−14.60	0.13	8.76
Japan	0.16	−0.41	−5.50	0.06	4.13

Note: This table contains the results of a multiple regression that analyzes changes in the IBES Long-Term Growth (LTG) forecast estimate over the next three years (t to $t + 3$) as the dependent variable versus the independent variables that include the LTG forecast level (at time t) and the P/E level (at time t). The earnings variable used in the P/E ratio is the IBES FY1 estimate (at time t). All variables are scored (ranked). For the U.S. Large Cap and U.S. Small Cap universes, the analysis period is from June 1986 through June 2009. For the U.K. and Europe ex-U.K. universes, the analysis period is from June 1995 through June 2009. For the Japan universe, the analysis period is from June 1997 through June 2009. The regression uses an annual frequency.
Source: Westpeak, based on data from IBES and MSCI Barra.

forward change in FY2 estimates. However, the beta coefficients for one-year past change in FY2 estimates are also highly significant in all markets, except Japan. The t-statistic values range from a high of 9.62 for U.S. Small Cap to 1.46 for Japan. The persistent significance of one-year past change in FY2 estimates in explaining one-year forward change in FY2 estimates, even in the presence of momentum, implies that price changes (momentum) only partially discount the systematic future changes in expectation.

The less significant results for the Japan universe are not surprising. As we have already documented, change in analyst short-term expectation exhibits little tendency to trend in the short run in Japan over the period studied. As a result, the multiple regression analysis shows that past changes in analyst expectation are not useful in explaining one-year forward change in analyst expectation. However, price changes still anticipate and explain future changes in analyst short-term earnings expectations in a significant manner.

Tables 6.2 and 6.3 analyze whether valuations price the systematic mean reverting behavior of long-term analyst growth expectations for the major developed markets. These tables present the results of two multiple regressions. In the first regression (Table 6.2), the dependent variable is one-year forward change in IBES long-term growth expectations, while in the second regression (Table 6.3) the dependent variable is three-year forward change in IBES long-term growth expectations. The independent variables in both regressions are the current (at time t) level of IBES long-term growth expectation and the P/E ratio. The objective of this analysis is to determine whether the current level of analyst long-term growth expectation is useful in predicting forward changes in analyst long-term growth expectation in the presence of current market valuation, or P/E ratio. As can be seen in Table 6.2, the t-statistic values for the beta coefficients of the level of P/E ratio are generally significant and range from 13.78 to 1.64. That is, current valuations discount, to some extent, one-year forward changes in the analyst long-term growth expectation. However, the t-statistic values for beta coefficients of the current level of analyst long-term growth expectation are more significant and range from −19.00 to −2.60.

When the investment horizon is extended from one-year forward change to three-year forward change in analyst long-term growth expectation (Table 6.3), the beta coefficients of the current level of analyst long-term growth expectation become even more significant. These results are consistent in each and every market studied. These results, in conjunction with the strong positive cross-sectional relationship documented in Figure 3.3 in Chapter 3 between valuation ratios and analyst long-term growth expectations, imply that current market valuations largely discount current analyst long-term growth expectation, but only partially discount the future changes in analyst long-term growth expectation. This is evidenced by the fact that the current level of analyst long-term growth expectation is highly significant in explaining one-year and three-year forward change in analyst long-term growth expectation, even in the presence of current market valuation.

Another way to analyze the pricing of the systematic behavior of earnings expectations is through the decomposition of high-momentum and high-value stock returns into the change in expectation and change in valuation components. This analysis is presented in Table 6.4 for the various stock market universes.

Table 6.4 decomposes the one-year forward returns of high-momentum and high-value stocks into the change in expectation and change in valuation components for various markets and market segments. In this table, high-momentum stocks are defined as the highest quintile of stocks based on a 12-month momentum ranking of the selection universe. The high-value stocks represent the lowest quintile of stocks based on a P/E ranking of the universe. Change in expectation is defined as the change in IBES FY2 estimates over the last year. The P/E ratio is calculated using the IBES FY2 earnings estimates at each point in time. At the start of June of each year, the

TABLE 6.4 Decomposing Momentum and Value Returns for Various Universes

Top Quintile	FY2 Estimate Change 1 Year Forward (%)	P/E Change 1 Year Forward (%)
U.S. Large Cap		
High Momentum	16.0	−5.7
High Value	−0.6	8.3
U.S. Small Cap		
High Momentum	17.0	−9.8
High Value	−2.9	10.8
United Kingdom		
High Momentum	12.6	−7.4
High Value	−0.2	8.3
Europe ex-U.K.		
High Momentum	9.3	−8.0
High Value	−4.1	8.0
Japan		
High Momentum	8.3	−15.3
High Value	−6.2	4.7

Note: The time periods illustrated in this table are as follows: U.S. Large Cap from 1985 through 2008, U.S. Small Cap from 1985 through 2008, United Kingdom from 1994 through 2008, Europe ex-U.K. from 1994 through 2008, and Japan from 1996 through 2008.
Source: Westpeak, based on data from IBES and MSCI Barra.

High-Momentum and High-Value Quintiles are identified and their median performance over the next year is decomposed in terms of a median change in expectation (change in FY2 estimates) contribution and a median change in valuation (change in P/E ratio) contribution to total returns. This process is repeated every year. Table 6.4 reports the average of the median returns coming from change in expectation and change in valuation.

We have already established in Chapter 4 that the change in expectation component is the main source of one-year forward returns for high-momentum stocks. High past-year momentum stocks represent those stocks that have exhibited high change in expectation over the last year. Because change in expectation trends in the short term, these stocks continue to experience increases in expectations. If the future trending behavior of change in expectation was fully discounted in current price changes, then prices will not rise as future expectations rise, leading to a corresponding decrease in the P/E ratio, all else being equal.

However, Table 6.4 indicates that the High-Momentum Quintile registers large positive changes in FY2 estimates and only modest decreases in the P/E ratio over the next year in all markets, except Japan. In the case of the U.S. Large Cap universe, for instance, the High-Momentum Quintile experienced a 16 percent increase in FY2 estimates and only a –5.7 percent decrease in the P/E ratio, leading to a 9.4 percent total return for this quintile.

Similarly, if the current P/E ratio of high-value companies fully reflects the anticipated mean reversion of analyst long-term growth expectation, then there should be no change in the P/E ratio going forward, all else being equal. However, as we see in Table 6.4, the High-Value Quintile registers large positive increases in P/E ratios in all universes.

The return decomposition analysis in Table 6.4 suggests that the trending behavior of change in analyst short-term expectation is not fully priced by price changes. Likewise, the mean reversion of analyst long-term growth expectation is also not fully priced in current valuations.

The preceding discussion on the pricing of the systematic behavior of earnings expectations needs to be viewed in the context of the constraint that true market expectations are not directly observable. Therefore, the conclusions derived from the analysis in Tables 6.1 through 6.4 cannot be viewed as definitive, especially if there are large divergences between true market expectations and analyst expectations. It is possible that true market expectations, and prices, fully incorporate the systematic behavior of earnings, even though analyst expectations do not. If this is the case, then momentum and value active returns will not be due to the systematic behavior of earnings, but rather caused by some other "unidentified" source.

However, based on the research we have conducted, we subscribe to the view that true market expectations and analyst expectations do not diverge significantly in a cross-sectional, relative-ranking sense. Furthermore, analysts and market participants appear to follow a conservative approach in the formation of their expectations and determination of prices. That is, current expectations and market prices reflect the systematic behavior of earnings only slowly over time.

PERSISTENCE OF THE SYSTEMATIC SOURCES OF ACTIVE EQUITY RETURNS

The active returns associated with value strategies were documented by Basu in 1977. Basu reported that, in the United States, low P/E stocks tended to have higher subsequent returns than high P/E stocks. However, pronounced academic and practitioner interest in value (and growth) investing did not materialize until the publication of two further research articles, Fama and French (1992) and Lakonishok, Shleifer, and Vishny (1994). The Fama and

French article, in particular, was viewed as a pronouncement on the "death of beta" and the Capital Asset Pricing Model and, as a result, quickly became the subject of heated debate and discussion in the world of finance.

The active returns related to momentum strategies were first documented by Jegadeesh and Titman (1993). Their research highlighted that stocks with higher relative returns in the past one year continued to deliver superior returns in the subsequent 12 months. The discovery of the momentum anomaly directly challenged the weak form of market efficiency, which asserts that past prices cannot predict future prices in an efficient market. Since the publication of this article, numerous other research articles have documented the persistence of short-term (up to one year) active returns associated with the so-called momentum anomaly in the major stock markets of the world (e.g., Rouwenhorst, 1998; Jegadeesh and Titman, 2001; Griffin, Ji, and Martin, 2005; Schwert, 2003; and Asness, Moskowitz, and Pederson, 2009).

After more than a decade of out-of-sample confirmation, there is now a general agreement in the academic and practitioner communities on the existence and persistence of momentum and value active returns. That is, these active returns do not appear to be the result of data-mining or data-snooping efforts of hundreds of researchers. So, why do these returns persist over time?

Explaining Momentum and Value Active Returns

Understanding the source of momentum and value active returns is essential to determining whether these active returns are likely to persist in the future. Unfortunately, there is still little or no agreement on the source of such active returns among academics or practitioners. Broadly speaking, two diametrically opposed explanations are offered. On the one hand, the advocates of efficient markets, such as Fama and French, argue that value securities represent higher-risk investments and, therefore, value active returns merely represent a compensation for bearing higher risk. On the other hand, the proponents of inefficient markets, such as Lakonishok, Shleifer, and Vishny, argue that behavioral biases of investors and various agency issues better explain the persistence of these anomalous active returns. Let us review these two explanations in more detail.

Rational Compensation for Risk   The efficient markets–based rational compensation for risk argument advocated by Fama and French asserts that value companies are more exposed to financial distress and, therefore, have higher risk and expected returns than growth stocks. Thus, the value premium constitutes a rational compensation for bearing higher risk. However, Fama and French also state that past losers (low-momentum stocks) have value-like characteristics (past price declines lead to lower valuation ratios). This would imply that past losers, not past winners (high-momentum stocks), should have higher expected risk and, therefore, higher expected and realized returns. This contradiction led Fama and French to conclude that their Value factor cannot explain momentum returns, as it would predict higher returns for past losers than for past winners. As a result, in another research article, Fama (1998) labeled price momentum as the "granddaddy" of market anomalies.

The rational compensation for risk argument would assert that the value premium should persist over time as it merely reflects a risk premium. However, in their current structure, the rational asset-pricing models cannot explain the existence and the persistence of momentum and value active returns simultaneously.

Behavioral Explanations Lakonishok, Shleifer, and Vishny (1994) argued against the rational compensation for risk arguments advocated by Fama and French. They showed in their research that value stocks do not possess higher risk, as measured by traditional risk metrics, such as market beta and standard deviation of returns. They further argued that if value (growth) stocks represent some other high- (low-) risk characteristics, which are not properly measured by traditional measures of risk, then another more direct test would be to look at the performance of value and growth stocks in periods when investor risk aversion is high. Such periods would correspond to times when the market experiences negative returns or the economy experiences negative growth. When investor risk aversion is high, one would expect value stocks (high-risk stocks) to underperform growth stocks (low-risk stocks). However, Lakonishok, Shleifer, and Vishny (1994) found that value stocks outperformed growth stocks in down markets and in periods of economic contraction, and provided similar returns to growth stocks in up markets and expansionary environments. They, therefore, concluded that the value premium over growth cannot be reasonably attributed to higher fundamental risk of such securities. They advocated behavioral and cognitive biases, as well as various agency issues related to delegated investment management, as the more likely source of the existence of the value premium.

The foundations of behavioral finance can perhaps be traced back to the Nobel Prize–winning work of Daniel Kahneman and Amos Tversky (1979) and to Richard Thaler (1985). Their work, as well as that of other researchers, suggests that investors tend to use simple heuristics (rules) in investment decision-making, which gives rise to behavioral biases. For example, investors tend to behave as if past growth will continue in the future for a long time period. That is, investors simply extrapolate past growth into the distant future. Since value (growth) companies have typically experienced low- (high-) growth rates in the past, this behavior creates a negative sentiment for value stocks and a favorable one for growth stocks. However, Chan, Karceski, and Lakonishok (2003) reported that there is no persistence in past growth rates. Consequently, investors are positively surprised when value (growth) stocks subsequently experience upward (downward) revisions in growth, leading to value stocks outperforming growth stocks. To provide a direct test of this hypothesis, Chan, Karceski, and Lakonishok looked at the past realized growth and future growth expectations of earnings embedded in current pricing. They argued that if price-book value (P/B) correctly reflects future growth expectations, then a direct relationship should exist between current P/B ratios and five-year forward realized earnings growth rates. However, they discovered that this relationship was weak. Yet, the relationship between past realized earnings growth and current P/B ratios was significantly positive. They concluded that this represents evidence that current valuation is driven by past growth and that investors overreact to past growth by extrapolating it into the future.

There are many behavioral explanations for the existence of the momentum active returns as well. For example, momentum returns are often attributed to investor underreaction. Research shows that investors are often slow to act on new information. This may be due to a behavioral trait known as "anchoring and adjustment," in which investors update their views only partially when new information becomes available. As a result, new information is discounted only slowly over time, which creates momentum in prices. Other researchers have attributed the momentum returns to the herding behavior of investors, who often invest in recent winners, thus giving rise to a bandwagon effect.

In a more recent study, Chen, Moise, and Zhao (2009) offer a myopic extrapolation explanation for the simultaneous existence of short-term price momentum and long-term price reversal. De Bondt, Werner, and Thaler (1985) first documented price reversal by showing that stocks with higher relative returns in the past five years tended to underperform stocks with lower relative returns over the next five years. This price reversal is closely linked to value, as stocks that have done poorly in the past five years also tend to have lower valuation multiples. As discussed, the risk-based explanations for value cannot reconcile the simultaneous existence of momentum and value (reversal) active returns. The behavioral explanations, on the other hand, offer one behavioral bias (short-term underreaction) as the primary source of momentum returns and another behavioral bias (long-term overreaction) as the source of value, or price reversal, active returns. These two behavioral biases are not necessarily contradictory, as they may relate to different time horizons. Chen, Moise, and Zhao attempt to reconcile these different perspectives by offering a myopic extrapolation hypothesis to explain how momentum and reversal (value) returns coexist and are realized. They argue that the tendency for prices to trend in the short run and reverse in the long run can be explained by earnings shocks to future cash flows in all horizons. In essence, there is momentum and then reversal in cash-flow shocks, which causes momentum and reversal in prices. This behavior arises because investors revise expected future cash flows period by period, as if current cash flow shocks were to last for a long time. Stated differently, "investors overweight current earnings shocks but underweight their predictable trends" (Chen, Moise, and Zhao, 2009). They call this behavior "myopic extrapolation."

In summary, the advocates of the behavioral explanations argue that momentum and value active returns should persist over time as they arise from deep-rooted behavioral biases of investors.

ActiveBeta Perspective   The ActiveBeta Framework provides some useful insights into the source of momentum and value returns. It highlights that momentum and value returns are driven by the systematic behavior of earnings growth and, as such, constitute systematic sources of active equity returns (or Active Betas). It further highlights that momentum active returns arise from the fact that positive change in expectation contributes more to future returns than the negative change in valuation. Value active returns, on the other hand, come from large positive change in valuation, which more than offsets the negative change in expectation.

Why do momentum and value active returns persist over time? They persist because (1) the systematic behavior of earnings growth persists over time, and (2) the systematic behavior of earnings growth is difficult to fully incorporate in current expectations and prices.

The systematic behavior of earnings growth to trend and then mean revert is the outcome of the fundamental way in which an open, competitive economic system works. In such a system, an individual company, such as Microsoft, may be able to sustain above-average earnings growth for a relatively long period of time. But, a large group of stocks, say 200 to 300, may be able to sustain above-average growth for only a short period of time. It is highly unlikely that above-average earnings growth for such a large group of stocks will continue indefinitely. Competitive forces will cause above-average growth rates to fall over time, on average, as new entrants appear to take advantage of above-average return on capital opportunities or existing competitors move to develop and bring to market competing products. Similarly, below-average growth rates tend to rise over time, on average, as companies restructure to become more efficient and profitable or exit from unattractive lines of business, thus raising their own profitability as well as the profitability of the companies that remain in those lines of business. Consequently, competitive forces, a fundamental driver of an open economic system, cause earnings for large groups of stocks to behave in a trending, and then mean-reverting, fashion. The existence and persistence of the systematic behavior of earnings and earnings expectations is the outcome of the fundamental way in which open and competitive systems work in free-market economies.

The systematic behavior of earnings is difficult to incorporate fully in current expectations and prices for two main reasons, as discussed previously. First, there is uncertainty related to the magnitude and timing of the systematic behavior at a given point in time. As a result, investors adopt a "conservative" approach in the formation of their expectations. They discount the systematic tendency only slowly over time as new information becomes available and provides more clarity on the magnitude and timing of the systematic behavior. Second, it is difficult to incorporate the average tendency of earnings to trend in the short run and mean revert in the long run in the pricing of individual securities. However, this average tendency can be effectively captured in broadly diversified momentum and value portfolios.

Chen, Moise, and Zhao (2009) argue that the failure of investors to reflect the systematic behavior of earnings in current expectations is a behavioral bias of market participants, caused by investors revising current expectations as if current cash flow shocks are more or less permanent. We would prefer to term this behavior "conservatism." In the face of uncertainty, a reasonable argument can be made that this conservatism represents rational behavior and that blindly discounting the observed historical average tendencies in current expectations and prices may entail more hazards than benefits.

MOMENTUM, VALUE, AND RISK AVERSION

Our research highlights that value is mainly a "growth-adjusted stock risk premium" (see Chapter 5) and that value and momentum relative returns are influenced by the risk aversion of investors. That is, when investor risk aversion is high (down markets), value stocks underperform momentum stocks. When investor risk aversion is low (up markets), value stocks outperform momentum stocks. Lakonishok, Shleifer, and Vishny (1994) did not find this behavior when they studied the relative returns of value and growth, which led them to conclude that value stocks do not represent high-risk stocks. But, with value and momentum, two properly specified systematic sources, the expected pattern of relative returns clearly emerges. Table 6.5 reports the relative performance of value and momentum active returns, based on ActiveBeta Momentum and Value Indexes (described in Chapter 8), for

TABLE 6.5 Relative Performance of Value and Momentum Active Returns in Up and Down Markets for Various Universes, 1992 through 2008

Universe	Up Markets Active Return Difference (%) (Value − Momentum)	Down Markets Active Return Difference (%) (Value − Momentum)
U.S. Large Cap		
Full Period	−0.37	1.63
Excluding Bubble/Post-Bubble	0.10	−2.98
United Kingdom		
Full Period	3.10	−8.06
Excluding Bubble/Post-Bubble	−0.41	−7.56
Europe		
Full Period	4.24	−6.10
Excluding Bubble/Post-Bubble	3.04	−8.55
Japan		
Full Period	3.39	5.54
Excluding Bubble/Post-Bubble	7.24	0.72

Note: Returns in this table are based on the ActiveBeta Indexes. Monthly active returns are first sorted into either up or down market categories based on the total return of the universe portfolio for the corresponding month. Next, the arithmetic average of the monthly active returns is computed for each index (Value and Momentum) within each category. Finally, the average active returns are annualized and the difference between the two indexes is presented in the table. The second row of each universe excludes the dot-com bubble/post-bubble period, which is defined as calendar years 1999, 2000, and 2001. Please refer to the Disclosures section for a detailed explanation of performance.
Source: Westpeak.

various universes from 1992 through 2008. In this table, the first row under each universe presents the average return differences (value − momentum) in up and down markets for the full period. However, the period from 1999 through 2001, which corresponds to the formation and bursting of the dot-com bubble, constitutes such an aberration that we also present the statistics when this period is excluded from the analysis. In all market universes, the relative performance of value is significantly better in up markets than in down markets when the bubble period is excluded.

The cyclicality of momentum and value returns has been well documented. Both momentum and value can experience prolonged periods of pronounced underperformance, characterized by large drawdown relative to the underlying market universe. Figure 6.2 depicts the cyclicality of momentum and value excess returns. This figure uses excess returns for the Fama-French Momentum and Value factors for U.S. stocks from 1927 through 2008. These returns are derived from long-short, market-neutral portfolios constructed by subtracting the returns of high-momentum and high-value stocks from the returns of low-momentum and low-value stocks. The portfolios are size neutralized in order to create more pure returns to the designated factor.

From the beginning of this return series, both the Momentum and Value factor portfolios have several negative years and even groupings of consecutive negative years. While both factors are quite powerful in the long run, their cyclical nature can cause unattractive drawdown of returns. Over the entire 82-year period, the momentum portfolio had negative returns in 17 years. The value portfolio, on the other hand, experienced 29 negative years and eight instances of at least two consecutive negative years.

Figure 6.2 also highlights the counter-cyclical nature (i.e., negative correlation) of momentum and value excess returns. Although momentum and value independently had a large number of negative years, there were only five years out of a total of 82 in which both momentum and value delivered negative returns at the same time. These five instances include a three-year stretch during the late 1930s.

The link of momentum and value relative returns with the risk aversion of investors explains both the cyclicality and the counter-cyclicality of momentum and value-active returns. The risk aversion of investors is linked to the overall economic environment and its impact on the predictability of future earnings. When the visibility of future earnings shortens and earnings predictability risk increases, such as during a period of economic contraction, investors tend to focus on companies that have high current relative short-term earnings growth. In times like these, when risk aversion is high, investors tend to favor short-horizon momentum strategies over long-horizon value strategies, as was the case in 2007 and 2008 (see performance charts for the ActiveBeta Momentum and Value Indexes in Chapter 8). On the other hand, when the visibility of future earnings lengthens and earnings predictability risk decreases, such as during a period of economic expansion or toward the end of an economic contraction, investors tend to focus on companies where the likely mean reversion of current relatively low long-term growth will cause significant expansion in P/E multiples. During these times, when risk aversion is low, investors tend to favor long-horizon value strategies over short-horizon momentum strategies, as was the case during 2001 through 2006 and in the second quarter of 2009 (see Chapter 8).

Realizing the Payoff to Risk

Even though momentum and value are simultaneously linked to the risk aversion of investors and, so, represent some form of higher *ex-ante* risk

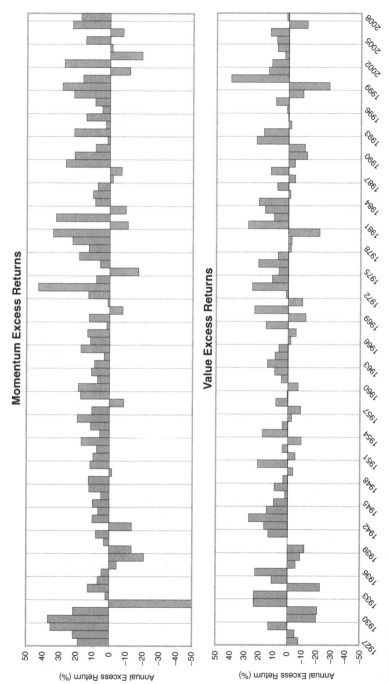

FIGURE 6.2 Fama-French Momentum and Value Factor Annual Excess Returns for U.S. Stocks, 1927 through 2008

Note: This figure illustrates annual excess returns discounted by an implementation cost assumption of 40 bps round trip and an assumed turnover of 150 percent for momentum and 50 percent for value.

Source: Westpeak, based on data from Kenneth French (http://mba.tuck.dartmouth.edu/pages/faculty/ken.french/data_library.html).

investments, the important question for an investor is, "What is the mechanism by which these potential risk premia will actually be earned over time?"

The payoff to a risk premium can materialize in two ways, through cash flow growth and/or reduction in risk. For instance, the overall risk of equities as an asset class is fairly stable over the long run. The equity risk premium, therefore, is earned through cash-flow growth. An asset class that has a high and stable risk over the long run, but no cash-flow growth, may not deliver a positive risk premium over time. Currencies might be an example of such an asset class. Thus, higher risk translates into higher returns only if a mechanism exists for the higher risk to be rewarded in some manner.

Momentum and value may represent higher *ex-ante* risk investments, but, more importantly, the mechanism by which investors are rewarded for bearing this higher *ex-ante* risk is through growth in cash flows (change in expectation) for momentum and a reduction in risk (expansion of valuation ratios) for value. Both these influences are driven by the systematic behavior of earnings growth over time, which is difficult to fully incorporate in current expectations and prices. This is why momentum and value active returns exist and persist over time.

Given the excessive noise that characterizes the marketplace, some portion of momentum and value active returns could certainly be attributable to investors' behavioral biases. Therefore, from a practical perspective, understanding the source of momentum and value active returns, in our opinion, provides more useful insights than a theoretical discussion on whether momentum and value active returns represent rational compensation for risk or behavioral inefficiencies, a debate that might be difficult to resolve.

A Diversification Free Lunch?

Our research findings discussed thus far suggest that the marketplace provides two levels of diversification opportunities, of which investors do not currently take full advantage. First, simply holding broadly diversified momentum and value portfolios significantly increases the probability of capturing the active returns associated with the average tendency of earnings growth to trend in the short run and mean revert in the long run, respectively. Concentrated momentum and value portfolios do not provide an efficient capture of this average tendency and rely more on a manager's stock-selection skill to generate active returns. Second, because of the link of momentum and value with investor risk aversion, the independently positive momentum and value active returns are negatively correlated. The negative correlation of active returns implies that by combining momentum and value into one strategy, investors can significantly improve the risk/return profile of the combined strategy, compared to independent momentum and value strategies.

ActiveBeta Indexes, therefore, have been developed to take advantage of the two levels of diversification benefits just mentioned. They provide (1) a broad and independent capture of the momentum and value systematic active returns, and (2) a combined capture of momentum and value active returns to improve the efficiency of capture.

ACTIVEBETA FRAMEWORK: A SUMMARY OF RELATIONSHIPS

The various relationships discussed in Chapters 3 through 6 are summarized in Figure 6.3. These relationships are central to the ActiveBeta Framework. The main tenets of the ActiveBeta Framework are:

- Change in expectation and change in valuation are the two primary drivers of price change.
- Change in valuation is driven by the change in the difference between the discount rate and the long-term growth expectation.
- The average tendency for change in analyst short-term expectation is to trend (positive serial correlation) in the short run (up to one year).

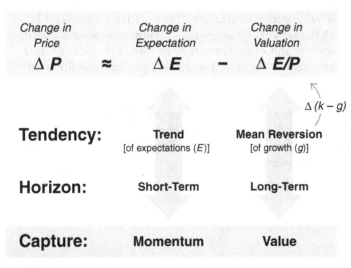

FIGURE 6.3 ActiveBeta Framework: Summary of Relationships
Source: Westpeak.

- The average tendency for P/E ratios is to mean revert (negative serial correlation) in the long run (within three to five years).
- This mean reversion in E/P ratios is caused by the mean reversion of long-term growth expectation, which causes the mean reversion of the growth-adjusted stock risk premium (SRP − g).
- Price momentum is contemporaneously linked to change in analyst short-term expectation. Momentum does not fully discount future systematic changes in analyst short-term expectation. Momentum strategies, therefore, represent one simple investment process whose active returns are driven by the undiscounted systematic behavior of change in short-term expectation to trend in the short run (up to one year). As such, momentum is a short investment horizon strategy.
- Value is contemporaneously linked to the level of analyst long-term growth expectation. Value does not fully discount future systematic changes in analyst long-term growth expectation. Value strategies, therefore, represent an investment process whose active returns are driven by the undiscounted systematic behavior of long-term growth expectation to mean revert in the long run (within three to five years) and the associated mean reversion of $k - g$ and valuation multiples. As such, value is a long investment horizon strategy.
- Broadly diversified momentum and value portfolios increase the probability of capturing the average systematic behavior of earnings expectations at a reasonable level of risk.
- Momentum and value generate positive active returns, independently. Momentum and value active returns are also negatively correlated because of their link to investor risk aversion. This implies that a combined capture of momentum and value active returns should provide superior risk-adjusted performance compared to an independent capture of either momentum or value.

These basic findings provide the rationale for and form the basis of the ActiveBeta Index Design and Methodology. Chapter 7 details the Active-Beta Index Construction Methodology, while Chapter 8 demonstrates the beneficial impact on performance.

Three

ActiveBeta Indexes

ActiveBeta Index
Construction Methodology

W hat are the characteristics of a good index? The answer depends on the context. That is, we have to first specify the objectives of an index, and its expected uses, and then evaluate whether the methodology used to create the index helps to achieve those objectives. If the index achieves its stated objectives, and fulfills its uses, then it is a good index; otherwise it is not. Take the example of the Dow Jones Industrial Average (DJIA). This index was created to serve as a simple barometer of the market, and it meets this objective. On the other hand, this index includes only 30 stocks that are price-weighted. Given this methodology, the index cannot serve as a performance benchmark or as the basis for creating investment vehicles. However, these points are neither objectives nor uses of this index. As intended, the DJIA, and its methodology, answers the question, "How did the stock market do today?" Therefore, the DJIA is a good index.

Contrast the Dow with the Wilshire 5000 Index. The objective of this index is to represent the performance of the entire U.S. stock market. With 5,000 or more constituents, this index obviously covers the broad equity universe comprehensively. It also offers a better proxy for the overall value changes of the market, with its capitalization-weighting scheme. Again, the Wilshire 5000 Index is a good index because it meets its objective. By including a large number of small stocks, the index does become less investable, and thus less useful for creating investment products. But, investability and full replicability are not the primary objectives of this index.

Therefore, the methods used to construct the index must match the objectives and uses of the index. The degree to which an index achieves its intended objectives and suits its prospective uses determines whether it is a good index.

INVESTMENT PROCESS INDEXES

This chapter approaches index construction from the perspective of investment process indexes, that is, indexes intended to be a proxy for the activities of active investment managers. Today's style indexes are examples of this genre of indexes. The ActiveBeta Indexes also fall in this category.

Therefore, before we discuss the details of the construction methodology, we first have to define the various active management styles.

Defining Investment Styles

A style, by definition, is a source of active return common to a large number of active managers. A common source of return that generates positive active returns that persist over time must have a systematic nature to it. Otherwise, it would not persist.

Active Betas provide a conceptual framework for the existence of persistent systematic sources of active equity returns emanating from the fundamental behavior of earnings growth to trend and mean revert over time. Momentum and value represent two investment strategies that are directly linked to this behavior of earnings. As such, we argue that value and momentum reflect the investment styles of active managers much better than value and growth.

At a conceptual level, Equation 3.5 in Chapter 3 highlights that price change is driven primarily by change in expectation and not directly by growth in earnings. Therefore, the choice of past or future levels of earnings growth as a variable to define an independent investment style (i.e., growth) lacks a theoretical or conceptual rationale. Furthermore, Figure 3.3 in Chapter 3 also clearly establishes that value is a good proxy for the prevailing consensus of expected growth. These findings mean the growth investment process is incorrectly specified and also indicate a mis-specification of the core investment style.

Since value and growth are mirror images of each other, defining the core investment style as a combination of the two simply implies that core managers have no value bias. Additionally, value and growth indexes typically add up exactly to the underlying parent or market index. This construction philosophy defines the opportunity set of core managers as the entire market. We believe that momentum, rather than growth, combines with value in defining the neutral portfolios of core managers.

The objective of a style index is to define and measure the performance of the opportunity set that is the most relevant or representative of a given style. As we show in Chapter 9, a performance decomposition of active manager returns highlights that:

- Growth managers are momentum players with a slight value bias.
- Value managers are essentially value players.
- Core managers incorporate combined momentum and value tilts.

In essence, therefore, core is an independent investment style. Core managers, as a group, clearly have style attributes and characteristics. By specifying their opportunity set as the entire market universe and benchmarking their performance to the market index, we assume that these managers are style-neutral and that market capitalization, or size, is the factor that best describes their investment process. But they are not style-neutral, and market capitalization certainly does not describe their investment process.

OBJECTIVES OF INVESTMENT PROCESS INDEXES

To capture the performance of active investment processes, an index requires certain properties in order to be effective. We have incorporated several of these key objectives into our ActiveBeta Index Construction Methodology. In some cases, conflicting objectives require reconciliation, and we make the appropriate trade-offs. This chapter details the objectives of the indexes, and demonstrates how these objectives are met.

In our opinion, a good investment process index must possess the following characteristics.

Representative of the Opportunity Set of a Style

For a style index to be useful, it must represent the opportunity set relevant to managers within that style, that is, the universe of constituents from which a style manager would typically select stocks. Focusing an index on an opportunity set not relevant to a style creates an unacceptable mismatch, rendering the index ineffective in assessing the results of managers following that style. Therefore, the first step in creating an investment process index is proper specification or definition of active styles.

The ActiveBeta Indexes are based on the following style specification principles:

- Momentum is a more accurate reflection of the so-called growth investment style.
- Momentum and value are two independent styles.
- Core is also an investment style, with momentum and value tilts.

These principles imply that:

- High momentum stocks better represent the opportunity set of the so-called growth managers than high earnings growth stocks.
- Momentum and value indexes need to be created independently of each other and not be defined in terms of each other.
- The entire market universe is not representative of the core managers' style, as these managers typically do not consider low momentum and low value stocks for investment.

With these concepts established, the ActiveBeta Indexes produce universes that better represent the group of stocks in which an active manager would typically invest.

Reflective of an Investment Process

Having identified the constituents of the opportunity set of the various styles—momentum, value, and core—we consider the next objective of an investment process index, that is, reflecting the characteristics of the investment process that it endeavors to capture.

Within the opportunity set, the investment process index needs to weight constituents and rebalance in similar fashion to an active manager employing the index style. By linking the exposure sought by an index to the investment activities of active managers, an index can serve as a true benchmark for the managers' returns.

Replicating an investment process is most effective when the essence of the process is captured by the proxy index. The effective capture of an investment process may require higher turnover than is typically found in current index offerings. For instance, momentum strategies, by their very nature, are characterized by high frequency of rebalancing and high turnover. Keeping an index timely in its informational value may require increasing turnover beyond what is deemed standard for an index.

The more exactly an index captures the returns associated with an investment process, the better proxy the index is for that style. For example, a core investment process focuses on stocks with attractive momentum or value characteristics. Stocks unattractive on both dimensions are avoided. Minimizing the exposure to these stocks in the selection universe is part of the *representative* objective. Weighting the remaining constituents in a scheme that reflects the investment process of core managers falls within the responsibility of this *reflective* objective.

A core manager would likely favor stocks with positive momentum and value characteristics above those with only one of these two aspects.

An index designed to reflect core manager actions needs to include this relative weighting. Thus, a stock that is appealing on both counts must have an increased index weight, indicative of its increased importance to an active core manager. By matching index weighting and overall construction to that of an investment process, the indexes can have added relevance in providing analysis of and alternatives to active style management.

Usable on a Wide Scale

While creating a representative and reflective index is critical, one clear objective remains. The index must also have wide-scale usability in order to serve as a true market benchmark. Only by making an index widely usable can the representative and reflective properties of the index become relevant in the marketplace. This objective requires the construction methodology to be:

- **Replicable.** Investors should be able to replicate an index fully and completely for the index to have credibility. In this regard, simplicity and transparency are two key considerations. An index that is too complicated to recreate cannot meet the needs of the investment community. Similarly, an index that does not provide complete transparency is less useful. For instance, the use of proprietary information in index construction is less desirable, as investors do not have access to the information necessary to duplicate the index.
- **Investable.** A useful equity index must be investable if it is to be replicable by all. Investors require the ability to hold the same constituents as the index at the same weight in order to obtain the same results. If size, access, or other constraints limit an index from being a market-wide solution, its utility is compromised.
- **Low-cost.** Style indexes, and the index products based on them, are designed to serve as a passive alternative to an active investment style. A passive investment generally implies a low-cost investment. Index construction should recognize this expectation and include limiting the expense of holding the index as a key part of the process.

By creating a replicable, transparent, and low-cost process, in combination with making capacity nearly unlimited and coverage as complete as possible, an index serves as a truly useful proxy for more active methods of acquiring the same exposure. With these properties, an investment process index can be the basis for investment products that provide a true, fair alternative to active management.

The ActiveBeta Index Construction Methodology strives to incorporate these objectives into the index structure. At the conclusion of this chapter, we assess how successful the ActiveBeta Index Construction Methodology is in achieving this goal. We start, however, by discussing the inherent conflicts that these objectives and other considerations create in the design of an index.

CONFLICTING OBJECTIVES

In creating an investment process index, some of the objectives just mentioned can be at odds. Because the representative objective defines the context for the reflective objective, these two objectives function largely in harmony. Building a widely usable index, however, does come into conflict with the first two objectives. In this section, we highlight some of the critical contradictions for which a balance must be struck in building these indexes.

The most straightforward way to discuss the conflicts between the objectives is to break down the usability objective into some of its sub-objectives. We will contrast these sub-objectives with the reflective objective to demonstrate the conflicts.

Reflective versus Replicability

For an index to gain acceptance in the marketplace, users must be able to replicate it. This means that building the index should involve a reasonable level of simplicity, so that interested parties can easily understand how to reproduce the index. Yet, investment process indexes should also fairly represent the investment process of a style, which at times can entail a certain level of complexity. In such a case, a more sophisticated, but less accessible, construction methodology might better represent the targeted investment process.

Consequently, an investment process index should capture a style as fully as possible without unduly complicating the process, which hinders wide-scale replicability.

Reflective versus Investability

A useful index needs to offer enough capacity for industry-wide usage and adoption. This invariably means employing a market capitalization weighting scheme to create the index from a given opportunity set. This weighting scheme is, of course, appropriate for the construction of market indexes. However, its use in an investment process index can, and often does, interfere with capturing the true essence of the style.

A balance must be struck between creating an index that embodies what active managers actually do and one that has sufficient capacity. Too large a divergence from a true investment process will make the index less relevant. Too little capacity will make the index less useful.

Reflective versus Low-Cost

Various users of indexes—investors, consultants, and managers—expect indexes to be as unencumbered by cost as possible. For example, in considering a passive investment, reduced expenses are part of the benefit realized by forgoing active management. On the other hand, improving the capture of a target style entails incorporating the most recent information. Including this timely data into an index often requires more frequent rebalancing and increased turnover, which adds to the overall expense. Thus, high turnover is considered somewhat undesirable from the perspective of a low-cost index.

An index designed to capture an investment process like momentum, a fast-moving signal requiring more frequent rebalancing, faces a particular quandary in this regard. Resolving these objectives requires employing methods to reduce turnover, while allowing the index to incorporate a reasonable amount of signal information on a timely basis. If accomplished, higher turnover strategies, such as momentum, can have a passive alternative. The resultant index can then be used to benchmark active managers who use, for example, momentum, while also providing the basis for investment products.

Reflective versus Coverage

In current style index construction methodologies, the sub-indexes typically sum to the core or parent index. For example, the Russell 1000 Index is a combination of the Russell 1000 Value Index and the Russell 1000 Growth Index. To accomplish this entirety of coverage, the style indexes must be defined in terms of each other. Additionally, a given stock must have its full and exact weight in the core index distributed to the value portion, growth portion, or some combination thereof. Completeness of coverage among the style indexes minimizes what is known as benchmark misfit, or the divergence between a policy benchmark used by an asset owner in asset allocation and portfolio structuring and the implementation benchmark used as the basis for active or passive portfolio management.

A measure of the conflict between reflectiveness and coverage is active risk. Assets owners generally prefer to eliminate the active risk that arises from benchmark misfit, at the expense of style purity and, hence, performance.

How far can a style index series reasonably stray from the core benchmark? Balancing these two attributes can create benchmark style indexes that reflect style without exposing investors to undue market risk. Additionally, just as indexes have to strike a balance between competing objectives, asset owners also may wish to reconsider their approach toward misfit management to strike a more appropriate balance between active risk and return.

TRANSPARENCY, UNDERSTANDING, AND RATIONALE OF THE ACTIVEBETA MOMENTUM INDEX

Transparency includes creating a clear understanding of both the *how* and the *why* of index construction. An index intending to capture the active returns associated with momentum faces a particular challenge with regard to the *why*. Unlike the widely accepted, if still debated, value effect, a lack of consensus exists on a reasonable rationale for explaining momentum active returns. This disagreement has constrained the development of momentum indexes. (See Chapter 6 for a more detailed discussion of this topic.)

In our opinion, and based on our research, the ActiveBeta Framework provides a simple, but robust, explanation of the source of momentum (and value) returns. Momentum is a proxy for the systematic behavior of changes in short-term earnings expectations and, hence, represents a systematic source of active equity returns, as has been demonstrated in previous chapters. Broadly diversified momentum strategies are an efficient way of capturing the average tendency of changes in short-term earnings expectations to trend in the short run. This insight provides a fundamental reason for investors to consider a passive implementation of momentum strategies via a market capitalization-weighted index, which can offer investors as transparent and cost-effective a capture of momentum as possible.

ACTIVEBETA INDEX CONSTRUCTION PROCESS

Now we enter the methodology portion of our discussion. We begin with a broad outline of our process for constructing ActiveBeta Indexes. Figure 7.1 depicts the basic steps involved in creating the ActiveBeta Indexes.

The construction process entails four steps. These steps are as follows:

1. Specify a selection universe from which the ActiveBeta Indexes will be created.

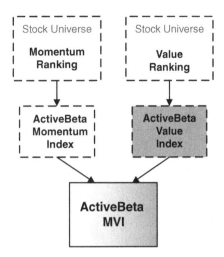

FIGURE 7.1 Index Construction
Process Overview
Source: Westpeak.

The reference universe can be a commonly used market or regional index. Alternatively, an investor may choose a uniquely created subset of stocks or a custom index.

2. Rank each stock in the given selection universe, from high to low, on the momentum and value signals, independently.
   - Momentum is defined as past 12-month total return.
   - Value is defined as a composite signal consisting of price-book value, price-sales, and price-cash flow (or price-forward earnings, where appropriate). The composite signal is an equally weighted average of the three valuation ratios.
3. Create independent ActiveBeta Momentum and ActiveBeta Value Indexes.

   These indexes are created using buy and sell thresholds, which we refer to as buffer-based construction and maintenance.

   A universe is first ranked by the momentum and value signals, independently.

   A stock is added to the style index if its style rank places it within the top third of the universe market capitalization, and is removed from the index when its style rank places it in the bottom third of the universe market capitalization. This limits turnover and results in about 50 percent market capitalization coverage of the underlying universe in

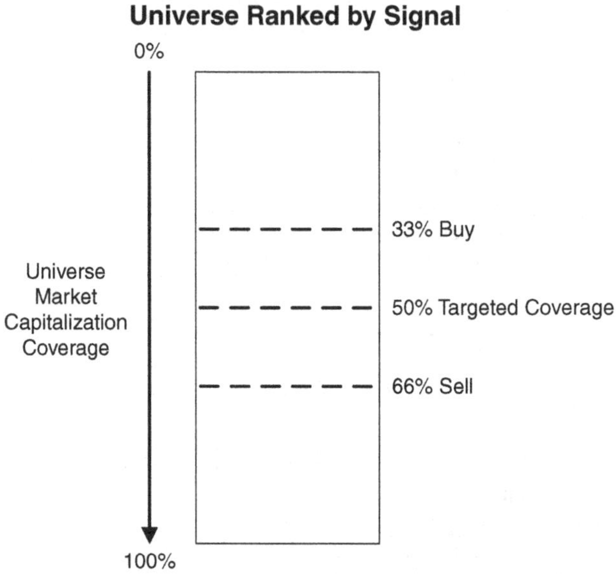

Universe Ranked by Signal

FIGURE 7.2   Buffer-Based Construction and Maintenance
of ActiveBeta Momentum and Value Indexes
Source: Westpeak.

each style index. The buffer-based construction methodology is depicted
in Figure 7.2.

The selected securities in each style index are then weighted according to their relative float-adjusted market capitalization.

4. Combine the ActiveBeta Momentum Index and ActiveBeta Value Index,
   in equal proportions, to create the ActiveBeta Momentum and Value
   Index (MVI).

   In the creation of the ActiveBeta MVI, independent security-level
   positions from each style index are added with a 50 percent weight.

DIFFERENCES IN CONSTRUCTION BETWEEN ACTIVEBETA INDEXES AND OTHER PUBLIC STYLE INDEXES

The ActiveBeta Index Construction Methodology presents a number of
important differences compared to the most common public equity style
indexes currently in use. This section focuses on three critical points of
variation: choice of signals used to create the independent ActiveBeta

Momentum and Value Indexes, the overall index design, and the frequency of rebalancing the indexes.

Specification of Styles

ActiveBeta Indexes differ from the traditional style indexes in terms of defining the so-called growth and core styles.

As mentioned previously, the use of earnings growth to define the growth style for style indexation is inappropriate. Active growth managers do not truly pursue *growth*, as defined by index providers. Rather, professional growth managers appear to focus on momentum in building their portfolios. Therefore, momentum and value better reflect the styles of active managers compared to the conventional classification of growth and value.

Furthermore, in the current practice of style investing and style index construction, the core style is simply defined as the market. This implies that core managers have no investment biases relative to the market. But, core managers clearly have momentum and value tilts in their portfolios. As such, a combination of two independent styles, momentum and value, better reflects the core investment style. The ActiveBeta Index Methodology takes this important consideration into account when defining the neutral portfolio and investment process of core managers.

Capturing of Styles: Index Design

In the prevailing style framework, there are only two styles, value and growth. Core is not considered a separate investment style. As a result, the index design that has been followed by the industry is one in which value and growth are defined in terms of each other. The combination of value and growth indexes fully and exactly covers the parent indexes, which are viewed as the appropriate benchmark for core managers.

The ActiveBeta Framework includes three, not two, separate investment styles, namely momentum, value, and blend. Momentum and value are independent styles. Blend is a combination of momentum and value, which is different from the underlying parent index. The relevant opportunity set for each style is, therefore, different and needs to be properly reflected in an index.

The ActiveBeta Indexes have been designed to achieve this goal. In the ActiveBeta family of indexes, momentum and value are independently defined and constructed. The two indexes are then combined to form the ActiveBeta MVI, which represents the opportunity set of core, or blend, managers, in a weighting scheme that mirrors their investment process.

Rebalancing Frequency

Rebalancing, or reconstitution, of most equity style indexes usually occurs semiannually or annually. The primary motivation for this rebalancing frequency is to control turnover, and the transaction costs related to turnover. The primary style in current style indexes is clearly value, as growth simply reduces to non-value. Value is a slow-moving, low-frequency investment strategy. Therefore, a semiannual or annual rebalancing of the style indexes does not necessarily interfere with an effective capture of the investment process of value.

When value and momentum are considered as two independent and equally important styles, the rebalancing frequency of the style indexes needs to be re-evaluated. This is because momentum is a fast-moving, high-frequency investment strategy. An annual rebalancing of the momentum index will not capture the true returns associated with this style. An effective capture of the investment process of momentum requires more frequent rebalancing. This is why ActiveBeta Indexes are reconstituted on a monthly basis.

We believe that the rebalancing frequency, *per se*, should not be the focus of investors. Ultimately, the focus should be on after-cost returns. These are the returns that investors will actually realize in their portfolios. If monthly rebalancing captures the true returns of an investment style, and if that capture can be combined with a technique to limit turnover, then investors have the best of both worlds, which ultimately delivers higher after-cost returns.

ACHIEVING OBJECTIVES

Having described the construction and design details, we now consider whether the ActiveBeta Index Construction Methodology achieves its goals and how it balances the various conflicting objectives.

Representative of the Opportunity Set of a Style

We believe that the ActiveBeta Indexes are more representative of the opportunity set of active style managers.

We redefine the *growth* investment style as *momentum*. Thus, the opportunity set of the growth style is respecified as the high-momentum stocks that cover about 50 percent of the underlying universe by market capitalization.

This opportunity set is a more accurate reflection of the growth managers' selection universe.

The opportunity set of value managers is specified as those high-value stocks that cover about 50 percent of the underlying universe by market capitalization. The opportunity sets of value and momentum (growth) managers are specified independently of each other. This independence also makes each opportunity set more reflective of its style.

We redefine the core investment style as a blend of momentum and value. Thus, the opportunity set of the blend style is obtained by combining the opportunity sets of the momentum and value styles. This opportunity set covers about 75 percent of the market capitalization of the parent index and is a more reasonable representation of the neutral portfolio of the so-called core managers.

Reflective of an Investment Process

We believe that the ActiveBeta Indexes more accurately reflect the investment processes of active style managers.

In order to properly reflect the momentum investment process, the indexes are rebalanced on a monthly basis. The monthly frequency, combined with a buffer-based rebalancing process, actually increases the return capture without significantly increasing turnover and implementation costs. The net result, as we discuss later, is higher after-cost returns.

The ActiveBeta MVI is a more reasonable reflection of the investment process for core managers than simply the market. Core managers, as a group, have a combined momentum and value bias. They do not favor stocks with both low-momentum and low-value characteristics and typically overweight stocks with both high-momentum and high-value attributes. Their performance benchmark should reflect this. An appropriate opportunity set and performance benchmark for core managers is one that combines stocks that have positive momentum and value attributes and, within that universe, overweights stocks that have both high-momentum and high-value scores. This is exactly what the ActiveBeta MVI delivers by combining the independently formed momentum and value indexes.

Usable on a Wide Scale

We believe that ActiveBeta Indexes have the properties required to serve as industry-wide benchmarks.

Our index construction process is transparent on multiple levels. The *why* of index construction is addressed through our conceptual explanation of momentum and value active returns and our research supporting the proposed concepts. We further enhance understanding and acceptance by selecting simple, straightforward, and commonly used definitions of momentum and value. The *how* of our construction methodology, though different from the current style index creation methods, is also simple, low-cost, and fully replicable.

The ActiveBeta Indexes are based on large and liquid universes and are market capitalization weighted. They offer high capacity and are easily replicated.

Next, we discuss how the ActiveBeta Index Design and Methodology strikes an appropriate balance, or makes compromises, between the most important conflicting objectives.

Reflective versus Low-Cost

We believe the ActiveBeta Indexes strike a good balance between capturing the essence of a high turnover strategy, such as momentum, and keeping implementation costs to a reasonable level. This is achieved through the use of the buffer-based construction methodology.

The impact of using market-capitalization-based buffers to construct and maintain the ActiveBeta Indexes is illustrated in Table 7.1.

When a momentum index is constructed using a 50 percent market capitalization cutoff for both inclusion in and exclusion from the index, and the index is rebalanced on an annual basis, the turnover is 45 percent and

TABLE 7.1 Impact of Market-Cap-Based Buffers on the Turnover of ActiveBeta Indexes for U.S. Large Cap Universe, 1992 through 2008

Rebalance Frequency	Buy Threshold	Sell Threshold	Turnover (%)	After-Cost Active Return (%)
Momentum				
Annual	< 50	> 50	45	1.15
Monthly	< 50	> 50	154	0.81
Monthly (buffer)	< 33	> 66	54	1.38
Value				
Annual	< 50	> 50	15	1.76
Monthly (buffer)	< 33	> 66	11	1.77

Note: Please refer to the Disclosures section for a detailed explanation of performance.
Source: Westpeak.

the after-cost active return is 1.15 percent per annum. When the index is rebalanced on a monthly basis with the same (50 percent) buy and sell thresholds, the turnover is more than three times higher (154 percent) and, even though the before-cost active returns are significantly higher, the after-cost active return (0.81 percent) falls below the annual rebalancing return (1.15 percent). When the 33 percent and 66 percent buy and sell thresholds are introduced, and the index is rebalanced monthly, the turnover (54 percent) drops to about the level of the annual rebalancing, and the after-cost returns increase to 1.38 percent per annum. The buffers make it possible to keep the index *current* by rebalancing on a monthly basis, without lowering after-cost active returns.

In the case of a value index, the buffer-based monthly rebalancing produces about the same turnover as an annual rebalancing without buffers and the same active return. These statistics highlight that value is a low-turnover, low-frequency strategy.

If the essence of a style is to be captured, then the style indexes must reflect the most recent readings of a signal, especially in the case of momentum. This will allow the style index to deliver the true return potential of a high-turnover investment style, by transferring the information contained in the fast-moving signal into the index. The degree to which the information contained in a signal is transferred into the index is measured by a statistic commonly referred to as the transfer coefficient (TC). The TC is the correlation of signal ranks with the active weights of the stocks in the core index. If the highest-ranked stocks have the highest active weights, then the correlation and the TC are high. When an index is rebalanced, the relationship between signal ranks and active weights is strong, and the TC is high. Between rebalancings, the TC can drop significantly, depending on the volatility of the signal, which could have an important impact on the return generation capability of the index.

The TC of the ActiveBeta Momentum Index is represented in Figure 7.3. As can be seen from this graph, the transfer coefficient for the monthly (dashed line) and annual (solid line) rebalancing, without buffers, is the same at the time the index is rebalanced. However, for the annual rebalancing, the TC drops to almost zero, and even below zero, between rebalancing dates. The monthly rebalancing clearly produces higher TCs and does so consistently. Therefore, in the case of momentum, monthly rebalancing is preferred if transaction costs can be controlled. This is exactly what the buffer-based rebalancing process accomplishes. The TC of the monthly rebalancing with buffers (dotted line) is very close to the TC of the monthly rebalancing without buffers.

The TCs of the value index are shown in Figure 7.4. This graph differs significantly from the momentum TC graph (Figure 7.3). First, the decline in

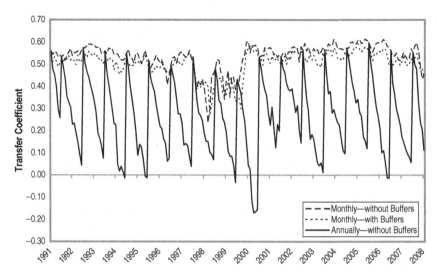

FIGURE 7.3 Transfer Coefficient of ActiveBeta Momentum Index for Monthly and Annual Rebalancing with and without Buffers for U.S. Large Cap, 1992 through 2008
Source: Westpeak.

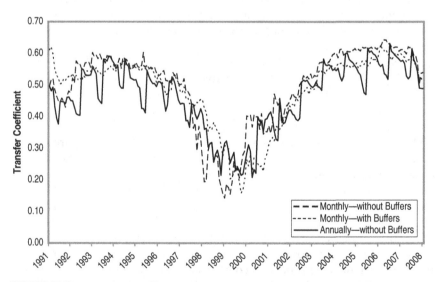

FIGURE 7.4 Transfer Coefficient of ActiveBeta Value Index for Monthly and Annual Rebalancing with and without Buffers for U.S. Large Cap, 1992 through 2008
Source: Westpeak.

the TC between rebalancings is far smaller for value compared to momentum when considering the annual rebalance frequency (without buffers). This result highlights the slow-moving nature of the value signal, which, thus, requires less frequent rebalancing. Second, the TCs for the value index drop regardless of rebalancing frequency during the formation of the dot-com bubble. This occurred as the growing concentration in the market disturbed the link between the value signal and the market capitalization weighting scheme used in the ActiveBeta Indexes. Finally, all the TCs move in a tight band.

The benefit of using a monthly buffer-based rebalancing process is that it produces TCs similar to the monthly rebalancing, but turnover similar to that of an annual rebalancing. This technique, therefore, allows the Active-Beta Indexes to strike a good balance between keeping the index current (reflective) and limiting turnover (low-cost).

Reflective versus Coverage

This is one area where we have found it difficult to strike a balance between the conflicting objectives, that is, an accurate reflection of all investment styles, on the one hand, and complete coverage of the underlying universe or parent index, on the other hand. The current style indexes have an index design in which the two style *pieces* add up to the parent *whole*. This is possible only because core is not considered a separate style from the market in the current paradigm.

In the ActiveBeta Indexes, we do not strive for completeness when capturing momentum and value in tandem. The ActiveBeta MVI does not completely cover the underlying parent index in terms of market capitalization or constituents. More specifically, the ActiveBeta MVI excludes those stocks that have both low-momentum and low-value characteristics. Our assertion is that a complete market index does not accurately reflect the core investment process. This active style is characterized by momentum and value tilts. Therefore, the trade-off is between a true representation of the core opportunity set versus holding all the stocks in the broad market index to eliminate benchmark misfit or tracking risk. We choose to favor mirroring the actions of active core managers.

Nevertheless, we are sensitive to the needs of asset owners to minimize any benchmark misfit that may arise from a combined capture of momentum and value. Therefore, we have created custom indexes that can shift the balance between these two competing objectives, such as covering more of the broad universe while sacrificing some style capture. Chapter 10 discusses these custom indexes in detail.

CONCLUSION

Active managers employ investment processes that exploit the systematic behavior of change in expectation—through momentum strategies—and change in valuation—through value strategies. Therefore, a properly constructed and internally consistent family of ActiveBeta Indexes provides a better reflection of the investment processes of active managers and constitutes more accurate performance benchmarks for active managers, including core managers.

The ActiveBeta Index Construction Methodology presents a unique approach to the capture of investment styles. With this methodology, we have created ActiveBeta Indexes that better meet the investment process index goals listed at the start of this chapter. By achieving these index objectives, we believe we have built a good suite of investment process indexes, which represent a clear improvement over current style index offerings.

APPENDIX: ACTIVEBETA INDEX CONSTRUCTION PROCESS EXAMPLE

In order to clarify the ActiveBeta Index construction process, we have provided a simplified example of the methodology. This example shows the steps from the initial scoring and index construction through rebalancing an existing ActiveBeta Index. The steps are as follows:

1. Constructing the initial index
   a. Rank the reference universe (1 = highest/best rank).

Stock	Weight (%)	Momentum Rank	Value Rank
A	14.3	1	2
B	14.3	2	4
C	14.3	3	6
D	14.3	4	1
E	14.3	5	3
F	14.3	6	5
G	14.3	7	7

   b. Create the ActiveBeta Momentum and Value Indexes, employing a buy threshold of 33 percent of reference universe weight coverage and a sell threshold of 66 percent of reference universe weight coverage.
   1. The ActiveBeta Momentum Index

Stock	Momentum Rank	Weight (%) Reference Index	Weight (%) Momentum Index
A	1	14.3	50
B	2	14.3	50

2. The ActiveBeta Value Index

Stock	Value Rank	Weight (%) Reference Index	Weight (%) Value Index
D	1	14.3	50
A	2	14.3	50

3. Combine into the ActiveBeta MVI.

Stock	Weight (%) Momentum Index	Weight (%) Value Index	Weight (%) MVI
A	50	50	50
B	50	0	25
D	0	50	25

2. **Rebalancing the index**
   a. Rerank the reference universe (1 = highest/best rank).

Stock	Weight (%)	Momentum Rank	Value Rank
A	14.3	3	1
B	14.3	5	2
C	14.3	1	3
D	14.3	2	4
E	14.3	4	5
F	14.3	6	6
G	14.3	7	7

   b. Re-create the ActiveBeta Momentum and Value Indexes, again employing a buy threshold of 33 percent of reference universe weight coverage and a sell threshold of 66 percent of reference universe weight coverage.
   1. The ActiveBeta Momentum Index

Stock	Momentum Rank	Weight (%) Reference Index	Weight (%) Momentum Index
C	1	14.3	33.33
D	2	14.3	33.33
A	3	14.3	33.33

Stock A remains in the index because it is above the 66 percent sell threshold, although below the 33 percent buy threshold.

2. The ActiveBeta Value Index

Stock	Value Rank	Weight (%) Reference Index	Weight (%) Value Index
A	1	14.3	33.33
B	2	14.3	33.33
D	4	14.3	33.33

Stock D remains in the index because it is above the 66 percent sell threshold, although below the 33 percent buy threshold.

3. Combine into the ActiveBeta MVI

Stock	Weight (%) Momentum Index	Weight (%) Value Index	Weight (%) MVI
A	33.33	33.33	33.33
D	33.33	33.33	33.33
C	33.33	0	16.67
B	0	33.33	16.67

CHAPTER 8

Historical Performance of ActiveBeta Indexes

T he index design and methodology outlined in Chapter 7 is used to create the ActiveBeta Indexes for various markets and market segments around the world. The ActiveBeta Index Methodology is completely transparent, which means that investors can independently fully replicate and verify the performance results presented in this chapter.

ACTIVEBETA INDEX CONSTRUCTION PROCESS OVERVIEW

Before we present the historical performance of ActiveBeta Indexes, we outline the process by which these indexes are created.

Defining Market Segments and Composites

The ActiveBeta Indexes discussed in this book are based on the following market segments and market composites:

- U.S. Large Cap
- U.S. Small Cap
- Europe ex-U.K.
- United Kingdom
- Japan
- Developed Markets World
- Developed Markets World ex-Europe
- Developed Markets World ex-Japan
- Developed Markets World ex-North America
- Europe

The segments and composites mentioned reflect the manner in which investors construct their portfolios in terms of domestic and nondomestic allocations. They are defined in similar fashion to commonly used market indexes for these segments. For example, in the United States, we define the large cap segment as the largest 500 stocks and the small cap segment as the smallest 2,000 stocks out of the largest 3,000 stocks. Thus, our U.S. selection universes are similar to the S&P 500 Index and the Russell 2000 Index. In the United Kingdom and Japan, our selection universes closely approximate the FTSE 350 Index and the Tokyo Stock Price Index (TOPIX), respectively. For other international markets and composites, we create each single-country universe (with Europe ex-U.K. considered as one country) by selecting stocks that constitute the top 85 percent of the float-adjusted market capitalization of the target country. A multi-country composite universe simply combines the relevant single-country universes in their market capitalization proportions. For example, Europe combines the U.K. and Europe ex-U.K. universes. This methodology closely mirrors that of well-known international index providers, such as FTSE and MSCI.

Creating ActiveBeta Indexes

The ActiveBeta Indexes are created from the selection universes just defined. For each selection universe, two independent ActiveBeta Indexes are constructed using the index methodology outlined in Chapter 7. These indexes are:

- The ActiveBeta Momentum Index, covering about 50 percent of the market capitalization of the underlying universe when ranked by the momentum signal (past 12-month total return).
- The ActiveBeta Value Index, covering about 50 percent of the market capitalization of the underlying universe when ranked by the value signal (an average of three valuation ratios, namely price-book value, price-sales, and price-cash flow (or price-forward earnings where appropriate)

The independent ActiveBeta Momentum and Value Indexes are then combined, in equal proportions, to create the ActiveBeta Momentum and Value Index (MVI).

The tables and figures presented in this chapter show the performance of the three ActiveBeta Indexes, that is, Momentum, Value, and MVI.

Performance Comparison

The history of the ActiveBeta Indexes for each market segment and composite is calculated from 1992 through 2008. In the calculation of the index history, we lag the fundamental historical data to match the data utilized in the construction of the index with the data that would have been available at the historical construction date, thus mitigating any look-ahead bias. We rebalance the ActiveBeta Indexes at the end of each month.

To determine the active return generation capability of ActiveBeta Indexes, we compare their performance to that of the selection universe from which they are created. Therefore, to conduct this comparison, we compute a selection universe index for each selection universe mentioned earlier. The selection universe index measures the performance of the selection universe over time. We then compare the performance of the three ActiveBeta Indexes with their respective selection universe indexes.

We note that our selection universe indexes produce risk and return characteristics similar to those of commonly used market indexes. For instance, from 1992 through 2008, the annualized total return differences between our Europe and U.S. Small Cap selection universe indexes and the FTSE Europe Index and Russell 2000 Index are 0.26 percent and –0.12 percent, respectively. This magnitude of divergence between our selection universe index returns and those of the commonly used S&P, Russell, FTSE, TOPIX, and MSCI indexes is consistent across the various universes. These results indicate that no particular bias exists in our selection universe indexes compared to well-known market indexes. Therefore, the return comparison of the ActiveBeta Indexes against either the selection universe indexes or the public market indexes should produce substantially similar results.

Adjusting for Implementation Costs

In order to make the performance analysis and comparisons more meaningful from a practical perspective, we present after-cost active and total returns for all the ActiveBeta Indexes. The implementation cost assumptions used in the calculation of after-cost returns are reported in Table 8.1. They range from a 40 basis points round-trip cost assumption for U.S. Large Cap to 80 basis points round-trip for U.S. Small Cap. We believe these implementation

TABLE 8.1 Implementation Costs

Universe	Implementation Cost Assumption (Round-Trip)
U.S. Large Cap	0.40%
U.S. Small Cap	0.80%
International Large Cap	0.60%
Global Large Cap	0.50%

Source: Westpeak.

cost assumptions are representative of the costs incurred in managing real-life portfolios.

ACTIVEBETA INDEX PERFORMANCE: HIGHLIGHTS

The four main characteristics of the historical performance of ActiveBeta Indexes are summarized as follows.

1. **Active return.** The ActiveBeta Indexes outperform the selection universe indexes on which they are based across all markets and regions from 1992 through 2008. For example, the ActiveBeta Developed Markets World MVI outperformed, net of implementation costs, the Developed Markets World universe by 131 basis points per annum.
2. **Information ratio.** The ActiveBeta Indexes not only offer positive active return, but do so at reasonable levels of active risk. The information ratios produced by the ActiveBeta Indexes compare favorably to those of other indexes and traditional active equity strategies. The ActiveBeta Developed Markets World MVI had an average active risk (tracking error) of only 2.17 percent, thus generating an attractive after-cost information ratio of 0.56.
3. **Return stability.** Momentum and value active returns exhibit a strong negative correlation in all regional markets and market segments, thus providing significant diversification benefits in a combined capture. The ActiveBeta MVIs, which provide this combined capture, have significantly lower active risk and active return maximum drawdown compared to the independent ActiveBeta Momentum and Value Indexes in all markets. The ActiveBeta Developed Markets World MVI has an active risk that is 40 percent lower than the corresponding ActiveBeta Value Index and 65 percent lower than the ActiveBeta Momentum Index. The reduction in active return maximum drawdown is even more dramatic. For Developed Markets World, the MVI maximum drawdown is 77 percent and 84 percent lower than the associated value index and momentum index, respectively. The diversification benefits produce highly stable and consistent positive active returns. The ActiveBeta Developed Markets World MVI outperforms its selection benchmark in 13 out of 17 years, a hit rate of over 76 percent. The maximum underperformance was only 72 basis points in 1995.
4. **Universe coverage.** The ActiveBeta Momentum and Value Indexes target 50 percent market capitalization coverage of the selection universe upon which they are based. However, the combination of momentum and value produces a much higher coverage of the selection universe.

The ActiveBeta MVIs cover, on average, around 80 to 85 percent of the names and 75 to 80 percent of the market capitalization of the underlying selection universe. This level of coverage implies that investing in an ActiveBeta MVI offers broad market exposure, while providing the potential for active returns and greater active return stability and efficiency. This is why we refer to the ActiveBeta MVI as a passive, broadly diversified alternative to traditional active strategies.

These features of the ActiveBeta Indexes provide universal empirical support for the ActiveBeta Framework and Index Construction Methodology.

ACTIVEBETA INDEX PERFORMANCE: DETAILED ANALYSIS

The following figures and tables analyze the return, risk, coverage, and turnover characteristics of the ActiveBeta Indexes.

Relative Return Analysis

We start the analysis of historical performance by first comparing the active risk and return characteristics of ActiveBeta Momentum and Value Indexes with the existing value and growth indexes published by various index providers.

Comparison with Value and Growth Indexes　　Table 8.2 presents this comparison. The ActiveBeta Value Indexes generate superior active returns and risk-adjusted performance (information ratios) in the U.S. market and similar performance compared to the value indexes for international markets. The ActiveBeta Momentum Indexes perform significantly better than the published growth indexes in all markets. The outperformance versus growth indexes ranges from 205 basis points per annum for the World ex-North America universe to 568 basis points for the U.S. Small Cap universe. Furthermore, the current growth indexes underperformed the core benchmarks in all markets and regions. We will discuss the shortcomings of the existing growth indexes in more detail in Chapter 9.

After-Cost Active Returns　　Table 8.3 summarizes the active return, active risk, active return maximum drawdown, and other key results of the ActiveBeta Indexes relative to the underlying universe benchmark for various markets of the world.

TABLE 8.2 Comparing ActiveBeta Indexes with Value and Growth Indexes, 1992 through 2008

Universe	After-Cost Active Return (%)		Active Risk (%)	After-Cost Information Ratio
U.S. Large Cap		*(Diff.)*		
ActiveBeta Value Index	2.06	*(1.57)*	4.90	0.41
S&P 500 Value Index	0.49		4.82	0.10
ActiveBeta Momentum Index	1.64	*(2.41)*	6.25	0.26
S&P 500 Growth Index	−0.77		4.49	−0.17
U.S. Small Cap				
ActiveBeta Value Index	4.36	*(1.30)*	7.52	0.58
Russell 2000 Value Index	3.06		7.36	0.42
ActiveBeta Momentum Index	2.02	*(5.68)*	6.92	0.30
Russell 2000 Growth Index	−3.66		6.67	−0.55
Japan				
ActiveBeta Value Index	3.46	*(0.38)*	4.88	0.70
MSCI Japan Value Index	3.08		5.32	0.58
ActiveBeta Momentum Index	−1.06	*(2.17)*	7.00	−0.15
MSCI Japan Growth Index	−3.23		5.48	−0.59
Europe				
ActiveBeta Value Index	1.25	*(−0.18)*	3.43	0.40
MSCI Europe Value Index	1.43		3.67	0.39
ActiveBeta Momentum Index	1.02	*(2.56)*	5.57	0.16
MSCI Europe Growth Index	−1.54		3.69	−0.42
World ex-North America				
ActiveBeta Value Index	1.92	*(−0.04)*	2.99	0.64
MSCI EAFE Value Index	1.96		3.29	0.60
ActiveBeta Momentum Index	0.06	*(2.05)*	4.75	0.01
MSCI EAFE Growth Index	−1.99		3.33	−0.60
World				
ActiveBeta Value Index	1.65	*(0.31)*	3.54	0.45
MSCI World Value Index	1.34		3.85	0.35
ActiveBeta Momentum Index	0.80	*(2.33)*	4.89	0.16
MSCI World Growth Index	−1.53		3.90	−0.39

Note: In this table, ActiveBeta Index active returns are relative to their respective universes. The public style indexes are relative to their respective core indexes. The ActiveBeta returns are reduced by implementation costs, while the public indexes do not reflect the deduction of implementation costs. Returns are annualized. Please refer to the Disclosures section for a detailed explanation of performance.

Source: Westpeak, based on data from MSCI Barra, Russell, and Standard & Poor's.

TABLE 8.3 Active Risk and Return Performance Summary, 1992 through 2008

Universe	After-Cost Active Return (%)	Active Risk (%)	After-Cost Information Ratio	Active Return Drawdown Max (log %)	Names Held from Universe (%)	Annual Turnover (%)
U.S. Large Cap						
ActiveBeta Value Index	2.06	4.90	0.41	20.38	63.02	30.92
ActiveBeta Momentum Index	1.64	6.25	0.26	27.12	43.53	85.59
ActiveBeta MVI	**1.99**	**2.85**	**0.64**	**5.60**	**81.42**	**56.14**
U.S. Small Cap						
ActiveBeta Value Index	4.36	7.52	0.48	44.52	51.26	45.12
ActiveBeta Momentum Index	2.02	6.92	0.30	37.16	37.16	112.48
ActiveBeta MVI	**3.40**	**3.26**	**0.87**	**7.60**	**71.27**	**76.97**
United Kingdom						
ActiveBeta Value Index	1.00	4.53	0.26	23.88	45.98	41.48
ActiveBeta Momentum Index	2.28	5.80	0.37	24.04	46.78	90.50
ActiveBeta MVI	**1.77**	**2.67**	**0.63**	**7.09**	**72.95**	**62.48**
Japan						
ActiveBeta Value Index	3.46	4.88	0.70	19.40	73.32	35.41
ActiveBeta Momentum Index	−1.06	7.00	−0.15	29.66	40.28	92.92
ActiveBeta MVI	**1.31**	**3.67**	**0.33**	**10.04**	**85.77**	**61.54**
Europe ex-U.K.						
ActiveBeta Value Index	1.42	3.76	0.41	14.63	58.63	34.49
ActiveBeta Momentum Index	0.69	6.26	0.09	30.26	42.11	87.62
ActiveBeta MVI	**1.17**	**2.89**	**0.37**	**7.17**	**78.52**	**58.59**

(*Continued*)

129

TABLE 8.3 (*Continued*)

Universe	After-Cost Active Return (%)	Active Risk (%)	After-Cost Information Ratio	Active Return Drawdown Max (log %)	Names Held from Universe (%)	Annual Turnover (%)
Europe						
ActiveBeta Value Index	1.25	3.43	0.40	13.59	58.33	36.47
ActiveBeta Momentum Index	1.02	5.57	0.16	27.17	42.80	88.31
ActiveBeta MVI	**1.24**	**2.49**	**0.46**	**5.48**	**78.58**	**59.66**
World ex-North America						
ActiveBeta Value Index	1.92	2.99	0.64	10.80	65.76	34.80
ActiveBeta Momentum Index	0.06	4.75	0.01	24.32	51.79	86.18
ActiveBeta MVI	**1.07**	**2.17**	**0.46**	**4.74**	**82.41**	**57.50**
World ex-Japan						
ActiveBeta Value Index	1.25	3.76	0.33	19.74	68.60	30.73
ActiveBeta Momentum Index	1.27	5.08	0.23	24.65	54.65	80.50
ActiveBeta MVI	**1.35**	**2.30**	**0.53**	**4.44**	**84.02**	**53.72**
World ex-Europe						
ActiveBeta Value Index	1.73	4.24	0.38	22.76	71.81	29.25
ActiveBeta Momentum Index	0.70	5.18	0.14	23.22	57.80	82.21
ActiveBeta MVI	**1.31**	**2.36**	**0.51**	**4.35**	**85.78**	**53.83**
World						
ActiveBeta Value Index	1.65	3.54	0.45	16.67	67.31	31.24
ActiveBeta Momentum Index	0.80	4.89	0.16	24.46	52.25	84.03
ActiveBeta MVI	**1.31**	**2.17**	**0.56**	**3.99**	**83.29**	**55.32**

Note: Returns are annualized. Please refer to the Disclosures section for a detailed explanation of performance.
Source: Westpeak.

In all the displayed countries and regions, except Japan, the ActiveBeta Momentum and Value Indexes provide positive after-cost active returns, independently. The underperformance of the ActiveBeta Japan Momentum Index should not be surprising, as we have already documented (in Chapter 4) that short-term earnings growth did not exhibit a trending behavior in Japan over the time period studied.

In all countries except the United Kingdom, the ActiveBeta Value Index provides higher after-cost active returns than the ActiveBeta Momentum Index. We believe that this relative result is a time-period-specific phenomenon, and not a fundamental truth of the market. We will discuss this point in more detail later in the chapter.

ActiveBeta MVIs produce positive after-cost active returns in all markets and regions. The active returns range from 107 basis points per annum for World ex-North America to 340 basis points per year for U.S. Small Cap.

The findings reported in Table 8.3 support the argument that the systematic sources of active equity returns, momentum and value, and the ActiveBeta Framework are universally effective both independently and in combination.

Active Risk   In Table 8.3, active risk represents the tracking error of the indexes relative to the selection benchmarks. The ActiveBeta Momentum and Value Indexes generate relatively high active risk readings. In general, for single countries, the active risk of the ActiveBeta Momentum Indexes is over 6 percent, while the active risk of the ActiveBeta Value Indexes is around 5 percent, except in U.S. Small Cap. The active risk levels of the ActiveBeta Momentum and Value Indexes are somewhat reduced when single countries are combined to form regional composites, indicating that a regional diversification benefit exists.

In every market and region, the ActiveBeta MVI has significantly lower active risk than the ActiveBeta Momentum and Value Indexes. The negative correlation of momentum and value active returns drives this reduction in active risk. (Indeed, momentum and value active returns are negatively correlated in all markets, as shown later.) For example, in the U.S. Large Cap universe, the active risk of the ActiveBeta MVI (2.85 percent) is 42 percent lower than the active risk of the ActiveBeta Value Index (4.90 percent) and 55 percent lower than the active risk of the ActiveBeta Momentum Index (6.25 percent). The active risk of regional ActiveBeta MVIs is also lower than the active risk of single-country MVIs. This also shows that international investing provides diversification benefits. However, it is clear from the data that, in the active risk space, the diversification *across* momentum and value provides more active risk reduction than diversification *within* momentum and value.

After-Cost Information Ratios   The significant reduction in active risk achieved by combining momentum and value greatly improves the efficiency of the ActiveBeta MVIs, generally allowing them to yield superior after-cost information ratios compared to the component ActiveBeta Momentum or Value Indexes. The improvement is the most pronounced in the cases of the United States and the United Kingdom. Japan is the only market where the after-cost information ratio of the ActiveBeta MVI is substantially lower than that of the value index. Again, this is not a surprising result, given the performance of momentum in Japan.

The after-cost information ratios for the ActiveBeta MVIs generate highly respectable readings. In the U.S. and U.K. large cap universes, they approach 0.65. For regional composites, they are above 0.45.

Active Return Maximum Drawdown   The advantage of combining the capture of momentum and value is even more apparent when considering the concept of active return maximum drawdown. In essence, this measure indicates the greatest magnitude by which the return of a portfolio trails its benchmark during a distinct period of time. Taking U.S. Large Cap as an example, the after-cost active return drawdown of the ActiveBeta Momentum and Value Indexes was 27.12 percent and 20.38 percent, respectively. In contrast, the after-cost active return drawdown was only 5.60 percent for the ActiveBeta MVI.

Looking at the ActiveBeta Momentum and Value Indexes for the large cap universes, one can see that maximum *relative* underperformance of over 30 percent is possible, and over 20 percent is common. The combined ActiveBeta MVI, however, produces a drawdown of only around 7 percent in any country, except Japan, during the analysis time period. The diversification benefits are even more significant in market composites. For instance, the ActiveBeta Developed Markets World MVI had an active drawdown (3.99 percent), which was 77 percent and 84 percent lower than the drawdown registered for value (16.67 percent) and momentum (24.46 percent).

Market Coverage   In addition to favorable return and risk characteristics, the ActiveBeta Indexes also provide extensive market exposure, which may be a critical feature for many investors. The ActiveBeta Momentum and Value Indexes target about 50 percent market capitalization coverage and tend to hold 35 to 65 percent of the names in the underlying selection universe. Given the negative correlation of momentum and value, which will be clearly highlighted in the performance charts included later in this chapter, the ActiveBeta MVIs generally hold around 80 percent of the selection universe constituents, with the percentage rising above 85 percent in some cases. The ActiveBeta MVIs also provide 75 to 80 percent market capitalization coverage of the selection universe. By investing in the ActiveBeta MVI for any market, an investor can rest assured that the index will cover the vast majority of the target universe.

Index Turnover   Finally, we consider turnover. The ActiveBeta Momentum and Value Indexes have differing turnover characteristics. The ActiveBeta Value Index typically turns over by 30 to 50 percent annualized, while the ActiveBeta Momentum Index typically turns over by 80 to 100 percent. By combining these two indexes into the ActiveBeta MVI, we generally hold turnover to 55 to 65 percent. This seems a reasonable turnover amount for an index that is rebalanced on a monthly basis. The turnover numbers are kept in a reasonable range by the use of the market cap-based buffers to rebalance the indexes. Also, as a reminder, the higher turnover of ActiveBeta Indexes is not a problem, *per se*, as its impact is already considered in the reported after-cost performance statistics.

Performance in Up and Down Markets

How do ActiveBeta Indexes perform in various market environments? To explore this question, we analyze the relative performance of ActiveBeta Indexes in rising markets and falling markets. This performance information is detailed in Table 8.4.

As discussed in Chapter 6, the relative performance of momentum and value is linked to investor risk aversion. Therefore, our intuition is that ActiveBeta Momentum Indexes, representing a short horizon strategy, should perform better when risk aversion is high (market declines) and the ActiveBeta Value Indexes, representing a long horizon strategy, should generate superior performance when risk aversion is low (rising markets). We see this relative behavior of momentum and value quite clearly in Europe and Japan. In the United Kingdom, Europe ex-U.K., and Japan, momentum generates negative active returns in up markets and positive active returns in down markets. The ActiveBeta Value Indexes depict the opposite return patterns, that is, positive active returns in up markets and negative active returns in down markets, except for Japan. The situation in the U.S. Large Cap and Small Cap universes appears to be somewhat different. The ActiveBeta Momentum Indexes perform better in up markets, while the ActiveBeta Value Indexes generate better active returns in down markets. The results in the United States are skewed by the formation and bursting of the dot-com bubble, which produced the most pronounced market movements in the United States. Once we adjust for this unusual time period, U.S. results become consistent with the other markets, as demonstrated in Chapter 6. That is, value performs much better in up markets, while momentum does better in

TABLE 8.4 Performance in Up and Down Markets, 1992 through 2008

	Up Markets		Down Markets	
Universe	Active Return (%)	Over (%)	Active Return (%)	Over (%)
U.S. Large Cap				
ActiveBeta Value Index	1.32	58	3.18	55
ActiveBeta Momentum Index	1.68	62	1.54	54
ActiveBeta MVI	**1.51**	**62**	**2.37**	**54**
U.S. Small Cap				
ActiveBeta Value Index	−4.57	45	16.56	77
ActiveBeta Momentum Index	2.83	59	0.95	49
ActiveBeta MVI	**−0.88**	**50**	**8.75**	**80**
Japan				
ActiveBeta Value Index	0.52	59	6.16	69
ActiveBeta Momentum Index	−2.87	49	0.62	53
ActiveBeta MVI	**−1.15**	**48**	**3.40**	**59**
United Kingdom				
ActiveBeta Value Index	2.60	62	−1.31	50
ActiveBeta Momentum Index	−0.50	53	6.75	57
ActiveBeta MVI	**1.07**	**56**	**2.74**	**54**
Europe				
ActiveBeta Value Index	2.75	60	−1.06	49
ActiveBeta Momentum Index	−1.49	46	5.04	55
ActiveBeta MVI	**0.64**	**62**	**2.02**	**50**
Europe ex-U.K.				
ActiveBeta Value Index	3.07	59	−1.01	39
ActiveBeta Momentum Index	−2.54	47	5.73	59
ActiveBeta MVI	**0.28**	**62**	**2.38**	**50**
World ex-North America				
ActiveBeta Value Index	1.98	59	1.83	60
ActiveBeta Momentum Index	−1.56	44	2.66	57
ActiveBeta MVI	**0.24**	**54**	**2.26**	**56**
World ex-Japan				
ActiveBeta Value Index	0.55	58	2.39	55
ActiveBeta Momentum Index	0.48	55	2.40	49
ActiveBeta MVI	**0.52**	**57**	**2.40**	**52**
World ex-Europe				
ActiveBeta Value Index	−0.68	56	5.14	63
ActiveBeta Momentum Index	0.75	57	0.74	54
ActiveBeta MVI	**0.05**	**54**	**2.96**	**63**
World				
ActiveBeta Value Index	0.28	53	3.81	62
ActiveBeta Momentum Index	0.58	52	1.11	55
ActiveBeta MVI	**0.46**	**56**	**2.46**	**58**

Note: Returns in this table are based on the ActiveBeta Indexes. Monthly active returns are first sorted into either up or down market categories based on the total return of the universe portfolio for the corresponding month. Next, the arithmetic average of the monthly active returns is computed for each index (Value and Momentum) within each category. Finally, the average active returns are annualized and the difference between the two indexes is presented in the table. The "Over" column represents the "hit rate," or the percentage of months where the active return was positive. Please refer to the Disclosures section for a detailed explanation of performance.
Source: Westpeak.

down markets. The composite ActiveBeta Momentum and Value Indexes simply reflect the combined effect of what we see in the individual country indexes.

Contrary to popular belief, value does not appear to provide a margin of safety in down markets. Momentum does.

Of course, the most important implications of this analysis come from applying it to the combined capture of momentum and value, that is, the ActiveBeta MVIs. Benefiting from diversification, the ActiveBeta MVIs posted positive active returns in nearly all regions in both up and down markets during the analysis period. Even when either momentum or value underperformed, the other factor more than made up the active return deficit. The only exceptions to these observations were in up markets in Japan, where we have noted the lack of effectiveness of momentum, and U.S. Small Cap, where momentum returns only partially offset the negative payoff to value in up markets. Finally, the hit rate of the ActiveBeta MVIs is often significantly higher than 50 percent in both up and down markets.

Total Return Analysis

Table 8.5 provides a different return perspective, in this case, looking at total return and risk, as opposed to the active return and risk shown in Table 8.3.

Higher Efficiency of ActiveBeta MVI In all markets and regions, the ActiveBeta MVI produces a superior after-cost total return compared to the underlying selection benchmark. Perhaps equally importantly, the ActiveBeta MVI achieves this result while exposing investors to equal or lower total risk than the underlying selection universe index.

With an improved return versus risk trade-off, the ActiveBeta MVIs generate higher after-cost Sharpe ratios in all cases than the respective selection universe indexes. For example, the ActiveBeta U.S. Large Cap MVI produced a Sharpe ratio of 0.43 versus 0.29 for the selection benchmark, while the ActiveBeta Europe MVI produced a Sharpe ratio of 0.36 versus 0.29 for the selection universe index. These Sharpe ratios represent the most direct measure of the efficiency of the ActiveBeta MVIs in the total return space.

Additionally, in the vast majority of cases, the maximum drawdown of the total return is lower for the ActiveBeta MVIs compared to the underlying selection benchmarks, even though, in some instances, the drawdown of the momentum and value components is higher than that of the universe. For example, for the U.S. Large Cap universe, the drawdown of the ActiveBeta Momentum Index and ActiveBeta Value Index is over 47 percent and 45 percent, respectively, while the drawdown of the selection universe index is

TABLE 8.5 Total Risk and Return Performance Summary, 1992 through 2008

Universe	After-Cost Total Return (%)	Total Risk (%)	After-Cost Sharpe Ratio	Maximum Drawdown (%)
U.S. Large Cap	6.73	14.17	0.29	40.66
ActiveBeta Value Index	8.79	14.64	0.42	45.06
ActiveBeta Momentum Index	8.37	14.89	0.39	47.20
ActiveBeta MVI	**8.72**	**13.95**	**0.43**	**38.44**
U.S. Small Cap	7.20	18.38	0.29	43.14
ActiveBeta Value Index	11.56	16.06	0.55	45.44
ActiveBeta Momentum Index	9.22	19.77	0.37	36.91
ActiveBeta MVI	**10.60**	**16.82**	**0.48**	**40.68**
United Kingdom	6.63	13.91	0.22	34.79
ActiveBeta Value Index	7.64	15.51	0.27	39.52
ActiveBeta Momentum Index	8.91	13.91	0.37	28.90
ActiveBeta MVI	**8.40**	**14.04**	**0.34**	**33.73**
Japan	−2.87	18.58	−0.11	50.78
ActiveBeta Value Index	0.59	18.25	0.08	46.24
ActiveBeta Momentum Index	−3.92	18.61	−0.16	60.57
ActiveBeta MVI	**−1.56**	**17.80**	**−0.04**	**47.72**
Europe ex-U.K.	8.04	17.49	0.28	45.87
ActiveBeta Value Index	9.46	18.72	0.35	51.30
ActiveBeta Momentum Index	8.72	17.07	0.32	52.07
ActiveBeta MVI	**9.21**	**17.40**	**0.35**	**45.98**
Europe	7.88	15.70	0.29	41.42
ActiveBeta Value Index	9.13	16.91	0.35	46.69
ActiveBeta Momentum Index	8.90	15.32	0.35	42.06
ActiveBeta MVI	**9.12**	**15.65**	**0.36**	**41.04**
World ex-North America	4.06	14.73	0.14	43.47
ActiveBeta Value Index	5.98	15.29	0.26	46.24
ActiveBeta Momentum Index	4.13	14.63	0.14	45.40
ActiveBeta MVI	**5.14**	**14.59**	**0.21**	**42.68**
World ex-Japan	7.13	14.06	0.30	41.13
ActiveBeta Value Index	8.38	14.43	0.37	45.08
ActiveBeta Momentum Index	8.40	14.15	0.38	42.91
ActiveBeta MVI	**8.48**	**13.77**	**0.39**	**39.90**
World ex-Europe	4.16	13.82	0.13	42.08
ActiveBeta Value Index	5.89	13.66	0.25	44.78
ActiveBeta Momentum Index	4.85	14.43	0.17	48.11
ActiveBeta MVI	**5.47**	**13.44**	**0.22**	**40.41**
World	5.24	13.76	0.20	41.91
ActiveBeta Value Index	6.89	13.97	0.31	45.43
ActiveBeta Momentum Index	6.05	13.93	0.25	45.14
ActiveBeta MVI	**6.56**	**13.46**	**0.30**	**40.65**

Note: Returns are annualized. Please refer to the Disclosures section for a detailed explanation of performance.
Source: Westpeak.

nearly 41 percent. But, the drawdown of the combined ActiveBeta MVI is only about 38 percent.

The ActiveBeta MVIs have a market beta of around one, equal or lower standard deviation of returns and maximum drawdown, and higher returns than the underlying selection benchmark. Thus, by incorporating both the power and negative correlation of momentum and value, the ActiveBeta MVIs offer investors the attractive blend of enhanced return with lower risk and drawdown.

Is Value a Lower Risk Strategy Compared to the Market? Previously published research would seem to suggest that value strategies have lower risk (standard deviation of returns) than the market. We do not find clear evidence of this in our results. The ActiveBeta Value Indexes have higher standard deviations of returns than the selection universe index for U.S. Large Cap, the United Kingdom, and Europe ex-U.K. Only in the U.S. Small Cap universe is the standard deviation of value returns substantially lower than the benchmark. But, more importantly, from a downside risk perspective, the maximum total return drawdown of ActiveBeta Value Indexes is higher than the drawdown of the market in all countries, except Japan.

Is Momentum a Higher Risk Strategy Compared to Value? Momentum is generally perceived to be a riskier strategy than value. But, once again, we find no clear evidence of this in our results. The standard deviation of momentum returns is higher than the standard deviation of value returns in some countries, but lower in others. A similar pattern exists with respect to the relative drawdown of momentum and value. In addition, compared to the benchmark, the total risk and total return drawdown of momentum is also higher in some countries, but lower in others.

Consistency of Active Returns

Our analysis of the stability of after-cost active returns begins with large capitalization stocks in the United States.

U.S. Large Cap Figure 8.1 shows the historical active return performance of ActiveBeta U.S. Large Cap Indexes.

This graph plots the cumulative active returns of the ActiveBeta U.S. Large Cap Indexes over the 1992 through 2008 time period. The negative correlation of momentum and value active returns is quite clear from the relative movement of the dotted lines. The box in the top left corner of the graph reports a –0.33 correlation between the active returns of the ActiveBeta U.S. Large Cap Momentum and Value Indexes. This is a very

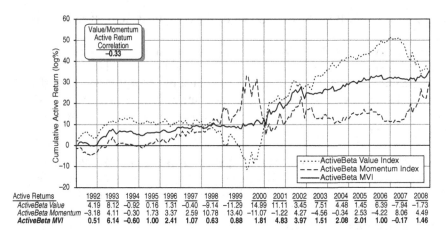

Active Returns	1992	1993	1994	1995	1996	1997	1998	1999	2000	2001	2002	2003	2004	2005	2006	2007	2008
ActiveBeta Value	4.19	8.12	-0.92	0.16	1.31	-0.40	-9.14	-11.29	14.99	11.11	3.45	7.51	4.48	1.45	6.39	-7.94	-1.73
ActiveBeta Momentum	-3.18	4.11	-0.30	1.73	3.37	2.59	10.78	13.40	-11.07	-1.22	4.27	-4.56	-0.34	2.53	-4.22	8.06	4.49
ActiveBeta MVI	0.51	6.14	-0.60	1.00	2.41	1.07	0.63	0.88	1.81	4.83	3.97	1.51	2.08	2.01	1.00	-0.17	1.46

FIGURE 8.1   ActiveBeta U.S. Large Cap Index Performance, 1992 through 2008
Note: Please refer to the Disclosures section for a detailed explanation of performance.
Source: Westpeak.

high and statistically significant level of negative correlation. Also evident from the graph is the fact that momentum and value depict highly cyclical and volatile active return patterns, but the ActiveBeta MVI combination of the two (the bold line) drastically reduces this cyclicality of returns, without sacrificing active returns.

Figure 8.1 also shows the year-by-year after-cost active performance of the ActiveBeta U.S. Large Cap Indexes. Over the entire period, both the ActiveBeta U.S. Large Cap Momentum and Value Indexes post reliably strong active returns. Still, in any given year, these indexes may underperform the core benchmark, and by a significant margin. For instance, the ActiveBeta U.S. Large Cap Value Index had a three-year stretch of negative returns from 1997 through the first quarter of 2000, which reduced the cumulative after-cost active returns of value to over −10 percent between 1992 and 2000. More recently, value also delivered significantly negative relative performance during the 2007 and 2008 recessionary years. Again, this is evidence that value is linked to the risk aversion of investors and that value strategies do not provide higher relative returns in down markets, barring excessively speculative periods.

The ActiveBeta U.S. Large Cap Momentum Index also had a few poor years, such as 2000, 2003, and 2006. However, over the entire 17-year period, there is only one year (1994) in which both momentum and value experienced negative active returns at the same time. The rest of the time, momentum and value active returns either diversify each other or, better still, reinforce each other. Indeed, there are five years in which ActiveBeta U.S. Large Cap Momentum and Value Indexes delivered positive active returns simultaneously.

Because of these diversification benefits, the ActiveBeta U.S. Large Cap MVI performance turns out to be remarkably stable. Year after year, the ActiveBeta U.S. Large Cap MVI provides consistent and stable positive active returns. There are only two negative years (1994 and 2007) over the entire history. The maximum underperformance of the ActiveBeta U.S. Large Cap MVI was only −60 basis points in 1994. Yet, there were six years in which the index outperformed the market by more than 200 basis points.

The benefits of diversification, and the resultant consistency of after-cost active returns, are further illustrated in Figures 8.2 and 8.3. Figure 8.2 depicts the reduction in active risk achieved by combining the ActiveBeta U.S. Large Cap Momentum and Value Indexes. This graph plots the 24-month rolling active risk of the ActiveBeta U.S. Large Cap Indexes, and depicts the reduced active risk of the ActiveBeta U.S. Large Cap MVI compared to the active risk of the momentum and value indexes.

Figure 8.3 shows the distribution of monthly active returns for the ActiveBeta U.S. Large Cap Indexes. This figure provides a graphical

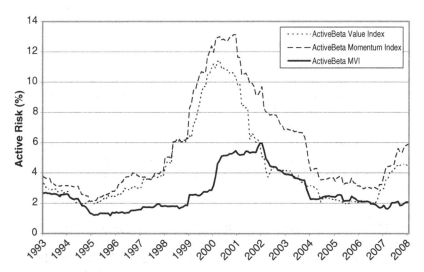

FIGURE 8.2 Twenty-Four-Month Rolling Active Risk for ActiveBeta U.S. Large Cap Indexes, 1993 through 2008
Note: Please refer to the Disclosures section for a detailed explanation of performance.
Source: Westpeak.

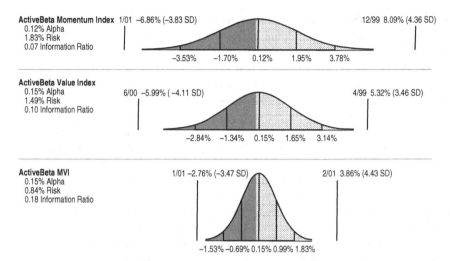

FIGURE 8.3 Distributions of Monthly Active Returns for ActiveBeta U.S. Large Cap Indexes, 1992 through 2008
Note: This figure depicts the normal distribution of monthly active returns for the ActiveBeta U.S. Large Cap Indexes. Bold vertical lines represent the most extreme observations, and show the date at which the observation occurred, the alpha, and the standard deviation from the mean of the distribution. Please refer to the Disclosures section for a detailed explanation of performance.
Source: Westpeak.

representation of the benefits of combining momentum and value. Compared to the ActiveBeta U.S. Large Cap Momentum and Value Index active return distributions, the ActiveBeta U.S. Large Cap MVI active return distribution has less pronounced tails (lower risk) and more height (higher return). More importantly, the left tail (negative active returns) shows more improvement than the right tail. That is, the combination of momentum and value compresses negative active returns more than it compresses positive active returns.

U.S. Small Cap Staying in the United States, Figure 8.4 displays ActiveBeta Index returns for small capitalization stocks.

Once again, both ActiveBeta U.S. Small Cap Momentum and Value Indexes produce independently positive active returns from 1992 through 2008. In addition, the returns to these two indexes remain strongly negatively correlated, with a correlation coefficient of –0.38. The result is an active return series with no years when both momentum and value

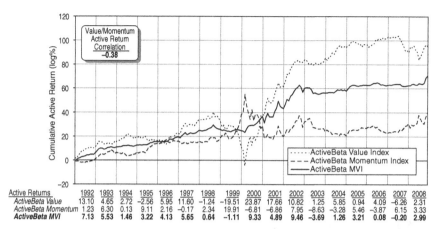

Active Returns	1992	1993	1994	1995	1996	1997	1998	1999	2000	2001	2002	2003	2004	2005	2006	2007	2008
ActiveBeta Value	13.10	4.65	2.72	−2.56	5.95	11.60	−1.24	−19.51	23.87	17.66	10.82	1.25	5.85	0.94	4.09	−6.26	2.31
ActiveBeta Momentum	1.23	6.30	0.13	9.11	2.16	−0.17	2.34	19.91	−6.81	−6.86	7.95	−8.63	−3.28	5.46	−3.87	6.15	3.33
ActiveBeta MVI	**7.13**	**5.53**	**1.46**	**3.22**	**4.13**	**5.65**	**0.64**	**−1.11**	**9.33**	**4.89**	**9.46**	**−3.69**	**1.26**	**3.21**	**0.08**	**−0.20**	**2.99**

FIGURE 8.4   ActiveBeta U.S. Small Cap Index Performance, 1992 through 2008
Note: Please refer to the Disclosures section for a detailed explanation of performance.
Source: Westpeak.

underperform the benchmark at the same time, and seven years when both factors outperform at the same time. As a result, the ActiveBeta MVI delivers positive active returns in 14 out of 17 years.

Europe Excluding the U.K. and United Kingdom   Moving outside the United States, in Figures 8.5 and 8.6, we present the historical performance of ActiveBeta Europe ex-U.K. and United Kingdom Indexes, respectively.

As in the United States, the ActiveBeta Europe ex-U.K. MVI active returns are reliably positive. Over 80 percent of the annual ActiveBeta Europe ex-U.K. MVI returns surpassed the returns of the benchmark, that is, only 3 negative years out of 17. In addition, in the event of annual underperformance, the magnitude of the deficit is a fraction of the potential benefit during the outperforming years. For example, the best year (2002) in Europe ex-U.K. was 5.90 percent over the benchmark, while the worst year (2000) was about half that amount, at −2.97 percent.

The negative correlation between the active returns of the ActiveBeta Momentum and ActiveBeta Value Indexes (about −0.40) remains a critical component in these regions, as it was in the United States. The ActiveBeta United Kingdom Index active return series plotted in Figure 8.6 is perhaps the best example of the benefits of combining momentum and value. The ActiveBeta United Kingdom Momentum and Value Indexes show significant volatility of returns as well as long stretches of underperformance.

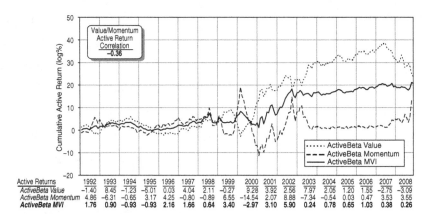

FIGURE 8.5   ActiveBeta Europe ex-U.K. Index Performance, 1992 through 2008
Note: Please refer to the Disclosures section for a detailed explanation of performance.
Source: Westpeak.

The value index, for instance, underperformed for four years in a row from 2005 through 2008, with a cumulative active return drawdown of almost 24 percent. Despite the volatility and the performance of the two components, there are no years when both momentum and value lag the

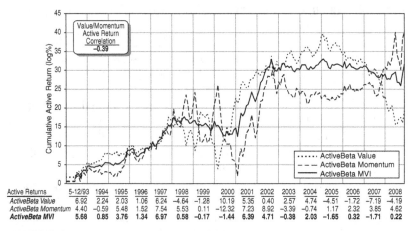

FIGURE 8.6   ActiveBeta United Kingdom Index Performance, 1993 through 2008
Note: Please refer to the Disclosures section for a detailed explanation of performance.
Source: Westpeak.

core index simultaneously. Additionally, the ActiveBeta United Kingdom MVI underperformed in only 5 out of the nearly 16 years, with the highest underperformance being limited to −1.71 percent in 2007. At the same time, the outperformance of the ActiveBeta United Kingdom MVI exceeded 3 percent in four different years. Further, despite the highly negative and prolonged active return performance of value, the MVI has delivered near-market returns during the 2003 through 2008 period, which is likely to result in a favorable comparison of the MVI with active core managers.

Japan   Japanese equities produce results, depicted in Figure 8.7, that differ somewhat from those of stocks in other regions.

The decreased effectiveness of the ActiveBeta Japan Momentum Index changes the dynamic between momentum and value active returns. However, the ActiveBeta Japan Momentum and Value Index active returns still retain their diversifying properties, with a correlation of −0.14. The negative payoff to momentum reduces the cumulative active return of the ActiveBeta Japan MVI compared to the ActiveBeta Japan Value Index. However, the negative correlation effect still provides some diversification benefits in a combined capture of these two systematic sources by reducing the active risk and the active return drawdown, compared to the individual momentum and value indexes. The diversification benefits are quite obvious in 1999, 2000, and 2003, when the highly negative active returns in one index are offset by the strong positive performance of the other index. As such,

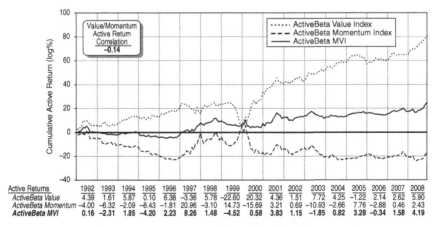

Active Returns	1992	1993	1994	1995	1996	1997	1998	1999	2000	2001	2002	2003	2004	2005	2006	2007	2008
ActiveBeta Value	4.39	1.61	5.87	0.10	6.38	−3.36	5.78	−22.60	20.32	4.36	1.51	7.72	4.25	−1.22	2.14	2.62	5.90
ActiveBeta Momentum	−4.00	−6.32	−2.09	−8.43	−1.81	20.96	−3.10	14.73	−15.69	3.21	0.69	−10.93	−2.66	7.76	−2.88	0.46	2.43
ActiveBeta MVI	0.16	−2.31	1.85	−4.20	2.23	8.26	1.48	−4.52	0.58	3.83	1.15	−1.85	0.82	3.28	−0.34	1.58	4.19

FIGURE 8.7   ActiveBeta Japan Index Performance, 1992 through 2008
Note: Please refer to the Disclosures section for a detailed explanation of performance.
Source: Westpeak.

the ActiveBeta Japan MVI still generates solidly positive active returns on a steady basis. In addition, we see some improvement from the combined capture, as both momentum and value indexes outperform in several years, while in no year do they both underperform. Further reinforcing the complementary nature of the factors, even if reduced to a degree, is that the three strongest years for momentum offset the only three years of the analysis period in which value underperformed.

The ActiveBeta Framework provides an explanation for the relative performance of momentum and value in Japan. As we show in Chapters 4 and 5, there is no tendency for change in short-term earnings expectation to trend over the time period studied. However, there is a strong tendency for long-term earnings expectation to mean revert, and to mean revert at a faster pace than that observed in other markets. As such, it is not surprising that value in Japan has delivered the best performance of all the major developed markets, while momentum has done extremely poorly.

Developed Markets World   Some investors may invest in world equities as a single investment. Figure 8.8 shows the active return performance of this investment through the ActiveBeta World Indexes.

By incorporating all the developed market countries into a cohesive whole, the most all-encompassing picture of ActiveBeta Index performance emerges. The benefits of strategy (momentum and value) and geographical

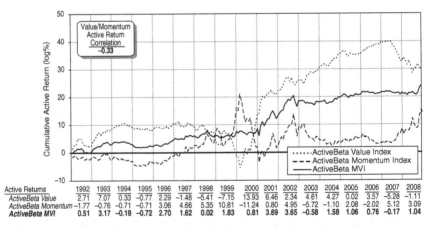

Active Returns	1992	1993	1994	1995	1996	1997	1998	1999	2000	2001	2002	2003	2004	2005	2006	2007	2008
ActiveBeta Value	2.71	7.07	0.33	–0.77	2.29	–1.48	–5.41	–7.15	13.93	6.46	2.34	4.61	4.27	0.02	3.57	–5.28	–1.11
ActiveBeta Momentum	–1.77	–0.76	–0.71	–0.71	3.06	4.66	5.35	10.81	–11.24	0.80	4.95	–5.72	–1.10	2.08	–2.02	5.12	3.09
ActiveBeta MVI	0.51	3.17	–0.18	–0.72	2.70	1.62	0.02	1.83	0.81	3.69	3.65	–0.58	1.58	1.06	0.76	–0.17	1.04

FIGURE 8.8   ActiveBeta Developed Markets World Index Performance, 1992 through 2008
Note: Please refer to the Disclosures section for a detailed explanation of performance.
Source: Westpeak.

diversification are highlighted. The individual ActiveBeta World Momentum and Value Indexes exhibit less volatile active return patterns. The combined ActiveBeta World MVI also has the lowest active risk (2.17 percent) and active return drawdown (3.99 percent) of all the indexes presented in this chapter.

The correlation between the active returns of the ActiveBeta Momentum Index and ActiveBeta Value Index is −0.33. This negative correlation allows for a diversifying pattern of returns, with only one year (1995) in which both momentum and value underperform at the same time. The ActiveBeta World MVI depicts a consistent and stable positive active return pattern. Only four years witnessed below-benchmark returns, and the largest deficit was only 72 basis points in 1995. Yet, in a number of years, the index delivered strongly positive active returns of 250 basis points or more.

This transparent and cost-effective investment in global equities should be of interest to many institutional asset owners looking to increase expected returns from asset portfolios to reduce funding gaps, at a reasonable level of active and total risk. By allocating to the ActiveBeta Developed Markets World MVI, asset owners can potentially increase the expected return for the equity asset class by 100 to 150 basis points, without taking undue risks.

Nondomestic Composite Indexes Next, we consider composites that investors commonly use to allocate to nondomestic equities as a group. The performance of the ActiveBeta Indexes for these composites is shown in Figures 8.9 through 8.12.

In similar fashion to the ActiveBeta Developed Markets World Indexes, these composites highlight the benefits of strategy and geographical diversification. In general, diversification reduces the risk and magnitude of underperformance, while retaining the potential upside. The ActiveBeta Indexes, particularly the ActiveBeta MVIs, for these universes produce consistent outperformance compared to the underlying market benchmarks. The diversification benefit is pronounced in these universes, as indicated by the correlations between momentum and value exceeding −0.30 in all cases. The main performance characteristics for these various composites are summarized as follows.

- For the World ex-Europe (Figure 8.9), World ex-Japan (Figure 8.10), and World ex-North America (Figure 8.11) universes, we observe a maximum of one year of simultaneous underperformance by momentum and value. In these universes, the MVIs underperform their respective benchmarks in only 4 years out of 17, and the maximum annual underperformance in any universe is 167 basis points.

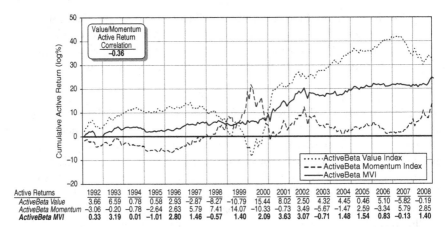

Active Returns	1992	1993	1994	1995	1996	1997	1998	1999	2000	2001	2002	2003	2004	2005	2006	2007	2008
ActiveBeta Value	3.66	6.59	0.78	0.58	2.93	-2.87	-8.27	-10.79	15.44	8.02	2.50	4.32	4.45	0.46	5.10	-5.82	-0.19
ActiveBeta Momentum	-3.06	-0.20	-0.78	-2.64	2.63	5.79	7.41	14.07	-10.33	-0.73	3.49	-5.67	-1.47	2.59	-3.34	5.79	2.85
ActiveBeta MVI	0.33	3.19	0.01	-1.01	2.80	1.46	-0.57	1.40	2.09	3.63	3.07	-0.71	1.48	1.54	0.83	-0.13	1.40

FIGURE 8.9 ActiveBeta World ex-Europe Index Performance, 1992 through 2008
Note: Please refer to the Disclosures section for a detailed explanation of performance.
Source: Westpeak.

- For the Europe (Figure 8.12) universe, we observe one year of simultaneous underperformance by momentum and value. The MVI underperforms in only 5 years out of 17, and the maximum underperformance is 228 basis points.

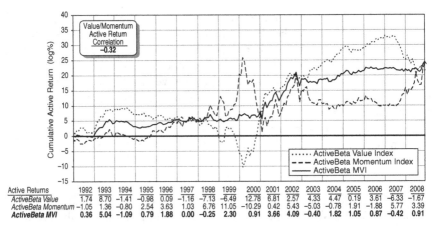

Active Returns	1992	1993	1994	1995	1996	1997	1998	1999	2000	2001	2002	2003	2004	2005	2006	2007	2008
ActiveBeta Value	1.74	8.70	-1.41	-0.98	0.09	-1.16	-7.13	-6.49	12.78	6.81	2.57	4.33	4.47	0.19	3.61	-6.33	-1.67
ActiveBeta Momentum	-1.05	1.36	-0.80	2.54	3.63	1.03	6.76	11.05	-10.29	0.42	5.43	-5.03	-0.78	1.91	-1.88	5.77	3.39
ActiveBeta MVI	0.36	5.04	-1.09	0.79	1.88	0.00	-0.25	2.30	0.91	3.66	4.09	-0.40	1.82	1.05	0.87	-0.42	0.91

FIGURE 8.10 ActiveBeta World ex-Japan Index Performance, 1992 through 2008
Note: Please refer to the Disclosures section for a detailed explanation of performance.
Source: Westpeak.

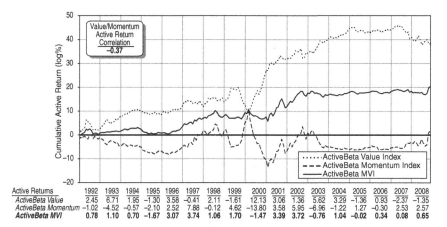

Active Returns	1992	1993	1994	1995	1996	1997	1998	1999	2000	2001	2002	2003	2004	2005	2006	2007	2008
ActiveBeta Value	2.45	6.71	1.95	−1.30	3.58	−0.41	2.11	−1.61	12.13	3.06	1.36	5.62	3.29	−1.36	0.93	−2.37	−1.35
ActiveBeta Momentum	−1.02	−4.52	−0.57	−2.10	2.52	7.88	−0.12	4.62	−13.80	3.58	5.95	−6.96	−1.22	1.27	−0.30	2.53	2.57
ActiveBeta MVI	0.78	1.10	0.70	−1.67	3.07	3.74	1.06	1.70	−1.47	3.39	3.72	−0.76	1.04	−0.02	0.34	0.08	0.65

FIGURE 8.11 ActiveBeta World ex-North America Index Performance, 1992 through 2008
Note: Please refer to the Disclosures section for a detailed explanation of performance.
Source: Westpeak.

Finally, Figure 8.13 shows the distribution of monthly active returns for the ActiveBeta Europe Indexes. As in the case of the U.S. Large Cap universe, the benefit of strategy diversification is clearly seen. Compared to the active return distributions of the ActiveBeta Momentum Index

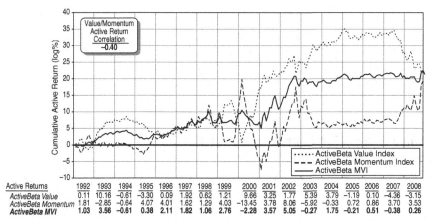

Active Returns	1992	1993	1994	1995	1996	1997	1998	1999	2000	2001	2002	2003	2004	2005	2006	2007	2008
ActiveBeta Value	0.11	10.16	−0.61	−3.30	0.09	1.92	0.62	1.21	9.66	3.25	1.77	5.39	3.79	−1.19	0.10	−4.36	−3.15
ActiveBeta Momentum	1.81	−2.85	−0.64	4.07	4.01	1.62	1.29	4.03	−13.45	3.78	8.06	−5.92	−0.33	0.72	0.86	3.70	3.53
ActiveBeta MVI	1.03	3.56	−0.61	0.38	2.11	1.82	1.06	2.76	−2.28	3.57	5.05	−0.27	1.75	−0.21	0.51	−0.38	0.26

FIGURE 8.12 ActiveBeta Europe Index Performance, 1992 through 2008
Note: Please refer to the Disclosures section for a detailed explanation of performance.
Source: Westpeak.

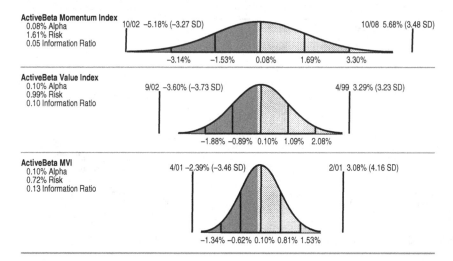

FIGURE 8.13   Distributions of Monthly Active Returns for ActiveBeta Europe Indexes, 1992 through 2008
Note: This figure depicts the normal distribution of monthly active returns for the ActiveBeta Europe Indexes. Bold vertical lines represent the most extreme observations, and show the date at which the observation occurred, the alpha, and the standard deviation from the mean of the distribution. Please refer to the Disclosures section for a detailed explanation of performance.
Source: Westpeak.

and ActiveBeta Value Index, the ActiveBeta MVI active return distribution has less pronounced tails (lower risk) and more height (higher return). Once again, the left tail (negative active returns) shows more improvement than the right tail. That is, the combination of momentum and value truncates negative active returns more than it truncates positive active returns.

Is Value a Superior Source of Active Return Compared to Momentum?

What has been displayed in the historical return analysis section may lead some investors to conclude that value is a more significant source of active returns than momentum. We believe that this relative result is a time period-specific phenomenon, not a fundamental truth of the market. The value outperformance in many universes essentially comes from the post-dot-com bubble environment, in which value stocks gained favor with investors, sparking a notably strong relative run through the middle of 2007.

This multiyear comparative rally in value stocks influences the 17-year time period of the analysis. In a different time period, the relative performance of the two factors could easily reverse.

In the U.S. Large Cap and Europe universes, the active returns of momentum and value are fairly close (see Table 8.3). In the United Kingdom, momentum provided significantly higher active returns than value. Additionally, from 1992 through 2000, we notice that many of the charts show near-equal cumulative active returns to the two systematic sources.

At this point, it might also be useful to review the long-term performance of momentum and value to put our own 17-year historical analysis in the right perspective. Figure 8.14 presents the performance of the Fama-French Momentum and Value factors for the U.S. market since 1927. These graphs depict the strong, consistent outperformance of both the momentum and value systematic sources of active equity returns. Before costs, the Momentum factor performance is higher than that of the Value factor from 1927 through 2008, but this advantage disappears once costs are considered.

The Fama-French factor performance since 1927 coincides with our view of these systematic sources. Over long periods of time, we expect momentum and value, independently, to outperform the market benchmark by similar amounts. Consequently, our passive index capture of momentum and value favors neither factor, but rather includes each systematic source in the ActiveBeta MVI at an equal weight.

Some investors could still reasonably argue that value is a more powerful and persistent source of active return than momentum, as it is a long horizon strategy that relies on the mean reversion of earnings growth in the long run. This mean reversion of earnings growth in the distant future may be more difficult to incorporate in current expectations and prices than the short-term trend in earnings growth, which drives momentum active returns. However, we would argue that even if value was considered to provide superior performance in the long run, investors are better served to capture that performance in combination with momentum, if risk considerations are important. The combined capture of momentum and value significantly reduces risk and drawdown compared to the independent capture of just value.

ACTIVEBETA INDEX EXPOSURES

The ActiveBeta Framework and its accompanying research establish and explain the nature of the systematic sources of active equity returns, that is, momentum and value. The ActiveBeta Index Construction Methodology has been designed to capture the positive active returns associated with these systematic sources. Accordingly, the primary focus of the ActiveBeta Indexes

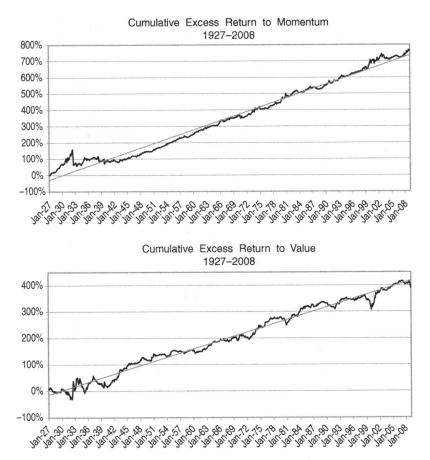

FIGURE 8.14 Fama-French Momentum and Value Cumulative Excess Returns, 1927 through 2008
Note: This figure illustrates the cumulative excess return for Momentum and Value portfolios. The accumulation is a straight addition of the monthly excess returns.
Source: Westpeak, based on data from Kenneth French (http://mba.tuck.dartmouth. edu/pages/faculty/ken.french/data_library.html).

is to gain exposure to the two systematic sources. Other exposures arise in conjunction with achieving as great an exposure to momentum and value as reasonable, but these exposures are secondary to the factor exposures. This section will summarize and review the relative index weights, that is, maximum underweight and overweight positions, to countries, sectors/industries, and individual stocks.

Table 8.6 shows the coverage and the average underweight and over-weight positions reflected in the ActiveBeta Indexes between 1992 and 2008.

Universe Coverage

The first item to note on the table pertains to coverage. As we discussed earlier, the ActiveBeta Indexes seek a reasonable representation of any given core universe. This representation is shown in Table 8.6 in terms of number of securities. Using the U.S. Large Cap universe as an example, we note that the ActiveBeta Value Index covers a minimum of 242 constituents or 48 percent of the 500 core index names, and a maximum of 404 or 81 percent of the constituents. The ActiveBeta Momentum Index covers a somewhat smaller, but still robust, percentage, ranging from 23 percent (115) to 64 percent (320). As noted before, these two indexes have a negative active return correlation in all regions. Therefore, the ActiveBeta MVI benefits from diversification by combining the capture of these systematic sources. The result is an ActiveBeta U.S. Large Cap MVI that holds a minimum of 71 percent (356) and a maximum of 93 percent (464) of the names in the selection universe.

Security Active Weights

In the single-country universes, the highest security underweight and overweight positions occurred in the United Kingdom, as reported in Table 8.6. These extreme positions of around +/–6 percent result from the highly concentrated nature of the U.K. market. Looking at the remaining markets, we observe that the maximum underweight and overweight active positions in the ActiveBeta MVI in any universe is less than 3.25 percent.

Sector/Industry Active Weights

Once again, the most extreme industry active positions occurred in the United Kingdom, a result of the stock and industry concentration that characterizes this market. Excluding the United Kingdom, the average industry active weights for the ActiveBeta MVIs were only around 2 percent, despite the fact that active industry positions were much higher in the component ActiveBeta Momentum and Value Indexes.

Country Weights

In the historical calculation of the ActiveBeta Indexes, the multiple-country indexes are rebalanced at the end of each month to match the country

TABLE 8.6 Average Exposures of ActiveBeta Indexes, 1992 through 2008

Universe	Number of Securities		Security Active Weight (%)		Industry Active Weight (%)		Country Active Weight (%)	
	Min	Max	Under	Over	Under	Over	Under	Over
U.S. Large Cap								
ActiveBeta Value Index	242	404	−3.09	2.93	−2.69	2.17	—	—
ActiveBeta Momentum Index	115	320	−2.62	3.09	−3.12	3.82	—	—
ActiveBeta MVI	356	464	−2.47	2.44	−2.07	1.97	—	—
U.S. Small Cap								
ActiveBeta Value Index	914	1,163	−0.36	0.28	−1.92	1.44	—	—
ActiveBeta Momentum Index	420	1,026	−0.26	0.38	−2.23	2.99	—	—
ActiveBeta MVI	1,175	1,615	−0.25	0.28	−1.36	1.42	—	—
Japan								
ActiveBeta Value Index	875	1,349	−4.09	1.97	−2.22	2.10	—	—
ActiveBeta Momentum Index	180	1,030	−3.21	3.35	−2.90	3.36	—	—
ActiveBeta MVI	1,040	1,557	−3.14	1.78	−2.04	1.95	—	—
United Kingdom								
ActiveBeta Value Index	87	236	−5.58	6.40	−3.44	2.65	—	—
ActiveBeta Momentum Index	81	254	−5.47	5.79	−3.70	4.03	—	—
ActiveBeta MVI	212	308	−4.03	4.96	−2.38	2.17	—	—
Europe								
ActiveBeta Value Index	216	423	−2.88	2.45	−2.54	1.74	−2.41	2.09
ActiveBeta Momentum Index	128	339	−2.47	2.77	−2.93	3.38	−2.83	2.98
ActiveBeta MVI	364	504	−2.05	2.06	−1.89	1.67	−1.67	1.60
Europe ex-U.K.								
ActiveBeta Value Index	161	328	−3.89	2.34	−2.59	1.92	−3.80	3.47
ActiveBeta Momentum Index	90	248	−2.94	3.43	−3.16	3.87	−4.41	5.06
ActiveBeta MVI	273	390	−2.92	2.11	−2.21	1.98	−2.61	2.72
World ex-North America								
ActiveBeta Value Index	578	824	−1.88	1.82	−2.09	1.57	−1.60	1.19
ActiveBeta Momentum Index	327	686	−1.72	1.85	−2.54	2.82	−1.52	1.76
ActiveBeta MVI	753	957	−1.43	1.53	−1.57	1.37	−1.09	0.95
World ex-Japan								
ActiveBeta Value Index	780	941	−1.99	1.84	−2.11	1.56	−0.72	0.66
ActiveBeta Momentum Index	410	950	−1.66	1.96	−2.63	2.99	−0.88	0.87
ActiveBeta MVI	874	1,232	−1.53	1.52	−1.66	1.41	−0.57	0.53
World ex-Europe								
ActiveBeta Value Index	643	851	−2.46	2.28	−2.15	1.81	−0.06	0.08
ActiveBeta Momentum Index	346	815	−2.04	2.43	−2.77	3.15	−0.08	0.06
ActiveBeta MVI	695	1,105	−1.90	1.97	−1.73	1.58	−0.04	0.03
World								
ActiveBeta Value Index	981	1,168	−1.71	1.57	−2.00	1.46	−0.61	0.58
ActiveBeta Momentum Index	480	1,113	−1.42	1.68	−2.57	2.86	−0.78	0.74
ActiveBeta MVI	1,102	1,526	−1.32	1.37	−1.57	1.36	−0.48	0.47

Note: The two columns under the "Number of Securities" heading provide the minimum and maximum number of month-end holdings across the analysis period. Average underweights (overweights) under the industry and country headings are computed by first taking the minimum (maximum) month end value across the analysis period for active positions in industries and countries. Next, these minimum (maximum) values are averaged across all industries and countries.
Source: Westpeak.

weights with those of the underlying universe. Consequently, the active country weights for composite ActiveBeta Indexes are typically extremely small, as shown in Table 8.6. Europe excluding the United Kingdom is an exception to this rule. As we consider Europe ex-U.K. as one country in the ActiveBeta Index Construction Methodology, active country positions arise. However, the maximum active country weights for the ActiveBeta MVI were still only around 2.5 percent.

CONCLUSION

The preceding tables and figures highlight the universal validity and applicability of the ActiveBeta Framework. The extensive analysis presented in this chapter provides the following evidence.

- Momentum and value independently outperform the universe benchmark in all markets, except Japan for momentum.
- Momentum and value are negatively correlated in all markets and regions, thus providing significant diversification benefits when captured in a combined fashion through the ActiveBeta MVI.
- The ActiveBeta MVIs outperform their selection benchmarks in each and every universe and generate highly respectable after-cost information ratios, especially from the perspective of a passive investment.
- The ActiveBeta MVI reliably lowers the risk and drawdown compared to the component momentum and value indexes.
- The ActiveBeta MVI outperforms the selection benchmark at least 70 percent of the time in all universes. The underperforming years are also muted in magnitude compared to the outperforming years in all universes.
- From a risk exposure perspective, the primary tilts in the ActiveBeta Indexes are toward the systematic sources, as intended. The ActiveBeta MVIs, in particular, achieve these exposures with extensive coverage of the selection universe, and only limited exposures to other risk factors, securities, sectors/industries, or countries.

Confronted with underfunded plans and growing funding gaps, institutional investors are looking for ways to increase the expected returns of their asset portfolios. The risk and return characteristics of the ActiveBeta Indexes provide a transparent, cost-effective, and passive investment alternative to achieve this goal.

CHAPTER 9

ActiveBeta Index Applications

The existence of systematic sources of active equity returns, and their efficient capture through the ActiveBeta Indexes, has many applications within the equity asset class related to style investing, performance attribution, portfolio structuring and asset allocation, performance benchmarking, research, and the creation of investment vehicles. These applications are discussed in this chapter.

STYLE INVESTING: A NEW FRAMEWORK

In a celebrated article, Fama and French (1992) created a three-factor model to explain the cross-sectional variation of average stock returns. In addition to the market beta, Fama and French added factors related to a stock's size (based on its market capitalization) and value (based on its book value–price ratio). Although the excess returns associated with size and value had been documented in previous research, the academic stature of the authors gave the Fama-French three-factor model added credence in the marketplace. The Fama-French empirical findings were used by consultants and mutual fund analysts, such as Morningstar, to argue for the existence of investment styles and to create "style boxes" to classify managers. A typical style box for equities is shown in Figure 9.1.

As one can see in this style box, large cap stocks and managers represent one end of the spectrum, with small cap stocks and managers representing the opposite end. By the same token, value stocks and managers find their mirror image in growth stocks and managers.

Index providers have taken a similar tack when creating their style indexes. Initially, index providers divided the universe in half, by market capitalization, according to a single factor, such as book value–price. The high book value–price half was defined as the value index. The other half became the growth index. Thus, the two styles and associated style indexes

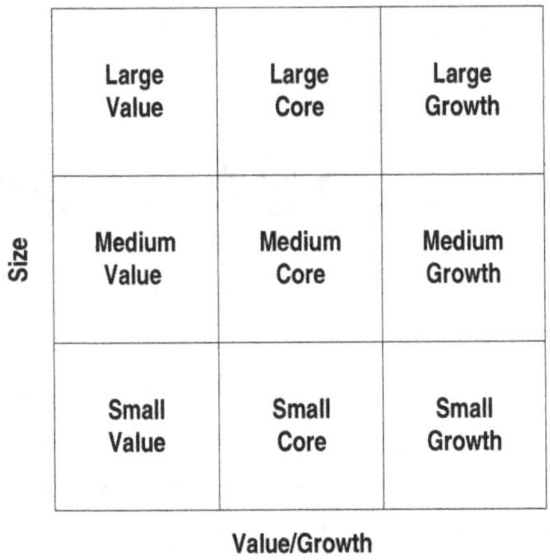

Large Value	Large Core	Large Growth
Medium Value	Medium Core	Medium Growth
Small Value	Small Core	Small Growth

Size

Value/Growth

FIGURE 9.1 Equity Style Box
Source: Westpeak.

were defined in terms of each other. Recently, index providers have evolved their methodology to define growth more explicitly, in terms of long-term realized growth and/or expected growth, thus creating a two-dimensional process for dividing the core universe into growth and value. However, as suggested by the highly significant relationship between valuation ratios and earnings growth rate documented in Chapters 3 and 5, the growth style continues to be defined as the mirror image of value. That is why we believe that growth is better referred to as simply non-value.

Is Growth an Investment Style?

A style, by definition, represents a source of return that is common across a large number of active managers. Therefore, a style investment process must capture some fundamental belief of managers about active return generation in the marketplace. In other words, styles represent some form of systematic sources of active equity returns, especially if they persist over time. Value is clearly an investment style, as it captures the systematic active equity returns associated with the mean reversion of long-term earnings growth expectation and anticipated risk, as we have already discussed. But, is growth an investment style? Which positive systematic source of active equity return does it capture?

The definition and construction methodology of growth indexes forces investors to buy high long-term actual and/or expected earnings growth companies. But the systematic tendency of long-term earnings expectations to mean revert (see Chapter 5) implies that a positive payoff to growth comes from buying current "low" growth companies, not "high" growth companies. If high long-term growth companies are bought, and long-term growth systematically mean reverts, then negative payoffs will be realized.

Table 9.1 shows the published historical performance of value and growth indexes provided by index providers for various market segments and geographical regions. Without exception, growth benchmarks provided negative active returns compared to the core index, while value benchmarks provided positive active returns. For example, in the case of the MSCI World universe, the MSCI World Value Index outperformed the underlying core index by 1.34 percent per annum between 1992 and 2008. Over the same period, the MSCI World Growth Index underperformed by 1.53 percent per annum. Furthermore, the sign and magnitude of active returns and information ratios generated by the value and growth indexes across all universes also point to the fact that growth simply delivers non-value returns.

Given this evidence, how can growth investing, as currently defined by index providers, be an investment style that a large number of active managers willingly follow?

Growth Style Redefined as Momentum

Growth benchmarks do not accurately specify and capture the investment process of so-called growth managers. These managers typically develop strategies to predict "short-term changes" in earnings expectation, not the "level of long-term" earnings expectation. In other words, growth managers follow momentum strategies.

Table 9.2 provides a correlation analysis of growth managers' active returns against the active returns of a long-term expected earnings growth index and a price momentum index. Growth manager active returns are obtained from the PSN manager database and correspond to a large cap growth universe. The IBES 5-year projected growth estimate is a proxy for long-term expected earnings growth. Price momentum refers to 12-month relative price change. The indexes for long-term growth and momentum are created using the ActiveBeta Index Methodology outlined in Chapter 7. The Russell 1000 Growth Index return is subtracted from all manager, growth index, and momentum index returns each month. The large cap growth manager universe is divided into five quintiles based on performance over the 10-year period from 1999 through 2008. Quintile 1 corresponds to the best-performing managers and Quintile 5 to the worst-performing managers. For each manager, we calculate the correlation of its active monthly return with the active monthly return of the long-term growth index. We repeat the procedure for the momentum index.

The last line of Table 9.2 shows the average correlation of all growth managers against the projected growth index (column 2) and the momentum

TABLE 9.1 Historical Returns of Published Core, Value, and Growth Indexes, 1992 through 2008

Universe	Active Return (%) (vs. Parent Index)	Active Risk (%)	Information Ratio	Total Return (%)	Total Risk (%)	Sharpe Ratio
S&P 500				6.73	14.25	0.21
S&P 500 Value	0.49	4.82	0.10	7.22	14.53	0.24
S&P 500 Growth	−0.77	4.49	−0.17	5.96	15.41	0.15
Russell 1000				6.83	14.40	0.22
Russell 1000 Value	1.61	5.86	0.27	8.44	13.63	0.34
Russell 1000 Growth	−2.11	5.51	−0.38	4.72	17.20	0.06
MSCI Japan				−2.63	18.81	−0.17
MSCI Japan Value	3.08	5.32	0.58	0.45	18.39	−0.01
MSCI Japan Growth	−3.23	5.48	−0.59	−5.87	20.74	−0.31
MSCI Europe				7.62	15.80	0.26
MSCI Europe Value	1.43	3.67	0.39	9.05	16.83	0.33
MSCI Europe Growth	−1.54	3.69	−0.42	6.07	15.59	0.17
MSCI EAFE				3.78	14.81	0.02
MSCI EAFE Value	1.96	3.29	0.60	5.74	15.21	0.15
MSCI EAFE Growth	−1.99	3.33	−0.60	1.79	15.13	−0.10
MSCI World				5.16	13.82	0.12
MSCI World Value	1.34	3.85	0.35	6.50	13.79	0.22
MSCI World Growth	−1.53	3.90	−0.39	3.63	14.91	0.02

Note: This table reports the core and style index returns for various public index series. Active return and active risk for the style indexes are compared to the appropriate core index. Indexes are unmanaged, and investors cannot actually make investments in an index. The performance of the indexes shown does not reflect the deduction of management fees or other expenses, which would reduce returns. Returns are annualized.

Source: Westpeak, based on data from MSCI Barra, Russell, and Standard & Poor's.

TABLE 9.2 Correlation of Growth Manager Active Returns versus Active Returns for Long-Term Growth Expectation and 12-Month Price Momentum Indexes, 1999 through 2008

Manager Performance Quintile	Long-Term Growth Expectation	12-Month Price Momentum
Q1	−0.13	0.37
Q2	−0.17	0.31
Q3	−0.33	0.24
Q4	−0.29	0.28
Q5	−0.12	0.20
All	−0.21	0.28

Note: This table reports the correlation between growth-style equity manager active returns and long-term growth expectation and 12-month price momentum. The long-term growth expectation estimate is defined as the IBES long-term earnings growth estimate. The 12-month price momentum is the total return of a stock over the given period. The quintiles, based on returns over the past 10 years of managers in the universe, are formed to include equal numbers of managers, and the quintile return is the median manager return in the given quintile.
Source: Westpeak, based on data from IBES and PSN.

index (column 3). It indicates that growth managers have a 0.28 correlation with high momentum and a −0.21 correlation with projected growth. The negative correlation with projected growth indicates that growth managers may tilt toward value within the growth universe.

The other lines in the table show the average correlations for managers within the specified quintile.

The best-performing managers (Quintile 1) produce an even more pronounced correlation with momentum active returns. Their active returns have a negative correlation of −0.13 with long-term growth active returns and a highly positive correlation of 0.37 with the active returns of the momentum index. These general relationships hold across all manager performance quintiles.

The evidence presented in Table 9.2 supports the claim that growth managers tend to follow momentum strategies and tilt toward value. As such, momentum appears to be a superior representation of the so-called growth investment style.

Redefining Investment Styles and Style Boxes

The ActiveBeta Framework suggests that value and momentum more accurately describe active management styles than value and growth. In essence,

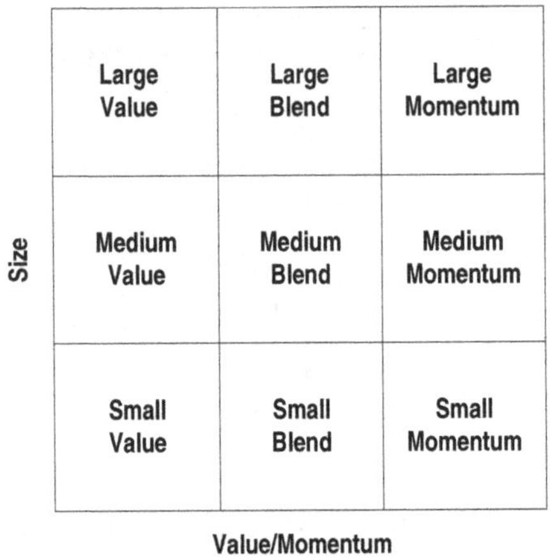

Large Value	Large Blend	Large Momentum
Medium Value	Medium Blend	Medium Momentum
Small Value	Small Blend	Small Momentum

Size

Value/Momentum

FIGURE 9.2 ActiveBeta Equity Style Box
Source: Westpeak.

value and growth capture just one systematic source of active equity returns, that emanating from the systematic behavior of long-term earnings growth. Value delivers the positive payoff associated with the average tendency for long-term earnings growth to mean revert, while growth provides the negative payoff. What is missing from the current style framework is the capture of the second (independent) systematic source of active equity returns, that emanating from the systematic behavior of change in short-term expectation to trend. Momentum provides an efficient capture of this systematic source. As such, momentum and value represent two independent systematic sources of active equity returns and provide a better framework for defining investment styles.

This conclusion leads to the potential development of a new style box to classify active managers, as shown in Figure 9.2.

In this classification, three distinct active manager styles are represented, namely value, momentum, and blend. The blend category better represents the so-called core managers, who have strong value and momentum tilts. Blend is also different from the market.

PERFORMANCE ATTRIBUTION: DECOMPOSING ACTIVE MANAGER RETURNS

If value and growth do not appropriately or fully reflect the investment styles of active managers, then a performance attribution analysis based only on

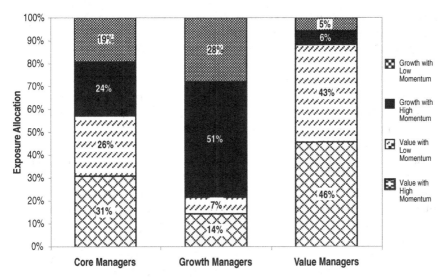

FIGURE 9.3 Active Manager Style Decomposition, 1999 through 2008
Source: Westpeak, based on data from PSN.

value and growth factors or indexes could lead to misleading conclusions. Incorporating momentum, the missing systematic source, or style, into the analysis may provide a better and more complete performance attribution.

Figure 9.3 provides the results of a return-based style analysis, which estimates the exposures of U.S. large-cap core, value, and growth managers to value, growth, and momentum over the 10-year period ending in 2008. The manager return data is obtained from the PSN U.S. Large Cap universe. In this analysis, we start with the Russell 1000 Value and Growth Indexes. Each month, these indexes are divided into two halves, one corresponding to high momentum stocks and the other representing low momentum stocks. Thus, each month, four independent indexes are created, namely:

1. Value/high-momentum index
2. Value/low-momentum index
3. Growth/high-momentum index
4. Growth/low-momentum index

The returns of each core, value, and growth manager are then regressed against the returns of these four indexes, using the regression methodology developed by William Sharpe for style analysis, in which the exposures to the four indexes are forced to add up to 100 percent. The first five years of the 10-year period are used to estimate the initial exposures, and thereafter, the exposures are estimated every month on a rolling five-year basis. Figure 9.3 depicts the average exposures of managers to the four indexes over the 10-year period.

To interpret and understand these statistics, we analyze the portfolio exposures along two dimensions, value versus growth and high momentum versus low momentum. This allows us to assess the value and momentum style tilts that active managers have in their portfolios. The exposures add up to 100 percent along each dimension. For example, if managers have an exposure of 60 percent to value, then by definition, they have a 40 percent exposure to growth. These exposures imply that 60 percent of the portfolio holdings of these managers are in value stocks. At the same time, if the same managers have an exposure of 70 percent to high momentum, then they have an exposure of 30 percent to low momentum. That is, 70 percent of their holdings are also in high momentum stocks. Therefore, these managers have an exposure to high value stocks and high momentum stocks of 60 percent and 70 percent, respectively. The exposures now exceed 100 percent because there is some overlap between high value and high momentum stocks.

Now let's look at the numbers in Figure 9.3. The core managers, on average, have an exposure to value of 57 percent (43 percent to growth). They also have an average exposure of 55 percent to high momentum (45 percent to low momentum). These exposures imply that core managers, as a group, have value and momentum biases in their portfolios. In addition, they have higher exposures to value and high-momentum stocks (31 percent) than to growth and low-momentum stocks (19 percent).

Growth and value managers, by definition, will have very high exposures to growth and value, respectively, when compared to the market as a whole. This is simply the result of how their benchmarks are defined relative to the market. That is, their high exposures to growth and value come from the selection universes are that is specified for them. Therefore, in analyzing growth and value managers the objective is to determine whether they have meaningful exposures to the various styles relative to their selection universe.

The growth managers have a very strong exposure to high momentum, with almost two-thirds of their portfolio holdings in high momentum stocks. They have a much smaller (21 percent) exposure to value. Value managers, on the other hand, have a small exposure to high momentum.

From these results, we can conclude the following:

- Core managers' investment processes have a substantial value and momentum tilt.
- Growth managers are essentially momentum players with a small value tilt.

■ Value managers are essentially value players with no meaningful bias to momentum or growth.

The analysis of Figure 9.3 can be extended to determine the pure alpha generation capability of managers. Figure 9.4 presents this decomposition of manager active returns. The methodology applied in this analysis is as follows. The first five years, that is, January 1999 through December 2003, are used to estimate the exposures of each manager to the four indexes. These exposures are then used to create a custom benchmark for each manager. The managers' returns in the month of January 2004 are then compared to the custom benchmark to determine if the manager provided returns in excess of the custom benchmark. Then, the return data from February 1999 through January 2004 is used to re-estimate the managers' exposures, which becomes the basis for a new custom benchmark for February 2004. The returns in February 2004 are then compared to this new custom benchmark, and so on. This process is repeated every month for each manager. Figure 9.4 reports the average contribution of systematic tilts to value and momentum to manager active returns, as well as the pure alpha contribution over the 10-year period. In analyzing these numbers, we must highlight that large active return contributions could arise even from small exposures, if value or momentum experience large return variation.

The value managers within the PSN U.S. Large Cap universe delivered an average alpha of 90 basis points per annum over the 10-year period. Of this total alpha, 17 basis points per year are attributable to a value tilt and

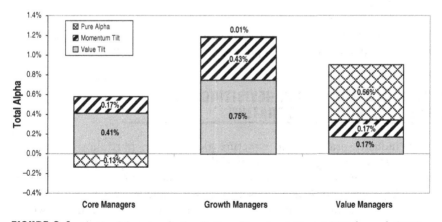

FIGURE 9.4 Active Manager Active Return Decomposition, 1999 through 2008
Source: Westpeak, based on data from PSN.

another 17 basis points per year to a momentum tilt. The remaining 56 basis points are considered pure alpha, representing manager skill.

- For value managers, 38 percent of the total alpha is attributable to systematic sources of active equity returns.

  The growth managers outperform their benchmark by an average of 119 basis points per year. However, nearly the entire outperformance is due to a tilt to value (75 basis points per annum) and to momentum (43 basis points per year). The pure alpha contribution amounts to only one basis point per annum.
- For growth managers, essentially 100 percent of the total alpha is attributable to systematic sources of active equity returns.

  The core managers' average alpha over this period amounts to 45 basis points per annum. However, the contribution from value and momentum tilts is 41 and 17 basis points per annum, respectively. This implies that the pure alpha component was negative 13 basis points per year.
- For core managers, over 100 percent of the total alpha is attributable to systematic sources of active equity returns.

These statistics paint a somewhat troubling picture for active management, especially when we consider the existence of significant selection and survivorship biases. Many studies have established that the survivorship bias in manager return databases averages at least 150 basis points per year. This bias and our analysis imply that active managers, on average, do not provide active returns over and beyond those provided by the systematic sources (momentum and value).

Asset owners can use the ActiveBeta Indexes to conduct an active return decomposition analysis of the active managers they employ. This analysis could help to quantify the pure alpha contribution of each manager.

PORTFOLIO STRUCTURING: REVISITING THE ALPHA-BETA RETURN SEPARATION

Current industry practice is to structure global equity portfolios in terms of a market beta component and an alpha component. The market beta component is implemented through a passive replication of a given market index. The alpha component aims to capture manager-specific skill and is implemented through active managers. The allocation between the two components is driven by asset owners' philosophical beliefs or views on the efficiency of various markets or market segments. However, to the extent that manager active returns largely originate from systematic sources, as depicted in Figure 9.3 and Figure 9.4, the decomposition of portfolio returns and structuring of portfolios into only market beta and alpha is incomplete and potentially misleading. Indeed, if alpha and market beta are the only two choices in decomposing portfolio returns, difficulties arise in distinguishing between systematic sources of active equity returns and a manager's true investment skill. In the alpha-beta return separation debate, therefore, a third source should be considered explicitly: Active Betas. This implies that asset owners should structure their overall equity portfolios in terms of three components:

1. Market beta, implemented through replication of market indexes.
2. Active Betas, implemented through ActiveBeta Indexes or similar vehicles.
3. Pure alpha, implemented through skilled active managers.

This suggested portfolio return decomposition structure is depicted in Figure 9.5.

Asset Allocation: Allocating to Active Betas

Just as the allocation between market beta and alpha is driven by an asset owner's philosophical beliefs about market efficiency, the allocation to

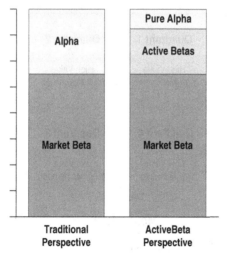

FIGURE 9.5 Equity Management Return Sources
Source: Westpeak.

Active Betas should be influenced by an investor's beliefs regarding the existence and persistence of systematic sources of active equity returns. However, independent of these philosophical beliefs, asset owners should realize that they are already exposed to systematic sources of active equity returns through the active managers they employ. Therefore, as a starting point, asset owners should view Active Betas as an efficient, transparent, and cost-effective alternative to capture that portion of active management returns attributable to systematic sources.

Through ActiveBeta Indexes, the asset owner has the option of allocating some portion of the current alpha component into a direct and more cost-effective capture of systematic sources. One way of allocating to ActiveBeta Indexes is to reduce or eliminate investments in those managers who lack the skill to deliver pure alpha. Thus, ActiveBeta Indexes provide a framework and a tool for asset managers to streamline their overall equity portfolio structure by alleviating the burden of maintaining numerous manager relationships, concentrating investments in truly skilled managers, and allocating active risk and management fee budgets more efficiently.

An allocation to ActiveBeta Indexes could also come from the passive component of the overall equity portfolio. The ActiveBeta Framework decomposes the overall selection universe into four distinct quadrants, represented in Figure 9.6. The ActiveBeta Value Index represents Quadrants 1 and 2. The ActiveBeta Momentum Index represents Quadrants 2 and 3. The

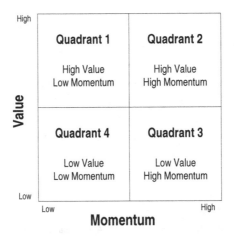

FIGURE 9.6 ActiveBeta Style Quadrants
Source: Westpeak.

ActiveBeta Momentum and Value Indexes combine to form the ActiveBeta MVI, which represents Quadrants 1, 2, and 3. In this index structure, the combination of ActiveBeta Value and ActiveBeta Momentum Indexes does not add up to the entire selection universe, as is the case with most traditional value and growth indexes. The securities that fall into Quadrant 4 are excluded from the ActiveBeta Indexes. These stocks have low momentum and low value characteristics. That is, they have low relative change in short-term expectation and high relative long-term growth expectation. These characteristics deliver the negative payoffs associated with the systematic behavior of earnings expectations.

Table 9.3 reports the historical performance of Quadrant 4 stocks for three universes, U.S. Large Cap, Europe ex-U.K., and Japan, for the 1992 through 2008 time period. On average, these stocks underperform the market universe by over 300 basis points per annum and have a very large maximum drawdown of active return.

Figures 9.7 through 9.9 show the long-term and year-by-year active returns of Quadrant 4 stocks for the U.S. Large Cap, Europe ex-U.K., and Japan universes, respectively. Not only do these stocks underperform the market, on average, by a significant margin, they do so on a consistent basis. In the case of the U.S. Large Cap universe, these stocks underperform in 12 of the 17 years under study. In Europe ex-U.K., they also underperform 12 out of 17 years. In Japan, they have negative performance in 14 out of 17 years.

Some researchers have argued that market capitalization weighting introduces a large performance drag on market indexes, by overweighting expensive stocks and underweighting cheap stocks. We argue, instead, that the performance drag comes from the Quadrant 4 securities that represent approximately 25 percent of the stocks in the universe.

TABLE 9.3 Historical Performance of Quadrant 4 for U.S. Large Cap, Europe ex-U.K., and Japan Universes, 1992 through 2008

Universe	Active Return (%)	Active Risk (%)	Active Return Drawdown Max (log%)
U.S. Large Cap	−3.18	5.90	45.37
Europe ex-U.K.	−3.51	6.52	45.01
Japan	−3.54	9.07	47.96

Note: Please refer to the Disclosures section for a detailed explanation of performance.
Source: Westpeak.

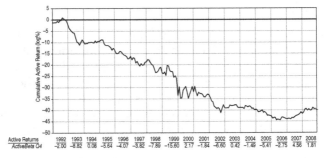

Active Returns	1992	1993	1994	1995	1996	1997	1998	1999	2000	2001	2002	2003	2004	2005	2006	2007	2008
ActiveBeta Q4	-2.00	-8.82	0.08	-5.64	-4.07	-3.82	-7.89	-15.80	2.17	-1.84	-6.60	0.42	-1.49	-5.41	-2.75	4.56	1.81

FIGURE 9.7 Historical Performance of Quadrant 4 for U.S. Large Cap Universe, 1992 through 2008
Note: Please refer to the Disclosures section for a detailed explanation of performance.
Source: Westpeak.

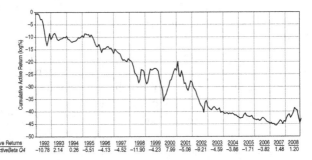

Active Returns	1992	1993	1994	1995	1996	1997	1998	1999	2000	2001	2002	2003	2004	2005	2006	2007	2008
ActiveBeta Q4	-10.78	2.14	0.26	-5.51	-4.13	-4.52	-11.90	-4.23	7.99	-5.08	-9.21	-4.59	-3.86	-1.71	-3.82	1.48	1.20

FIGURE 9.8 Historical Performance of Quadrant 4 for Europe ex-U.K. Universe, 1992 through 2008
Note: Please refer to the Disclosures section for a detailed explanation of performance.
Source: Westpeak.

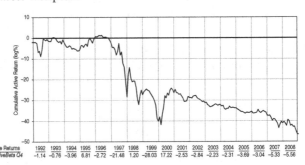

Active Returns	1992	1993	1994	1995	1996	1997	1998	1999	2000	2001	2002	2003	2004	2005	2006	2007	2008
ActiveBeta Q4	-1.14	-0.76	-3.96	6.81	-2.72	-21.48	1.20	-28.03	17.22	-2.53	-2.84	-2.23	-2.31	-3.69	-3.04	-5.33	-5.56

FIGURE 9.9 Historical Performance of Quadrant 4 for Japan Universe, 1992 through 2008
Note: Please refer to the Disclosures section for a detailed explanation of performance.
Source: Westpeak.

Table 9.4 shows the total return and risk characteristics of ActiveBeta MVIs for various markets and market segments. The statistics highlight that ActiveBeta MVIs have similar or lower standard deviations of returns and drawdown compared to the market indexes. Yet, ActiveBeta MVIs provide higher returns in every universe. In addition, although not reported in the table, each ActiveBeta MVI also has a market beta of about one.

Therefore, the ActiveBeta MVI could constitute a more efficient way of capturing both the market beta and Active Beta components for those investors who are willing to bear the risk that Quadrant 4 securities outperform the market on an occasional basis. If not holding 25 percent of the securities is considered too high a risk, then the number of securities not held can be reduced to below 10 percent through an innovative ActiveBeta Custom Index Methodology, which is discussed in more detail in Chapter 10.

PERFORMANCE BENCHMARKING

When asset owners decide to invest in certain styles, they are consciously, or unconsciously, acknowledging the presence of systematic sources of return in the market, which drive the active returns of these styles. As we have shown, momentum and value better represent these systematic sources and the styles of active managers, compared to the traditional choices of growth and value. Therefore, the ActiveBeta Momentum and ActiveBeta Value Indexes represent more appropriate performance benchmarks for active style managers.

In the current style index construction methodology, the style indexes typically combine to form the market index. As a result, the performance benchmark of core managers is typically the market index. But, should the market index be the performance benchmark for core active managers?

There are two ways to approach this question. First, by making the market index the opportunity set of core managers, the assumption is that core managers are style neutral. But are they? The style decomposition analysis depicted in Figure 9.3 highlights that core managers have substantial momentum and value tilts. In addition, they have a much higher exposure to high-value/high-momentum stocks than they do to low-value/low-momentum stocks. An appropriate performance benchmark for these managers could be one that limits the exposure to low value and low momentum stocks. This is exactly what the ActiveBeta MVI does. And, as such, it is perhaps a better representation of the neutral portfolio of core managers compared to the market index.

TABLE 9.4 Total Risk and Return of ActiveBeta Indexes Compared to Market Indexes, 1992 through 2008

Universe	Total Return (%)	Total Risk (%)	Sharpe Ratio	Maximum Drawdown (%)
ActiveBeta U.S. Large Cap MVI	8.72	13.95	0.43	38.44
S&P 500	6.73	14.25	0.21	40.66
ActiveBeta U.S. Small Cap MVI	10.60	16.82	0.48	40.68
Russell 2000	7.32	18.53	0.19	43.14
ActiveBeta United Kingdom MVI	8.40	14.04	0.34	33.73
FTSE 350	6.63	13.91	0.22	34.79
ActiveBeta Japan MVI	−1.56	17.80	−0.04	47.72
TOPIX	−3.13	18.59	−0.20	50.78
ActiveBeta Europe ex-U.K. MVI	9.21	17.40	0.35	45.98
MSCI Europe xUK	7.94	17.58	0.25	45.87
ActiveBeta Europe MVI	9.12	15.65	0.36	41.04
MSCI Europe	7.62	15.80	0.26	41.42
ActiveBeta World ex-North America MVI	5.14	14.59	0.21	42.68
MSCI EAFE	3.78	14.81	0.02	43.47
ActiveBeta World ex-Japan MVI	8.48	13.77	0.39	39.90
MSCI KOKUSAI	7.09	14.11	0.25	41.13
ActiveBeta World ex-Europe MVI	5.47	13.44	0.22	40.41
MSCI World Ex Europe	4.28	13.86	0.06	42.08
ActiveBeta World MVI	6.56	13.46	0.30	40.65
MSCI World	5.16	13.82	0.12	41.91

Note: This table reports the annualized total return and risk statistics for various ActiveBeta Indexes compared to an appropriate public index. The performance of the public indexes shown does not reflect the deduction of management fees or other expenses, which would reduce returns. Returns for the ActiveBeta Indexes do reflect the deduction of implementation costs. Please refer to the Disclosures section for a detailed explanation of performance.
Source: Westpeak, based on data from FTSE, MSCI Barra, Russell, Standard & Poor's, and TSE.

Second, core managers currently are evaluated against a market benchmark. For example, an active U.S. Large Cap manager may be evaluated against the S&P 500 Index. This performance benchmarking paradigm is consistent with an alpha-beta portfolio return separation structure, which implies that any return in excess of the market index represents alpha. However, our discussion on alpha-beta return separation argues that all alphas are not created equal. Some represent manager skill, while others are merely a capture of systematic sources of active equity returns. Therefore, portfolio return decomposition structures should consist of not two but three components, namely market beta, Active Betas, and pure alpha. Each component in this hierarchical structure builds on the previous one. Therefore, the appropriate performance benchmark for the ActiveBeta MVI is the market index. By extension, for core active managers, one could argue that the appropriate performance benchmark should be the underlying ActiveBeta MVI.

By making the ActiveBeta MVI the opportunity set and the performance benchmark for all core managers, the asset owner must have a strong philosophical belief in the ActiveBeta Framework, which identifies the relevant systematic sources and suggests a methodology for capturing them. In cases where the asset owner is reluctant to show such faith in Active Betas, the asset owner can allow the core active managers to use the market index (e.g., the S&P 500) as the selection universe, while keeping the ActiveBeta MVI as the performance benchmark. In instances where the asset owner is unwilling to use the ActiveBeta MVI as the (primary) performance benchmark, the asset owner may still wish to consider the ActiveBeta Indexes and Framework as an additional (secondary) benchmark to negotiate at least a fairer deal on investment management fees, as discussed below.

Investment Management Fees: A Fairer Deal

Asset owners have long felt that they are paying management fees that far exceed the pure alpha generation capability of active managers. But, they have lacked a simple, but effective, framework for arguing for a fairer deal with active managers. Active Betas represent a credible solution.

To the extent that ActiveBeta Indexes represent a cost-effective alternative to the systematic source portion of active management excess returns, they can be used to create a fairer investment management fee structure for asset owners and asset managers. As demonstrated in Figure 9.3 and Figure 9.4, an active portfolio's returns can be decomposed into a systematic source component and a pure alpha component. This decomposition allows asset owners to argue that the portion of a portfolio's active return that comes from systematic sources should be rewarded at lower fees. In return, asset owners should be willing to pay higher fees to those managers who have a demonstrated ability and skill to deliver returns that are in excess of and uncorrelated with the returns from the systematic sources.

These suggestions are unconventional. However, we believe they represent a step in the right direction and may work to the benefit of both the asset owner and the asset manager in the long run. In using ActiveBeta Indexes as a tool for structuring active management fees, asset owners will ensure that they are not paying alpha fees for an investment process that delivers systematic sources of active equity returns in a disguised manner. This fee structure, over time, may also force asset managers to innovate and restructure their investment processes to deliver a higher proportion of pure alpha, a development that should serve the best interests of both asset owners and asset managers.

RESEARCH AND ANALYSIS

The ActiveBeta Methodology provides a conceptual framework for understanding the existence and nature of systematic sources of active equity returns. ActiveBeta Indexes provide a vehicle for capturing the active returns associated with these systematic sources. As such, these indexes fulfill an important research and analysis need. The historical performance of ActiveBeta Indexes can be used to quantify the magnitude of the active returns generated by each systematic source (momentum and value), the manner in which this active return is earned over time (absolute and relative risk characteristics and maximum drawdown), the way in which the independent active returns from each source interact (correlation properties), and the potential benefits of implementing a combined capture of the two systematic sources (ActiveBeta MVI).

Apart from providing a historical perspective on the performance of systematic sources of active equity returns, which may be useful for asset allocation purposes, ActiveBeta Indexes can also prove helpful in understanding the market environment at a given point in time. For example, consider the data presented in Figure 9.10, relating to European equity markets. The data shows the monthly distribution of active returns for the ActiveBeta Momentum Europe and ActiveBeta Value Europe Indexes for the period January 1992 through August 2009. From the start of 2007 up to April 2009, the ActiveBeta Momentum Index outperformed the ActiveBeta Value Index and the selection universe index, as uncertainties relating to the prevailing economic environment led investors to favor short investment horizon strategies over long investment horizon strategies. In April 2009, as the first signs of a potential economic recovery appeared, a significant rotation out of momentum and into value strategies took place. This rotation caused the ActiveBeta

Momentum Index to underperform the selection benchmark by 9.55 percent, which was the most extreme negative monthly active return for this index over the analysis period, representing a negative 5.44 standard deviation event (depicted by the bar on the extreme left of the top graph). The ActiveBeta Value Index, on the other hand, outperformed the market index by 6.79 percent in April 2009, also the most extreme positive monthly active return experienced by this index, representing a positive 6.98 standard deviation event (depicted by the bar on the extreme right of the bottom graph). Since the momentum underperformance was far more pronounced than the value outperformance, the ActiveBeta MVI also delivered negative returns compared to the market. A quantification of the market environment through the active return patterns of the ActiveBeta Indexes provides a useful background for understanding the performance of European active managers in the month of April 2009. Value managers had a good month, while momentum and blend managers significantly lagged the market index. In fact, over 80 percent of all European blend managers in the PSN Europe universe had negative active returns in April 2009.

Figure 9.11 depicts an active return distribution chart for the U.S. market. It shows that April 2009 was not the most extreme month, as was

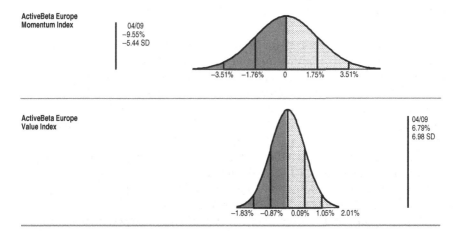

FIGURE 9.10 Distributions of Monthly Active Returns for ActiveBeta Europe Indexes, January 1992 through August 2009

Note: This figure depicts the normal distribution of monthly active returns for the ActiveBeta Europe Indexes. Bold vertical lines represent the most extreme observations, and show the date at which the observation occurred, the alpha, and the standard deviation from the mean of the distribution. Please refer to the Disclosures section for a detailed explanation of performance.

Source: Westpeak.

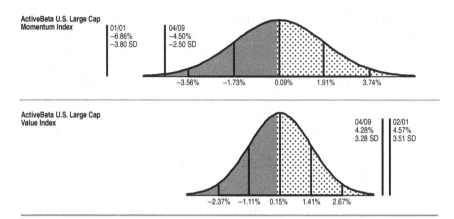

FIGURE 9.11   Distributions of Monthly Active Returns for ActiveBeta U.S. Large
Cap Indexes, January 1992 through August 2009
Note: This figure depicts the normal distribution of monthly active returns relative
for the ActiveBeta U.S. Large Cap Indexes. Bold vertical lines represent the most
extreme observations, and show the date at which the observation occurred, the
alpha, and the standard deviation from the mean of the distribution. Please refer to
the Disclosures section for a detailed explanation of performance.
Source: Westpeak.

the case in Europe. The ActiveBeta Momentum Index did underperform the
market by 4.50 percent, representing a negative 2.5 standard deviation event
(the most extreme month was January 2001, which returned –6.68 percent
[–3.80 standard deviations]). However, the ActiveBeta Value Index offset
the negative performance of momentum by providing a positive active return in April 2009 of 4.28 percent. As a result, the ActiveBeta MVI delivered
performance in line with the selection universe index.

Similar analysis can be conducted for other markets, regions, or market
segments and can be extended to study the performance of sectors or industries. Investors currently do not have the tools, that is, an internally consistent family of momentum and value indexes for global equity markets, that
provide potentially useful insights into the prevailing market environment
and foster a better understanding of the performance of active managers.

INVESTMENT VEHICLES

ActiveBeta Indexes are designed to be investable and replicable. They can
be based on any selection universe. Therefore, they are well-suited for the
creation of a wide variety of investment vehicles, including mutual funds,

exchange traded funds (ETFs), and derivatives. Investment products based on ActiveBeta Indexes would provide investors an efficient, transparent, and cost-effective capture of systematic sources of active equity returns.

The ActiveBeta MVI provides a vehicle, in a single investment, for the combined capture of the two systematic sources in an internally consistent family of ActiveBeta Indexes. The ActiveBeta MVI takes advantage of the significant diversification benefits offered by the counter-cyclical excess return patterns of momentum and value. This efficient capture of Active Betas significantly lowers risk compared to the ActiveBeta Momentum and Value Indexes, such as tracking error and downside risk relative to the underlying selection universe. The current value and growth benchmarks do not provide this opportunity, as (1) growth indexes generate negative active returns, which almost completely offset the positive active returns generated by value, and (2) the combination of value and growth benchmarks simply adds up to the core index and, hence, provides only market returns.

The improved risk/return trade-off of the ActiveBeta MVI suggests that investors should implement a combined passive capture, as opposed to an individual passive capture, of systematic sources, or styles. For instance, the sole capture of value appears to be quite risky, as returns similar to value may be generated through the ActiveBeta MVI, but without the significant downside risk associated with value investing. Given the amount of assets currently invested in pure value and growth strategies or linked to value and growth indexes, this is potentially a very meaningful insight provided by the ActiveBeta Framework.

Four

ActiveBeta
Customizable Solutions

CHAPTER **10**

Alternative Solutions for Capturing Active Betas

A ctiveBeta Indexes offer a straightforward, high-capacity vehicle for capturing the systematic sources of active equity returns. However, the capture of Active Betas can also be offered through a variety of alternative solutions, which may better meet the specific investment needs of some investors. These alternative solutions fall into two broad categories: Active-Beta Custom Indexes and ActiveBeta Custom Solutions. In this chapter, we discuss additional innovative and patent-pending techniques developed by Westpeak Global Advisors to create customized indexes and solutions for sophisticated asset owners and investors.

ACTIVEBETA CUSTOM INDEXES

Customization of ActiveBeta Indexes falls into two broad categories: selection universe and universe coverage.

Selection Universe

The ActiveBeta Index Methodology, discussed in previous chapters, and the customization techniques, discussed in this chapter, can be applied to any selection universe specified by the investor, as long as the selection universe offers enough breadth to make the efficient capture of Active Betas possible.

For example, the ActiveBeta Methodology can be applied to any single-country market index or multiple-country composite market index. It can also be applied to a universe of constituents that adheres to the Islamic principles of investing (e.g., an Islamic index) or to the principles of socially responsible investing (e.g., a socially responsible index). Similarly, the methodology and customization techniques can be applied to custom indexes that some asset owners may use in their asset allocation process or as the policy benchmark for their overall equity portfolio. A GDP-weighted world equity index, as opposed to a market capitalization–weighted index, would be an example of such a custom index.

Universe Coverage

As discussed in Chapter 9, the ActiveBeta MVI more accurately reflects the relevant opportunity set of core managers than the underlying market index. Core managers follow investment strategies that have a combined momentum and value tilt. Thus, the ActiveBeta MVI reflects these characteristics of the investment process of active core managers. But, in doing so, it also creates a benchmark misfit (tracking risk) between the parent index and the ActiveBeta MVI, as the securities that have low momentum and low value attributes are excluded from the index.

We view the elimination of benchmark misfit more as a convenience for asset owners than as a fundamental investment principle of structuring portfolios. Nevertheless, we have designed and developed a new methodology that allows for constructing ActiveBeta Indexes at various levels of coverage of the underlying selection universe in an internally consistent manner. This methodology does not eliminate benchmark misfit, but allows asset owners to vary and choose the level of tracking risk they feel comfortable assuming.

The index construction and maintenance rules used to create the ActiveBeta Public Indexes, discussed in Chapter 7, can be modified to create additional families of high-coverage and low-coverage ActiveBeta Custom Indexes based on the same underlying selection universe. The methodology for creating these additional custom indexes is depicted in Figure 10.1. The ActiveBeta Momentum and Value Public Indexes are created using 33 percent market capitalization coverage of the underlying parent index as the buy threshold and 66 percent coverage as the sell threshold. That is, a security is included in the style index when its style rank places it in the top third of stocks ranked by market value and excluded from the index when it falls into the bottom third. This methodology achieves about a 50 percent market capitalization coverage of the underlying universe in the independent ActiveBeta Momentum and ActiveBeta Value Indexes. The coverage of the underlying universe in the ActiveBeta Momentum and Value Indexes can be increased or decreased by changing the buy and sell thresholds. As shown in Figure 10.1, a 50 percent buy and 75 percent sell threshold increases the coverage of the underlying index, while a 25 percent buy and 50 percent sell threshold decreases the coverage of the underlying universe.

Once the independent ActiveBeta Momentum and Value Custom Indexes are created at various levels of universe coverage, they are then

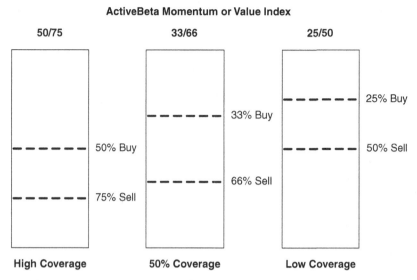

FIGURE 10.1 High- and Low-Coverage ActiveBeta Custom Indexes
Source: Westpeak.

combined (50/50) to form the ActiveBeta Custom MVI. Table 10.1 reports the coverage, active return, and active risk characteristics of the ActiveBeta Public and Custom MVIs for various selection universes. The ActiveBeta U.S. Large Cap Public MVI holds about 81 percent of the names in, and covers almost 76 percent of the market capitalization of, the selection universe. The high-coverage MVI includes over 91 percent of the names and provides an 88 percent market capitalization coverage of the selection universe. Because of higher coverage, the active risk of this index (2.22 percent) is lower than the active risk of the public MVI (2.90 percent). However, lower active risk also leads to lower active returns, as the increase in coverage is achieved by including securities with less favorable momentum and value attributes. The low-coverage MVI, in contrast, has lower coverage of names and market capitalization of the selection universe, and higher active risk and return.

This ability to capture styles at various levels of coverage and active risk is currently not available in the construction of traditional value and growth style indexes. In the prevailing style index construction framework, a given methodology is applied to create a single set of value and growth indexes. As a result, the coverage, active risk, and active return characteristics of the value and growth indexes simply derive from the construction methodology. Investors currently do not have the option of capturing investment styles at various levels of coverage and active risk (or tracking error) for

TABLE 10.1 Coverage, Active Return, and Active Risk of ActiveBeta Public and Custom Indexes for Various Universes, 1992 through 2008

Universe	Names Held (%)	Market Cap Coverage (%)	After-Cost Active Return (%)	Active Risk (%)
U.S. Large Cap				
ActiveBeta MVI (Public)	81.42	75.81	1.59	2.90
ActiveBeta MVI (Custom High-Coverage)	91.08	87.77	1.08	2.22
ActiveBeta MVI (Custom Low-Coverage)	69.78	59.83	2.46	3.95
United Kingdom				
ActiveBeta MVI (Public)	72.95	78.07	1.46	2.68
ActiveBeta MVI (Custom High-Coverage)	85.14	89.33	0.95	2.21
ActiveBeta MVI (Custom Low-Coverage)	60.47	64.60	1.66	3.20
Europe ex-U.K.				
ActiveBeta MVI (Public)	78.52	77.39	1.04	2.85
ActiveBeta MVI (Custom High-Coverage)	88.04	88.92	0.35	2.23
ActiveBeta MVI (Custom Low-Coverage)	65.75	60.50	1.33	3.41
Japan				
ActiveBeta MVI (Public)	85.77	75.73	0.94	3.67
ActiveBeta MVI (Custom High-Coverage)	93.11	87.54	0.79	2.78
ActiveBeta MVI (Custom Low-Coverage)	75.13	60.26	1.31	4.20

Note: Please refer to the Disclosures section for a detailed explanation of performance.
Source: Westpeak.

a given family of value and growth indexes. Yet, this option may prove useful for many purposes, such as the risk-controlled capture of systematic sources, asset allocation research and analysis, performance benchmarking, and performance attribution. In addition, the coverage, active risk, and active return characteristics of the high-coverage and low-coverage ActiveBeta Indexes offer investors a way to assess the trade-off that exists between coverage/active risk and active return within a given selection universe, and, hence, to quantify the cost of avoiding benchmark misfit risk.

ACTIVEBETA CUSTOM SOLUTIONS

The capture of Active Betas can be made more efficient through a series of refinements. The first step in refining the capture entails improving the specification of the momentum and value signals. Next, we use these improved signals in a new portfolio construction methodology designed to build more informationally efficient portfolios. The resultant increase in efficiency through these refinements is meaningful, but is achieved at the expense of more complexity. Therefore, these refinements, which are offered with complete transparency, are intended for sophisticated investors.

Signal Specification

In the creation of ActiveBeta Indexes, the momentum and value signals are specified using simple and commonly accepted definitions. The momentum signal is defined as past 12-month total return, and the value signal is defined as the average of three valuation ratios, namely price-book value, price-sales, and price-cash flow (or price-forward earnings, where appropriate). These straightforward specifications for momentum and value are appropriate in a family of public indexes to demonstrate the systematic nature of momentum and value returns and to highlight the effectiveness of the ActiveBeta Framework at a basic level.

The specification of momentum and value signals can be refined to accomplish a more efficient risk-adjusted capture of Active Betas. For example, when nonindustry-relative valuation ratios are used, industry exposures cannot be effectively controlled. One way to overcome this is to use industry-relative value measures. Making value measures industry-relative minimizes structural industry bets and reduces active and total risk, as shown in Table 10.2.

The analysis in Table 10.2 is based on a long-short portfolio construction technique, which provides the pure factor payoffs. As can be seen from this table, industry-relative value measures have slightly lower excess returns over cash, compared to nonindustry-relative value measures. This implies that a small portion of value returns comes from a structural industry component. The industry-relative value measures, however, produce a significant reduction in the standard deviation of returns. In all cases, the standard deviation of returns is reduced by more than 50 percent. This highlights that a large portion of the risk of nonindustry-relative value strategies comes from a structural industry component. The Sharpe ratio of the industry-relative value measures is significantly higher for the three valuation ratios. This result would imply that the structural industry exposures embedded

TABLE 10.2 Impact of Industry Adjustment on Value Measures for U.S. Large Cap Universe, 1992 through 2008

Value Measure	Excess Return over Cash (%)	Total Risk (%)	Sharpe Ratio
Book/Price	3.81	13.63	0.28
Book/Price Relative	3.00	6.57	0.46
Sales/Price	4.56	16.07	0.28
Sales/Price Relative	3.97	7.12	0.56
FCF/Price	9.21	8.64	1.07
FCF/Price Relative	6.65	4.26	1.56

Note: Please refer to the Disclosures section for a detailed explanation of performance.
Source: Westpeak.

in nonindustry-relative value strategies increase risk much more than they increase return.

Informationally Efficient Capture of Active Betas

In the construction of ActiveBeta Indexes, the selection of securities to be included in the indexes is based on the momentum and value signals, but the selected securities are weighted in the final index by their respective market capitalizations. Consequently, the relationship between the momentum and value signals and the active weights of securities relative to the parent index is weakened. This results in a loss of investment efficiency, as the information contained in the momentum and value signals is not transferred into the index in an efficient manner. The capture of Active Betas can be significantly improved by constructing informationally efficient ActiveBeta Portfolios.

The efficient capture of a signal is achieved by maximizing the transfer coefficient (TC) of the active portfolio. The TC reflects the degree to which the information contained in a signal is actually transferred in an active portfolio. It is measured by the correlation between the signals and the active weights in the portfolio. When there is a direct relationship between the signal and the active weight in the portfolio, that is, the highest-ranked security has the highest active weight, the second-highest-ranked security has the second-highest active weight, and so on, then a high degree of the information contained in the signal is transferred into active weights, and the TC approaches 100 percent.

The TC, as a measure, was developed by Clarke, de Silva, and Thorley (2002) as an extension of the fundamental law of active management advocated by Grinold (1989). The TC is a central concept in the management of active portfolios, as it directly impacts the information ratio (IR) of an active strategy. The IR is defined as active return divided by active risk. The IR can also be decomposed as the product of three fundamental variables as shown in the following equation.

$$IR = TC \times IC \times \sqrt{N} \qquad (10.1)$$

where: IR = Information ratio
TC = Transfer coefficient
IC = Information coefficient, defined as the correlation between expected alphas (signal) and realized returns
N = Number of independent bets, or securities, from which to choose

Equation 10.1 is referred to as the *fundamental law of active management*. It states that the expected IR of an active strategy depends on how much information is contained in the manager-derived expected alphas (IC), how many independent bets the manager can take (N), and how much of the information contained in expected alphas is actually transferred into the active portfolio (TC).

The fundamental law of active management highlights the critical role that the TC plays. A manager's research process may generate highly meaningful alpha signals (IC), but, if the portfolio construction process is unable to transfer the information contained in the alpha signals into the portfolio, then no active returns would be generated. Further, for two active managers using the same alpha signal, constructing portfolios at the same level of risk, and selecting securities from the same universe, the manager who is able to create more informationally efficient portfolios (higher TC) will have a higher IR. Given the importance of the TC, it is surprising how little attention investors pay to this critical aspect of portfolio construction. Many active managers, asset owners, and consultants do not even know the TC of their active portfolios.

The TCs of ActiveBeta Momentum and Value Indexes for various universes are graphically represented in Figure 10.2, as of December 31, 2008.

The graphs depict the relationship between the momentum and value signals used to construct the indexes and the final active weights of securities in the ActiveBeta Momentum and Value Indexes relative to the selection universe. The TC of each index in each universe is reported in the top left corner of the graphs. In general, the TCs range between 0.30 and 0.60, indicating that no more than half of the information in the signals is actually

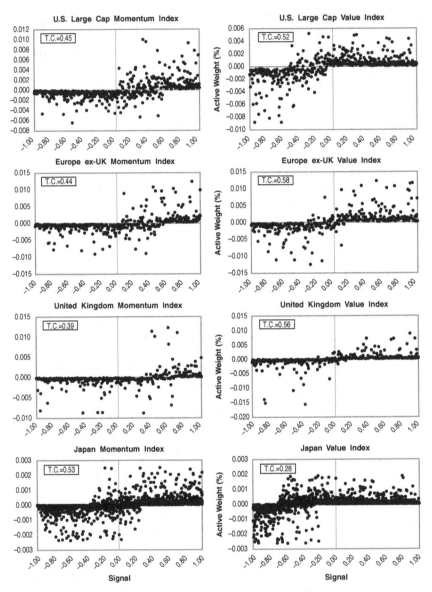

FIGURE 10.2 Transfer Coefficients of ActiveBeta Momentum and Value Indexes for Various Universes, as of December 31, 2008
Note: In this figure each graph plots the signal score vs. the active weight for both momentum and value across multiple ActiveBeta Indexes. The data in the graphs are winsorized, eliminating the top and bottom 2.5 percent of the observations based on active weight.
Source: Westpeak.

transferred into the indexes. However, we must remember that the objective of the ActiveBeta Index Methodology is not to maximize the TC of the indexes, but to create low-cost, high-capacity indexes.

To provide an informationally efficient alternative to capturing Active Betas, Westpeak Global Advisors has developed an innovative, patent-pending portfolio construction technique. This new technique maximizes the TC of the portfolio by converting ordinal security ranks directly into active portfolio weights, in order to implement a pure capture of any given signal. This technique also allows for the creation of informationally efficient ActiveBeta Portfolios at various levels of targeted active risk. The construction methodology does not employ an optimizer, thus providing complete transparency to investors.

The process of constructing ActiveBeta Portfolios is as follows. First, the ActiveBeta Momentum and Value Portfolios are constructed, independently, using the new portfolio construction technique. Then, these two portfolios are combined in equal proportions (50/50) to create the ActiveBeta Momentum and Value Portfolio (MVP).

The TCs of the ActiveBeta Portfolios generated by the new portfolio construction technique are reported in Table 10.3 and compared to the TCs of the ActiveBeta Indexes.

The TCs of ActiveBeta Portfolios range from about 0.65 to 0.75, which are high levels of information transfer, as a practical matter. The ActiveBeta

TABLE 10.3 Comparison of the Transfer Coefficients of ActiveBeta Indexes and ActiveBeta Portfolios for Various Universes, as of December 31, 2008

	ActiveBeta Index Transfer Coefficient	ActiveBeta Portfolio Transfer Coefficient	Increase (%)
U.S. Large Cap			
ActiveBeta Value	0.52	0.76	46.15
ActiveBeta Momentum	0.45	0.64	42.22
United Kingdom			
ActiveBeta Value	0.56	0.70	25.00
ActiveBeta Momentum	0.39	0.70	79.49
Europe ex-U.K.			
ActiveBeta Value	0.58	0.69	18.97
ActiveBeta Momentum	0.44	0.70	59.09
Japan			
ActiveBeta Value	0.28	0.70	150.00
ActiveBeta Momentum	0.53	0.73	37.74

Source: Westpeak.

Portfolios achieve a higher TC than ActiveBeta Indexes in each and every case. With respect to the capture of value, the increase in TC for the Active-Beta Value Portfolio ranges from almost 19 percent for Europe ex-U.K. to 150 percent for Japan. For the ActiveBeta Momentum Portfolio, the increase in TC ranges from almost 38 percent for Japan to about 79 percent for the United Kingdom.

The comparison shown in Table 10.3 is only as of a point in time (December 31, 2008). It does not highlight the consistency of the improvement in TC over time. This is shown in Figure 10.3 for the U.S. Large Cap universe.

Figure 10.3 highlights that the TCs of the ActiveBeta Indexes can vary significantly over time, as evidenced by the variation between the 1998 through 2003 time period. The ActiveBeta Portfolios consistently achieve a high level of information transfer, as shown by the consistently significant improvement in TCs relative to the ActiveBeta Indexes.

In general, our new portfolio construction technique achieves a TC of 1.00 in a long-short portfolio. The TCs of long-only, signal-weighted portfolios average around 0.75. The long-only constraint causes a 25 percent loss of information transfer, as securities cannot be underweighted beyond their benchmark weight. The TCs of long-only, market capitalization–weighted portfolios average around 0.50. Thus, market capitalization weighting causes another 25 percent loss in information transfer.

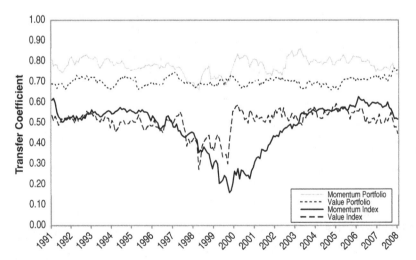

FIGURE 10.3   Transfer Coefficients of ActiveBeta Indexes and ActiveBeta Portfolios for U.S. Large Cap Universe, 1992 through 2008
Source: Westpeak.

Does the higher transfer of signal information improve the performance of ActiveBeta Portfolios?

The simulated historical performance of ActiveBeta Portfolios is reported in Table 10.4 for various universes.

In all universes, the ActiveBeta MVP provides positive after-cost active returns, which range from 127 basis points per annum for Japan to 264 basis points per year for U.S. Small Cap. In all cases, the combination of momentum and value provides significant diversification benefits. This can be seen in the fact that the active risk, as well as maximum drawdown, of the ActiveBeta MVP is lower than that of the two components in all universes, except the United Kingdom. The reduction in active risk results in highly respectable after-cost information ratios for the ActiveBeta MVPs. These are in excess of 0.60, except in Japan (0.47).

The ActiveBeta MVPs are also highly diversified, holding a large number of names from the selection universe. The percentage of names held varies from 66 percent for the World ex-North America universe to 82 percent for the U.S. Large Cap universe.

Table 10.5 compares the historical performance of ActiveBeta Indexes and ActiveBeta Portfolios for various universes.

In all universes, except U.S. Small Cap, the ActiveBeta MVP generates a higher level of after-cost active returns. In all universes, except Japan, the ActiveBeta Portfolios also have a lower level of active risk. The combination of higher after-cost active returns and lower active risk produces significantly higher after-cost information ratios for the ActiveBeta Portfolios in all markets and composites. Finally, ActiveBeta Portfolios also have similar or lower active return maximum drawdown.

The ActiveBeta Indexes and ActiveBeta Portfolios use the same momentum and value signals (i.e., identical IC) and selection universe (i.e., identical N). Therefore, the superior risk-adjusted performance (i.e., IR) of ActiveBeta Portfolios over ActiveBeta Indexes is solely a result of higher informational efficiency (i.e., higher TC) of ActiveBeta Portfolios. Again, these results highlight the critical importance of TC and the need to create informationally efficient active portfolio construction processes.

The ActiveBeta Portfolios achieve a very high level of TC by significantly limiting the concentration in individual securities and taking a very large number of active bets. A comparison of the maximum underweight and overweight active positions for the ActiveBeta Indexes and ActiveBeta Portfolios is shown in Table 10.6.

The top half of Table 10.6 shows the extreme active positions reflected in the ActiveBeta Indexes and ActiveBeta Portfolios at any point in time over the 1992 through 2008 time period. These extreme positions have a temporary nature and are caused by specific security, industry, or market events.

TABLE 10.4 Simulated Historical Active Return Performance of ActiveBeta Portfolios for Various Universes, 1992 through 2008

Universe	After-Cost Active Return (%)	Active Risk (%)	After-Cost Information Ratio	Active Return Drawdown Max (log %)	Names Held from Universe (%)	Annual Turnover (%)
U.S. Large Cap						
ActiveBeta Value Portfolio	1.92	2.84	0.66	17.08	60	38
ActiveBeta Momentum Portfolio	1.54	3.49	0.40	11.68	58	52
ActiveBeta MVP	1.78	1.76	0.94	4.74	82	43
U.S. Small Cap						
ActiveBeta Value Portfolio	3.59	3.81	0.81	19.26	57	45
ActiveBeta Momentum Portfolio	1.94	4.50	0.39	16.53	58	66
ActiveBeta MVP	2.64	2.30	0.97	5.40	80	67
United Kingdom						
ActiveBeta Value Portfolio	0.85	1.93	0.44	5.89	52	33
ActiveBeta Momentum Portfolio	1.81	4.36	0.39	24.17	50	51
ActiveBeta MVP	1.36	1.96	0.65	7.81	72	43
Japan						
ActiveBeta Value Portfolio	2.28	4.00	0.61	14.66	53	33
ActiveBeta Momentum Portfolio	−0.68	3.10	−0.24	19.12	50	53
ActiveBeta MVP	1.27	2.84	0.47	9.68	76	39

Europe ex-U.K.						
ActiveBeta Value Portfolio	1.31	2.53	0.46	13.29	52	39
ActiveBeta Momentum Portfolio	1.58	3.46	0.38	9.19	51	51
ActiveBeta MVP	**1.47**	**2.02**	**0.61**	**5.70**	**73**	**46**
Europe						
ActiveBeta Value Portfolio	1.70	2.85	0.56	11.28	50	52
ActiveBeta Momentum Portfolio	1.57	3.64	0.37	12.14	48	66
ActiveBeta MVP	**1.71**	**1.97**	**0.77**	**4.31**	**71**	**54**
World ex-North America						
ActiveBeta Value Portfolio	2.23	3.32	0.66	11.41	50	82
ActiveBeta Momentum Portfolio	0.83	4.03	0.19	14.77	49	107
ActiveBeta MVP	**1.64**	**2.01**	**0.77**	**4.01**	**66**	**87**
World ex-Japan						
ActiveBeta Value Portfolio	1.72	3.40	0.50	17.86	56	55
ActiveBeta Momentum Portfolio	1.74	4.23	0.38	14.63	55	73
ActiveBeta MVP	**1.81**	**2.21**	**0.76**	**4.94**	**74**	**60**
World ex-Europe						
ActiveBeta Value Portfolio	1.59	3.56	0.45	19.30	61	55
ActiveBeta Momentum Portfolio	0.87	4.21	0.21	13.09	61	77
ActiveBeta MVP	**1.32**	**2.05**	**0.62**	**6.77**	**78**	**61**
World						
ActiveBeta Value Portfolio	1.79	3.17	0.56	16.16	55	56
ActiveBeta Momentum Portfolio	1.28	3.99	0.31	13.96	54	77
ActiveBeta MVP	**1.62**	**1.99**	**0.77**	**3.87**	**73**	**61**

Note: Please refer to the Disclosures section for a detailed explanation of performance.
Source: Westpeak.

TABLE 10.5 Historical Performance of ActiveBeta Portfolios Compared to ActiveBeta Indexes for Various Universes, 1992 through 2008

Universe	After-Cost Active Return (%)	Active Risk (%)	After-Cost Information Ratio	Active Return Drawdown Max (log %)
U.S. Large Cap				
ActiveBeta MVI	1.08	2.22	0.43	4.99
ActiveBeta MVP	1.78	1.76	0.94	4.74
U.S. Small Cap				
ActiveBeta MVI	2.82	3.30	0.70	13.03
ActiveBeta MVP	2.64	2.30	0.97	5.40
United Kingdom				
ActiveBeta MVI	0.95	2.21	0.39	6.70
ActiveBeta MVP	1.36	1.96	0.65	7.81
Japan				
ActiveBeta MVI	0.79	2.78	0.23	7.92
ActiveBeta MVP	1.27	2.84	0.47	9.68
Europe ex-U.K.				
ActiveBeta MVI	0.35	2.23	0.11	7.64
ActiveBeta MVP	1.47	2.02	0.61	5.70
Europe				
ActiveBeta MVI	1.24	2.49	0.46	5.48
ActiveBeta MVP	1.71	1.97	0.77	4.31
World ex-North America				
ActiveBeta MVI	1.07	2.17	0.46	4.74
ActiveBeta MVP	1.64	2.01	0.77	4.01
World ex-Japan				
ActiveBeta MVI	1.35	2.30	0.53	4.44
ActiveBeta MVP	1.81	2.21	0.76	4.94
World ex-Europe				
ActiveBeta MVI	1.31	2.36	0.51	4.35
ActiveBeta MVP	1.32	2.05	0.62	6.77
World				
ActiveBeta MVI	1.31	2.17	0.56	3.99
ActiveBeta MVP	1.62	1.99	0.77	3.87

Note: In certain cases, the construction parameters were adjusted in one or both of the MVI/MVP simulations in order to achieve comparable active risk levels. Therefore, the values in this table may not match values contained in other tables. Please refer to the Disclosures section for a detailed explanation of performance.
Source: Westpeak.

TABLE 10.6 Maximum Underweight and Overweight Positions of ActiveBeta Indexes and ActiveBeta Portfolios for Various Universes, 1992 through 2008

Universe	Security Active Weight (%)		Industry Active Weight (%)		Country Active Weight (%)	
	Extreme Underweights and Overweights					
U.S. Large Cap						
ActiveBeta MVI	−4.39	4.91	−8.11	8.07	—	—
ActiveBeta MVP	−0.98	0.73	−2.31	2.91	—	—
U.S. Small Cap						
ActiveBeta MVI	−1.19	0.52	−5.06	6.00	—	—
ActiveBeta MVP	−0.32	0.34	−3.53	3.89	—	—
United Kingdom						
ActiveBeta MVI	−8.49	10.45	−15.18	14.69	—	—
ActiveBeta MVP	−0.76	0.60	−4.34	2.71	—	—
Europe ex-U.K.						
ActiveBeta MVI	−5.12	5.13	−9.23	8.29	−10.04	10.44
ActiveBeta MVP	−0.78	0.53	−3.86	4.42	−4.80	3.87
Japan						
ActiveBeta MVI	−7.24	3.85	−14.07	5.77	—	—
ActiveBeta MVP	−0.44	0.64	−2.08	3.94	—	—
	Average Underweights and Overweights					
U.S. Large Cap						
ActiveBeta MVI	−2.47	2.44	−2.07	1.97	—	—
ActiveBeta MVP	−0.71	0.57	−0.93	1.04	—	—
U.S. Small Cap						
ActiveBeta MVI	−0.25	0.28	−1.36	1.42	—	—
ActiveBeta MVP	−0.21	0.27	−1.02	0.89	—	—
United Kingdom						
ActiveBeta MVI	−4.03	4.96	−2.38	2.17	—	—
ActiveBeta MVP	−0.50	0.43	−0.98	1.14	—	—
Europe ex-U.K.						
ActiveBeta MVI	−2.92	2.11	−2.21	1.98	−2.61	2.72
ActiveBeta MVP	−0.52	0.40	−0.98	1.20	−1.74	1.90
Japan						
ActiveBeta MVI	−3.14	1.78	−2.04	1.95	—	—
ActiveBeta MVP	−0.30	0.14	−0.61	0.60	—	—

Note: Extreme underweights (overweights) represent the minimum (maximum) observation within each category (security, industry, country), and across the entire analysis period. Average underweights (overweights) are computed by first taking the minimum (maximum) month end value across the analysis period for active positions in industries and countries. Next, these minimum (maximum) values are averaged across all industries and countries.
Source: Westpeak.

In all cases, the extreme security, industry, or country active positions taken by the ActiveBeta Portfolios are a fraction of those reflected in ActiveBeta Indexes. For instance, in the case of U.S. Large Cap, the extreme security overweight position for ActiveBeta MVI was 4.91 percent. The extreme security overweight position for ActiveBeta MVP was only 0.73 percent. The differences become even more pronounced in the case of concentrated markets, such as the United Kingdom (10.45 percent vs. 0.60 percent).

The average underweight and overweight active positions are more reflective of what happens in the MVIs and the MVPs on a long-term basis. As shown in the bottom half of Table 10.6, the same picture emerges. ActiveBeta Portfolios have significantly lower security, industry, and country active positions.

The main point to highlight from Table 10.6 is the small active positions that the ActiveBeta MVPs take. On average, the maximum security overweight ranges from 57 basis points for the U.S. Large Cap to only 14 basis points for Japan. The range in maximum underweight is 71 basis points for U.S. Large Cap to only 21 basis points for U.S. Small Cap. The average maximum industry active positions are around 100 basis points. Finally, the maximum country active weights, on average, are below 200 basis points. And yet, ActiveBeta Portfolios produce after-cost active returns and information ratios that compare highly favorably to alpha processes that take concentrated bets.

A WORD ON TRADITIONAL ACTIVE MANAGEMENT

Many studies have documented that over 65 percent of traditional active managers underperform the market, on average. Since ActiveBeta Indexes outperform the market indexes in each and every universe for the period 1992 through 2008, we can safely assume that even a higher percentage of active managers would not compare favorably to these vehicles. This is a surprising (and somewhat disturbing) result, especially when we consider the fact that active managers, on average, seem to have very high exposures to the momentum and value signals used in the construction of MVIs. The market capitalization weighting of the MVIs, while providing high capacity and transparency, also sacrifices some investment efficiency as the link between momentum and value signals and the active weights of securities in the index is disturbed. Active managers presumably do not operate under the same constraints as market indexes, so they should be able to provide a more efficient capture of the momentum and value systematic returns. So, why isn't the typical active management process effective in capturing the systematic returns associated with momentum and value strategies?

The ActiveBeta Indexes are based on the same selection universe that active managers use as their performance benchmarks (i.e., identical N). Therefore, the fundamental law of active management would indicate that active managers, who, as a group, have high exposures to momentum and value, underperform the ActiveBeta Indexes for two potential reasons. First, the IC of active management signals may be lower than the IC of ActiveBeta Index signals. An investment process based on only two signals (momentum and value) would be considered too simple for an alpha product by many asset managers, consultants, and asset owners, which would make it difficult to argue for alpha fees. Therefore, active managers typically use many factors in their research and alpha signal generation process. However, it is not clear that the more complex multifactor process actually adds value relative to the two-factor momentum and value model presented here. To the contrary, it seems that the multiple factors introduce noise, resulting in a diluted, as opposed to pure, capture of momentum and value active returns.

Second, the TC of actively managed portfolios may be even lower than the 50 percent achieved by ActiveBeta Indexes, on average. Again, this is a surprising result because the ActiveBeta Indexes do not aim to maximize the TC. Active managers' investment process objective, on the other hand, should be to maximize the TC of the active portfolio at a given level of active risk, that is, to construct more informationally efficient active portfolios than the market capitalization–weighted indexes. But, active managers, in general, appear to fail in this endeavor. One reason for this could be that active managers, driven by their own interests, approach the capture of factors such as momentum and value as an alpha capture as opposed to a beta or systematic source capture. As a result, they create investment processes and construct active portfolios that may be inconsistent with the capture of systematic sources, as depicted in Figure 10.4.

This diagram shows that an active portfolio's excess return over cash can be broken down into a market return premium component, an additional systematic source component, and a pure alpha component. The source of return for each component, namely market beta, Active Betas, and manager skill, indicates the risks that need to be taken for an efficient capture of the return source. For example, the efficient capture of Active Betas requires a high exposure to the systematic sources (i.e., high TC), low stock-specific risk (i.e., small active positions), high level of diversification (i.e., a large number of small active bets), and no transparency risk (i.e., no investment process risk). This is exactly what ActiveBeta Portfolios achieve.

When active managers and asset owners approach the capture of systematic sources from the perspective of an alpha capture, inappropriate risks, such as concentrated stock bets, low diversification, and lack of transparency, are invariably assumed. This need not be the case. Active Betas

Portfolio (Excess Return) =	Market Return Premium	+	Active Returns		Pure Alpha
			Additional Systematic Sources of Return	+	
Source of Return	Market β		Active β		Manager Skill
Nature of Risk	Market Exposure		Systematic Source Exposure		Stock Exposure
Level of Specific Stock Risk	None		Low		High
Level of Diversification	Perfect		High		Low
Transparency Risk (Investment Process Risk)	None		None		High
Implementation	Passive Replication		ActiveBeta-Type Strategies		Active Manager

FIGURE 10.4   Capturing Various Components of Portfolio Returns
Source: Westpeak.

can be captured more efficiently while avoiding most of these risks. For instance, stock-specific risk is a major source of portfolio return instability, as evidenced by the market environment in 2007 and 2008. ActiveBeta Portfolios, targeting 3 percent active risk, typically have a maximum security overweight position of 50 basis points compared to as much as 500 basis points for a typical active manager, and yet produce superior returns.

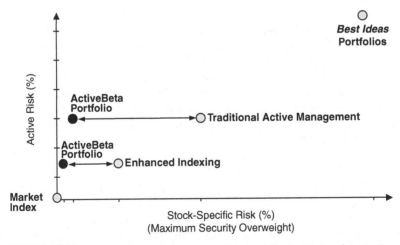

FIGURE 10.5   Comparison of Maximum Overweight Positions of ActiveBeta Portfolios and Traditional Active Portfolios
Source: Westpeak.

In other words, ActiveBeta Portfolios can deliver a capture of the systematic sources at a significantly lower level of stock-specific risk, compared to traditionally managed active portfolios, without sacrificing returns. This is depicted in Figure 10.5.

CONCLUSION

From an industry-wide application perspective, ActiveBeta Indexes provide a low-cost, high-capacity vehicle for capturing the systematic sources of active equity returns. These indexes have many more applications, as discussed in Chapter 9. Individual investors seeking a more efficient capture of Active Betas may wish to consider ActiveBeta Portfolio strategies as an alternative solution. ActiveBeta Portfolios are based on an innovative portfolio construction technique, which produces significantly more informationally efficient active portfolios. Complete transparency is also offered to those investors wishing to pursue the ActiveBeta Portfolio approach.

CHAPTER **11**

Concluding Remarks

The systematic behavior of change in short-term earnings expectation to trend and long-term earnings growth expectations to mean revert gives rise to systematic sources of active equity returns. Two simple investment strategies, namely momentum and value, are contemporaneously linked to short-term and long-term earnings growth, respectively. The returns to momentum and value strategies are, therefore, driven partly by the average tendency of short-term earnings growth to trend and long-term earnings growth to mean revert. We refer to these systematic sources of active equity returns as Active Betas and have created a family of ActiveBeta Indexes to capture these sources efficiently, transparently, and cost-effectively.

A style analysis of active managers, based on ActiveBeta Indexes, shows that growth managers are really momentum players, value managers are truly value players, and core managers have momentum and value tilts. A return decomposition analysis of active managers further shows that systematic momentum and value tilts account for a significant portion of traditional active equity returns. Given this evidence, the current value and growth style definitions and index construction appear to be suboptimal, if not misleading.

The role of a style benchmark is to identify the common investment process of active style managers and to represent the universe of securities that corresponds to that investment process. In this context, growth, as presently defined, is not an accurate representation of the growth investment process. Growth managers do not invest in high long-term growth securities. Rather, they invest in high change in expectation, or momentum, securities. Further, core managers' benchmark universe currently is defined as the capitalization-weighted market index, which would imply that core managers are style-neutral and simply follow a size-based investment process. This is clearly not the case, as core managers have higher exposure to securities that have attractive momentum and value characteristics than to securities with undesirable momentum and value attributes. Consequently,

199

in the current style framework, both growth and core managers are compared to inaccurately defined benchmarks.

The ActiveBeta Momentum Index, ActiveBeta Value Index, and ActiveBeta MVI more accurately reflect the investment processes and investable universes of active growth, value, and core managers, respectively. Therefore, they represent more appropriate performance benchmarks for active style managers, including core managers. ActiveBeta Indexes have many other applications, such as asset allocation research and analysis, performance attribution, portfolio structuring, and creation of investment products.

The ActiveBeta Indexes provide positive after-cost active returns relative to the universes upon which they are based in all markets and regions of the world that we have studied, except for momentum in Japan. In all markets and regions, the active returns of the ActiveBeta Momentum and Value Indexes exhibit strong negative correlation. The ActiveBeta MVIs, benefiting from this negative correlation, have lower active risk and active return drawdown compared to the ActiveBeta Momentum and Value Indexes. They generate after-cost information ratios that generally exceed 0.50. The momentum-value diversification also results in stable active returns for the ActiveBeta MVIs, as these indexes outperform the market benchmark at least 70 percent of the time in our study. Also, the magnitude of negative active returns in the underperforming years is highly muted compared to the positive active returns in outperforming years. In the relative return space, these results indicate that strategy diversification between momentum and value provides more meaningful risk reduction benefits than geographical diversification within either momentum or value.

The ActiveBeta Framework provides reasonable explanations to solve many of the puzzles in the current investment literature and practice. For example, it sheds light on the source of momentum and value returns. It explains why momentum has not worked in Japan for the past two decades. Active Betas provide a conceptual framework for explaining the relative performance of momentum and value returns. And it puts forth a rationale for why growth, as currently defined, is not an investment style, something that many practitioners have found puzzling for years.

The investment industry needs to take a critical look at the current state of traditional active management and style investing. With this book, we hope to initiate this discussion. We present our views on the matter, which we believe are well-supported by the research. We look forward to both the coming debate on the ActiveBeta Framework and the improved opportunities for investors that we expect will emerge from this give-and-take. Only by scrutinizing our long-held notions can we advance to the next level of investing. We trust that the questions and answers in this book will aid in this analysis.

Disclosures

The performance results shown for the ActiveBeta Indexes are not actual results. The results were achieved from historical simulation based on the rules used in creation of the indexes. Returns include a combined transaction cost and execution delay penalty assessed against monthly turnover as follows:

- U.S. Large Cap: 0.40 percent
- U.S. Small Cap: 0.80 percent
- International Large Cap: 0.60 percent
- Global Large Cap: 0.50 percent

The performance results shown for the ActiveBeta Portfolios are not actual results. The results were achieved from historical simulation and do not represent actual trading. As a consequence, they do not reflect the impact that material economic and market factors might have had on the decision-making if clients' money had actually been managed during the period shown. Simulated performance results are purely hypothetical and are achieved by means of the retroactive application of a model developed with the benefit of hindsight. Simulated portfolios have inherent limitations. Material economic and market factors may affect investment decisions differently when managers are investing actual client assets. Simulated portfolios do not reflect the impact of actual portfolio trading, which may affect the price and availability of securities.

Performance results are presented gross of management and performance fees, administrative fees, and withholding taxes. Returns reflect the reinvestment of dividends, and include a combined transaction cost and execution delay penalty assessed against monthly turnover as follows:

- U.S. Large Cap: 0.60 percent
- U.S. Small Cap: 1.50 percent
- International Large Cap: 0.80 percent
- Global Large Cap: 0.70 percent

The analysis period is May 1, 1993 through December 31, 2008 for the ActiveBeta United Kingdom Indexes and Portfolios, and January 1, 1992 through December 31, 2008 for all other ActiveBeta Indexes and Portfolios.

The simulated performance results shown are not indicative of any specific investment and are not a guarantee of future results. Current performance may be lower or higher than the performance results shown. Potential for profit is accompanied by the possibility of loss.

Although the information presented in this material has been prepared internally and/or obtained from sources that the authors believe to be reliable, the authors do not guarantee the accuracy or completeness of such information.

Sources of data include FTSE, IBES, MSCI Barra, PSN, Russell, Standard & Poor's, and TSE. FTSE, IBES, MSCI Barra, PSN, Russell, Standard & Poor's, and TSE assume no responsibility for the accuracy or completeness of the data and disclaim all express or implied warranties in connection therewith.

The London Stock Exchange Plc and the Financial Times Limited are the owners of trademarks relating to the FTSE Indices. I/B/E/S is a registered trademark of Thomson Reuters (Markets) LLC. Morgan Stanley Capital International Inc. is the owner of trademarks relating to the MSCI Indixes. Frank Russell Company is the owner of trademarks relating to the Russell Indexes. S&P 500 is a trademark of the McGraw-Hill Companies, Inc. TOPIX is a registered trademark of Tokyo Stock Exchange, Inc.

Bibliography

Asness, Clifford S. "The Interaction of Value and Momentum Strategies." *Financial Analysts Journal* 53, no. 2 (1997): 29–36.

Asness, Clifford S., Tobias J. Moskowitz, and Lasse Heje Pedersen. "Value and Momentum Everywhere." National Bureau of Economic Research Working Papers, 2009.

Baer, Gregory, and Gary Gensler. *The Great Mutual Fund Trap.* New York: Broadway Books, 2002.

Banz, Rolf W. "The Relationship between Return and Market Value of Common Stock." *Journal of Financial Economics* 9, no. 1 (1981): 3–18.

Basu, Sanjoy. "Investment Performance of Common Stocks in Relation to Their Price-Earnings Ratios: A Test of the Efficient Market Hypothesis." *The Journal of Finance* 32, no. 3 (1977): 663–682.

Black, Fischer. "Beta and Return." *Journal of Portfolio Management*, 20, no. 1 (1993): 8–18.

Black, Fischer, Michael Jensen, and Myron Scholes. "The Capital Asset Pricing Model: Some Empirical Tests." In *Studies in the Theory of Capital Markets*, edited by Michael C. Jensen, 79–121. New York: Praeger, 1972.

Bogle, John C. "As the Index Fund Moves from Heresy to Dogma ... What More Do We Need to Know?" Bogle Research Center (2004). www.vanguard.com/bogle_site/sp20040413.html.

Bogle, John C. "The First Index Mutual Fund: A History of Vanguard Index Trust and the Vanguard Index Strategy." Bogle Research Center (1997). www.vanguard.com/bogle_site/lib/sp19970401.html.

Callaghan, Joe, Austin Murphy, Mohinder Parkash, and Hong Qian. "Empirical Relationship between Stock Prices and Long-Term Earnings." *Journal of Investing* 18, no. 3 (2009): 49–52.

Carhart, Mark M. "On Persistence in Mutual Fund Performance." *Journal of Finance* 52, no. 1 (1997): 57–82.

Chan, Louis K. C., Yasushi Hamao, and Josef Lakonishok. "Fundamentals and Stock Returns in Japan." *The Journal of Finance* 46, no. 5 (1991): 1739–1764.

Chan, Louis K. C., Narasimhan Jegadeesh, and Josef Lakonishok. "Momentum Strategies." *The Journal of Finance* 51, no. 5 (1996): 1681–1713.

Chan, Louis K. C., Narasimhan Jegadeesh, and Josef Lakonishok. "The Profitability of Momentum Strategies." *Financial Analysts Journal* 55, no. 6 (1999): 80–90.

Chan, Louis K. C., Jason Karceski, and Josef Lakonishok. "The Level and Persistence of Growth Rates." *Journal of Finance* 58, no. 2 (2003): 643–684.

Chan, Louis K. C., and Josef Lakonishok. "Value and Growth Investing: Review and Update." *Financial Analysts Journal* 60, no. 1 (2004): 71–86.

Chen, Long, Claudia Moise, and Xinlei Zhao. "Myopic Extrapolation, Price Momentum, and Price Reversal." Working paper, Washington University, 2009.

Chordia, Tarun, and Lakshmanan Shivakumar. "Momentum, Business Cycle, and Time-Varying Expected Returns." *The Journal of Finance* 57, no. 2 (2002): 985–1019.

Clarke, Roger, Harindra de Silva, and Steven Thorley. "Portfolio Constraints and the Fundamental Law of Active Management." *Financial Analysts Journal* 58, no. 5 (2002): 48–66.

Coggin, T. Daniel, and Frank J. Fabozzi. *The Handbook of Equity Style Management*. New Hope, PA: Frank J. Fabozzi Associates, 1995.

Copeland, Tom, Aaron Dolgoff, and Alberto Moel. "The Role of Expectations in Explaining the Cross-Section of Stock Returns." *Review of Accounting Studies* 9, no. 2 (2004): 149–188.

Daniel, Kent, David Hirshleifer, and Avanidhar Subrahmanyam. "Investor Psychology and Security Market Under- and Overreaction." *The Journal of Finance* 53, no. 6 (1998): 1839–1885.

Daniel, Kent, and Sheridan Titman. "Evidence on the Characteristics of Cross-Sectional Variation in Stock Returns." *The Journal of Finance* 52, no. 1 (1997): 1–33.

Davis, James L., Eugene F. Fama, and Kenneth R. French. "Characteristics, Covariances, and Average Returns: 1929–1997." *Journal of Finance* 55, no. 1 (2000): 389–406.

De Bondt, F. M. Werner, and Richard Thaler. "Does the Stock Market Overreact?" *Journal of Finance* 40, no. 3 (1985): 793–805.

Edesess, Michael. *The Big Investment Lie*. San Francisco: Berrett-Koehler Publishers, 2007.

"Efficient Markets Hypothesis: History." www.e-m-h.org/history.html.

Elton, Edwin J., Martin J. Gruber, and Mustafa Gultekin. "Expectations and Share Prices." *Management Science* 27, no. 9 (1981): 975–987.

Fama, Eugene F. "Market Efficiency, Long-term Returns, and Behavioral Finance." *Journal of Financial Economics* 49, no. 3 (1998): 283–306.

Fama, Eugene F., and Kenneth R. French. "Common Risk Factors in the Returns on Stock and Bonds." *Journal of Financial Economics* 33, no. 1 (1993): 3–56.

Fama, Eugene F., and Kenneth R. French. "The Cross-Section of Expected Stock Returns." *Journal of Finance* 47, no. 2 (1992): 427–466.

Fama, Eugene F., and Kenneth R. French. "Dissecting Anomalies." *Journal of Finance* 63, no. 4 (2008): 1653–1678.

Fama, Eugene F., and Kenneth R. French. "Multifactor Explanations of Asset Pricing Anomalies." *Journal of Finance* 51, no. 1 (1996): 55–84.

Fama, Eugene F., and Kenneth R. French. "Size and Book-to-Market Factors in Earnings and Returns." *Journal of Finance* 50, no. 1 (1995): 131–155.

Fama, Eugene F., and Kenneth R. French. "Value versus Growth: The International Evidence." *Journal of Finance* 53, no. 6 (1998): 1975–1999.

Ferri, Richard A. *All about Index Funds: The Easy Way to Get Started*. New York: McGraw-Hill, 2002.

Fisher, Kenneth L., and Meir Statman. "Cognitive Biases in Market Forecasts." *Journal of Portfolio Management* 27, no. 1 (2000): 72–81.

Frazzini, Andrea. "The Disposition Effect and Underreaction to News." *Journal of Finance* 61, no. 4 (2006): 2017–2046.

Griffin, John M., Xiuqing Ji, and J. Spencer Martin. "Global Momentum Strategies: A Portfolio Perspective." *Journal of Portfolio Management* 31, no. 2 (2005): 23–39.

Grinblatt, Mark, Sheridan Titman, and Russ Wermers. "Momentum Investment Strategies, Portfolio Performance, and Herding: A Study of Mutual Fund Behavior." *American Economics Review* 85, no. 5 (1995): 1088–1105.

Grinold, Richard C. "The Fundamental Law of Active Management." *Journal of Portfolio Management* 15, no. 3 (1989): 30–37.

Jegadeesh, Narasimhan. "Evidence of Predictable Behavior of Security Returns." *Journal of Finance* 45, no. 3 (1990): 881–898.

Jegadeesh, Narasimhan, and Sheridan Titman. "Profitability of Momentum Strategies: An Evaluation of Alternative Explanations." *Journal of Finance* 56, no. 2 (2001): 699–720.

Jegadeesh, Narasimhan, and Sheridan Titman. "Returns to Buying Winners and Selling Losers: Implications for Stock Market Inefficiency." *Journal of Finance* 48, no. 1 (1993): 65–91.

Kahneman, Daniel, and Amos Tversky. "Judgement under Uncertainty: Heuristics and Biases." *Science* 185, no. 4157 (1974): 1124–1131.

Kahneman, Daniel, and Amos Tversky. "Prospect Theory: An Analysis of Decision under Risk." *Econometrica* 47, no. 2 (1979): 263–291.

Klein, Robert A., and Jess Lederman. *Equity Style Management*. Chicago: Irwin, 1995.

Lakonishok, Josef, Andrei Shleifer, and Robert W. Vishny. "Contrarian Investment, Extrapolation, and Risk." *Journal of Finance* 49, no 5 (1994): 1541–1578.

La Porta, Rafael. "Expectations and the Cross-Section of Stock Returns." *Journal of Finance* 51, no. 5 (1996): 1715–1742.

McWhinney, James E. "A Brief History of the Mutual Fund." www.investopedia. com/articles/mutualfund/05/MFhistory.asp?partner=aol-d&viewed=1.

Moskowitz, Tobias J., and Mark Grinblatt. "Do Industries Explain Momentum?" *Journal of Finance* 54, no. 4 (1999): 1249–1290.

Pensions & Investments. "P&I/Watson Wyatt World 500: The World's Largest Managers." www.pionline.com/article/20081013/CHART2/810069995/-1/WWTOPMANAGERS.

Reilly, Frank K., and Keith C. Brown. *Investment Analysis and Portfolio Management*, 6th ed. Orlando, FL: Harcourt, 2000.

Rouwenhorst, K. Geert. "International Momentum Strategies." *Journal of Finance* 53, no. 1 (1998): 267–284.

Scott, James, Mark Stumpp, and Peter Xu. "Behavioral Bias, Valuation, and Active Management." *Financial Analysts Journal* 55, no. 4 (1999): 49–57.

Siegel, Laurence B. *Benchmarks and Investment Management.* Charlottesville, VA: Research Foundation of AIMR, 2003.

Shleifer, Andrei. *Inefficient Markets: An Introduction to Behavioral Finance.* New York: Oxford University Press, 2000.

Schwert, G. William. "Anomalies and Market Efficiency." In *Handbook of the Economics of Finance*, 937–972. Amsterdam: North-Holland, 2003.

Standard & Poor's. "A History of Standard & Poor's," www2.standardandpoors. com/spf/html/media/SP_TimeLine_2006.html.

Thaler, Richard. "Anomalies: The Winner's Curse." *Journal of Economic Perspectives* 2, no. 1 (1985): 191–202.

van Dijk, Ronald, and Fred Huibers. "European Price Momentum and Analyst Behavior." *Financial Analysts Journal* 58, no. 2 (2002): 96–105.

Vanguard 500 Index Fund Investor Shares Overview. www.vanguard.com.

About the Authors

KHALID GHAYUR

Mr. Ghayur is Chief Executive Officer and Chief Investment Officer of Westpeak Global Advisors, L.P. Prior to joining Westpeak, Mr. Ghayur was employed by Morgan Stanley Capital International (MSCI) Barra, in New York, where he was a member of its Global Executive Committee and Chairman of the MSCI Index Policy Committee. As Director of Research Policy, he was responsible for MSCI Barra's global markets and benchmarking research, and new product development. From 1994 to 2000, Mr. Ghayur was Global Head of Quantitative Research and Strategy for HSBC Asset Management, in London, where he was responsible for supervising and coordinating the development and application of all quantitative research efforts globally. These research efforts concentrated in the areas of strategic and tactical asset allocation, fixed income modeling, stock selection techniques, portfolio construction and analysis, and risk management. From 1992 to 1994, he was a Senior Quantitative Analyst at Credit Lyonnais Asset Management, in Paris, and from 1987 to 1991, he held the position of Portfolio Manager at Union National Bank in Abu Dhabi, where he was responsible for managing the bank's U.K. and U.S. investment portfolios. Mr. Ghayur is a member of the FTSE Academic Advisory Board. He has served on the Board of Governors of the CFA Institute, the Board's Nominating Committee, and as Chairman of the Board's External Relations and Volunteer Involvement Committee. He is also a former trustee of the CFA Institute Research Foundation. Mr. Ghayur was a member of the Editorial Board of the *Financial Analysts Journal* and was the founding President of the U.K. Society of Investment Professionals. Mr. Ghayur received an M.B.A. in Finance and International Business from the École Nationale des Ponts et Chaussées, Paris (1992), and an M.A. (1984) and B.A. (1982) in Economics from the University of Karachi. He is a CFA charterholder, a member of the CFA Institute, and a Fellow of the Society of Investment Professionals (FSIP). He is also a Diplomaed Associate of the Institute of Bankers Pakistan.

RONAN G. HEANEY

Mr. Heaney is Director of Research at Westpeak Global Advisors, L.P. Before joining Westpeak, he was employed by Multum Information Services, in Denver, Colorado, as a Software Architect. From 1992 to 1996, he held the position of Senior Software Developer at Swiss Bank Corporation, in Chicago, where he developed and supported a global equity options/futures trading system. Mr. Heaney received an M.S. in Computer Science from Purdue University (1992), where he was awarded a Fulbright Fellowship, and a B.S. in Applied Physics from Dublin City University, Ireland (1990).

STEPHEN A. KOMON

Mr. Komon is Senior Portfolio Manager at Westpeak Global Advisors, L.P. Prior to joining Westpeak, he was Vice President, Foreign Exchange & Commodities, at J.P. Morgan & Company, Inc., in New York, where he developed expertise in foreign exchange and derivatives. From 1993 to 1998, Mr. Komon was Director, Foreign Exchange, at UBS AG/Swiss Bank Corporation, in various locations, including the United States, Asia, and Europe, where he priced, structured, and administered foreign exchange options. From 1989 to 1991 he was employed by Dean Witter Reynolds, Inc., in New York, as a Corporate Finance Analyst. Mr. Komon received an M.B.A., with honors, in Finance and Accounting from the University of Chicago Graduate School of Business (1993) and a B.S., with distinction, in Commerce with a concentration in Finance from the University of Virginia (1989). He is a CFA charterholder and a member of the CFA Institute and the Denver Society of Security Analysts.

STEPHEN C. PLATT

Mr. Platt is Director of Portfolio Management at Westpeak Global Advisors, L.P. Prior to joining Westpeak, Mr. Platt was a co-founder and Senior Vice President of Cordillera Asset Management, in Denver, Colorado. While at Cordillera, his responsibilities included portfolio management, research, and marketing. He codeveloped and implemented the quantitative investment process, and was responsible for performance attribution analysis and backtesting. He also gained experience in trading technology. From 1990 to 1992, he worked as a Senior Research/Marketing Associate at Vogelzang & Associates, in Denver. Mr. Platt received a B.S. in Finance from the University of Colorado Leeds School of Business (1988). He is a CFA charterholder and a member of the CFA Institute and the Denver Society of Security Analysts.

Index

209